Revolutionary Acts

PARALLAX  RE-VISIONS OF CULTURE
AND SOCIETY

Stephen G. Nichols, Gerald Prince, and Wendy Steiner
SERIES EDITORS

Revolutionary Acts

Theater, Democracy, and the
French Revolution

Susan Maslan

The Johns Hopkins University Press
Baltimore

This book was brought to publication with the generous
assistance of the President's Research Fellowships in the
Humanities, University of California.

The Johns Hopkins University Press
2715 North Charles Street
Baltimore, Maryland 21218-4363
www.press.jhu.edu

Library of Congress Cataloging-in-Publication Data

Maslan, Susan, 1963–
  Revolutionary acts : theater, democracy, and the French
revolution / Susan Maslan.
      p.   cm.—(Parallax, re-visions of culture and society)
  Includes bibliographical references and index.
  ISBN 0-8018-8125-0 (hardcover : alk. paper)
      1. Theater—France—History—18th century.
2. France—History—Revolution, 1789–1799—Theater and
the revolution.   3. French drama—18th century—History
and criticism.   I. Title.   II. Parallax (Baltimore, Md.)
  PN2633.M37 2005
  792'.0944'09033—dc22   2004025489

A catalog record for this book is available from the
British Library.

Contents

Illustrations appear on pages 171–182

Preface

This book explores the relation of art and politics during the complicated and violent birth of mass political participation, mass culture, and modern democracy in late-eighteenth-century France. Jacques-Louis David's paintings are widely recognized as the most important art created during the Revolution, but the now obscure revolutionary theater was an art form central to the Revolution, and despite its aesthetic shortcomings, the story of the theater constitutes an important lost chapter in the literary and cultural history of France. Recovering long-forgotten plays might seem an antiquarian's project, but the French revolutionary theater was the first modern experience of the interaction of mass culture and mass politics. It was, therefore, the inauguration of our own cultural moment.

In chapter 1, "Resisting Representation: Theater and Democracy in Revolutionary France," I show how newly emerging liberal political institutions came into conflict with a popular conception of participatory democracy that was coming into being in the theater. Scholars interested in the development of public expression and the growth of a public sphere have focused their attention almost exclusively on print culture, but print was only one mode of publicity and, indeed, was considered a far safer mode by revolutionary liberals who feared the form of publicity created in the theater. Books, they argued, were read in isolation, free from the contagion of emotion; plays, by contrast, were experienced in the presence of a crowd. For these reasons readers could assess books rationally, whereas spectators' judgments were clouded by the "electricity" of the group. Advocates of the theater, on the other hand, embraced theater's direct impact on the senses, as well as its communal dimension; these qualities, they claimed, made theater a more powerful and more important mode of publicity than print. This chapter examines the ways in which a certain conception of theater lined up with a popular movement to exert direct audience control over theatrical production in such a way as to make the theater not only a major crucible for the development of public opinion but also a central institution of direct democracy. I read Marie-Joseph

Chénier's tragedy *Charles IX, ou l'École des rois* (1789) in this context and study the debates and riots it spurred; I also analyze the riots caused by Jean-François Laya's play *L'Ami des lois* (1793) and by certain Théâtre de Vaudeville parodies of Chénier in order to show both how audiences successfully gained authority over theatrical production and why it was so important for them to do so. Theater audiences came to wield a power over theatrical representation far greater than the power citizens wielded over their political representatives. At least until 1794 audiences continued to exert extraordinary control over the conditions of theatrical production and performance. For this reason the economy of power that audiences established in theaters posed a direct challenge to the form of political representation—in which the empowering citizens are subsumed by their representatives—liberal politicians sought to institutionalize at the outset of the Revolution.

In chapter 2 I turn from tragedy to comedy. In "The Comic Revolution: Molière, Rousseau, Fabre d'Eglantine, and Revolutionary Antitheatricalism" I revisit the heated debate over the moral and social status of theater that exploded with the publication of Rousseau's *Lettre à M. d'Alembert sur les spectacles* in 1758. Rousseau argues that theater can never correct behavior or improve morals; instead, it confirms the audience's previously held beliefs. For Rousseau the most telling and egregious example of theater's structural impotence is Molière's *Le Misanthrope. Le Misanthrope,* Rousseau argues, immorally and cruelly mocks the honest Alceste and celebrates the hypocritical code of conduct championed by Philinte because Philinte represents the audience members and their beliefs. I show that Fabre d'Eglantine, in an effort to rescue high comedy from the decadence into which he and many critics believed it had fallen, made Rousseau's antitheatrical theories the basis for a novel dramatic practice. Fabre rewrote *Le Misanthrope,* a play that explicitly stages theatricality and its relation to the preservation of social bonds, along Rousseauian lines. In Fabre's enormously successful *Le Philinte de Molière, ou la suite du misanthrope* (1790), the fanatically sincere Alceste becomes not only the model for the new citizen but also the ideal sympathetic spectator, perpetually moved to action by affecting tableaux that exist only in his own imagination. The conventionally hypocritical Philinte stands for the bankruptcy not only of Old Regime society but also of Old Regime comedy. Fabre, perhaps paradoxically, sought to restructure the relationship between theater and society—and thus to regenerate the theater and create a truly republican culture—by detheatricalizing theater itself.

In chapter 3, "Robespierre's Eye: Revolutionary Surveillance and the Modern Republican Subject," I turn from the antitheatricality of Fabre's theater to the antitheatricalism of revolutionary politics and develop an important revision of the Foucauldian model of surveillance. Theatricality itself—the production of opaque, alienating relations between performers and spectators—remained deeply troubling to a radical political movement committed to building an entirely transparent society. Robespierre and other revolutionary politicians were as influenced by Rousseau's antitheatricalism as was Fabre. Radical republicans associated theatricality with the moral and social corruption of the Old Regime. Kings, they believed, manipulated and oppressed their subjects with theatrical displays because they had everything to hide. But the National Assembly—the very center of the Revolution—seemed to Robespierre to be disturbingly vulnerable to theatricalization: here the people were spectators and the deputies performers. Robespierre's solution to the theatrical threat was to subject politics to popular surveillance. Robespierre dreamed that the National Assembly would deliberate in a hall so vast it could accommodate ten thousand to twelve thousand observers, a hall so well-designed that every corner was visible and every whisper audible. Robespierre repeatedly imagined an overwhelming, total vision—the vision of all the French people—that pierced every mask, illuminated every shadow, and left no room for theatricality to occupy. Robespierre identified himself with the people precisely by conflating his chief political task with theirs: he, too, above all, was a surveillant of other politicians. The all-seeing gaze of the French people, according to Robespierre's theory, constituted a form of *democratic* surveillance dedicated to exposing counterrevolutionary theatricality. Furthermore, Robespierre's insistence that only vigilant popular surveillance could ensure the purity and safety of the Republic corresponded to a widespread popular demand for the right to surveil all authorities. For ordinary citizens surveillance over elected officials offered the best means to reconcile political representation with direct democracy and to safeguard the bedrock of the Republic: popular sovereignty.

In chapter 4, "The Home and the World: Domestic Surveillance and Revolutionary Drama," I explore the representation of surveillance on the revolutionary stage. I argue that the Revolution invented a new genre, the drama of domestic surveillance, in which we see the political practice of surveillance translated from the National Assembly into the neighborhood and the home. These extremely popular plays were staples of several of the theaters that sprang up quickly after the abolition of theatrical privilege in 1791. In the drama of domestic surveillance the adulterous spouses and villainous suitors who threaten the family are also revealed to be counterrevolutionary conspirators who threaten the nation. These domestic menaces are undone by careful surveillance (explicitly named as such) carried out by household members or neighborhood friends. The same surveillance that protects the Republic protects the happiness of its citizens. Popular revolutionary drama, I show, linked personal and political disaster and portrayed the home as wholly continuous with the larger public world. When popular sovereignty transformed subjects into citizens—that is, parts of the sovereign—it also transformed them from private individuals into public persons. The home was therefore just as much a locus of state importance as the Assembly and, consequently, just as much in need of careful scrutiny. The pitched battles that erupted during the performance of a Vaudeville play called *La Chaste Suzanne* demonstrate widespread popular support for such a conception of surveillance. For that play represented surveillance of the home as perversion masquerading as compelling state interest and portrayed the politicians who practiced surveillance as exploitative tyrants. The volunteer soldiers who interrupted the play, threatened the actors, and took a complaint to the municipal government were defending their belief in surveillance as the safeguard of both the Revolution and the home.

Acknowledgments

I have found these acknowledgments surprisingly difficult to write; it is impossible, I have come to realize, to fully convey the degree and kind of help I received as I worked on this book. Oliver Arnold was the sine qua non for the book. He helped me conceive the dissertation project that was its basis; he listened as I tried out arguments; he suggested avenues of research; most important, he read every word of this book in every one of its many drafts. I cannot thank him enough for that rigorous and generous intellectual labor, which has improved the book on every score. Mark Maslan inspired me to go to graduate school and has been a vital and crucial presence every step of the way since. His clarity and logic made our discussions of many of my central arguments extraordinarily valuable and productive. Michael Fried, the director of my dissertation, was not only a great intellectual exemplar, he was unfailingly helpful and enthusiastic. Lynn Hunt, with great generosity, read many drafts of chapters, and her suggestions always improved and refined my work. Sharon Marcus has been at once an important interlocutor and profound support; she read and criticized several chapters with enormous attention and always made my work better. Dorothy J. Hale and Jeffrey Knapp also helped transform my dissertation into this book; they asked sharp, difficult questions that forced me to clarify my thoughts and arguments. Their intellectual toughness was matched only by their constant enthusiasm, support, and good cheer. Karl Britto and Margaret Cohen read early versions of chapters, offered detailed comments, and asked important questions. I am grateful to Jim Creech, Mitchell Greenberg, Jonathan Strauss, and Marie-Claire Vallois for conversations early in the formulation of this project that helped to direct and shape it. I am also grateful to the anonymous readers for the Johns Hopkins University Press who read the manuscript with such attention and provided such helpful advice.

The University of California made research and writing possible through a President's Research Fellowship in the Humanities, a Humanities Research Fellowship, a Regent's Junior Faculty Fellowship, and a Junior Faculty Research Grant. I am grateful to the university not only for these all-important means of financial support but also for its culture of interdisciplinary investigation, its extraordinarily open community of scholars, and its commitment to junior faculty.

Introduction

This is a book about theater and democracy during the French Revolution. It is a book, in other words, about two things that disappeared from historical view. It may seem counterintuitive to claim that democracy lost out in the historical struggle for existence, but the democracy that I explore here is the direct popular democracy that burst forth in 1789 and was soon overwhelmed and replaced by the more practical, manageable system of political representation, that is to say, the hegemonic form of government in our own time.

The theater of the Revolution produced a body of plays that have remained unread and unperformed for nearly two hundred years. This book is, therefore, elegiac in a sense. It mourns the loss of two singular moments: the thrilling if terrifying moment when Jean-Jacques Rousseau's dream of a people acting, debating, and willing in their own persons seemed to come to life and the moment when an aesthetic institution that had always been the most prestigious, the most aristocratic of aesthetic pleasures suddenly exploded and was, for a time, at the center of a new mass revolutionary culture. But this book is more than an elegy, not only because the people and the culture that have been lost to view shaped much of the history that succeeded them but because the story of the relation between revolutionary politics and revolutionary theater offers a lesson for cultural studies and literary historicism. Revolutionary theater was no mere extension of revolutionary politics, nor can revolutionary politics be read as a theatrical text or performance. Revolutionary theater and revolutionary politics did not transform themselves one into the other. On the contrary, theater and politics were important to each other during the Revolution because both were distinct and powerful fields that had their own ambitions, dynamics, and history and that, in different ways, created new meanings, new practices, and new possibilities. Both were in the process of re-making themselves. In a time of great urgency and great invention theater *and* politics mattered, so when they came into contact, they sometimes cooperated and sometimes collided. The friction between these two, unequal, parties proved both creative and disastrous. This is not a book about the felicitous alliance of theater and politics; it is an account of a messy, uneven, tumultuous but essential cultural and historical intersection.

By *theater* I mean Parisian theaters as artistic, social, and public institutions; plays as performances and as literary texts; and the reception of plays and performances by audiences, critics, and spectators. By *politics* I mean the actions and discourses of the newly formed National Assembly, the Parisian neighborhood assemblies, the political clubs, and less organized forms of political action and thought. This study is limited to Paris because it was the theater capital as well as the political capital of France. I do not want to suggest that the theatrical and political lives of other areas were identical to that of Paris; each region had its own literary and political history. But the relation of Parisian theaters to national and local politics was the most significant and the most complex in revolutionary France.

During the Revolution the representative practices of the theater came into conflict with revolutionary politicians' attempts to theorize and practice representative politics, and the conflict was sometimes violent. Turmoil in revolutionary theaters was profoundly and increasingly meaningful; the theater was perhaps the most significant crucible for the formation and expression of public opinion. In the theater the public could express its judgment immediately and actively, but in the National Assembly public judgment was mediated by representatives. Theater and representative political assemblies institutionalized public opinion in radically different ways, and theater's importance as a site for the production and exercise of the public's judgment expanded exponentially as it participated energetically in the creation of democratic political culture and revolutionary sensibility.

This book's ambition is to uncover and interpret theater's participation in the creation of modern French democratic culture and democratic subjectivity and, conversely, to explore the role of revolutionary politics in shaping French theater. The two central issues around which this book unfolds are the nature of political representation—more specifically the problematic relationship between direct and representative democracy—and the correlative problem of transparency and its relation to theatricality. Precisely because neither the politics nor the theater of the Revolution was determined by the other, their relationship is critical. The relationship between revolutionary politics and theater was not simply one between two discourses; instead, as investigating theater and politics together reveals, there were manifold relations among linguistic, social, artistic, intellectual, and political discourses and practices that were themselves unstable.

The relation between representative and direct democracy was an urgent problem during the Revolution and has remained one of the central topoi of revolutionary historiography. The defining feature of the Revolution in its earliest days was the overwhelmingly effective entrance of the masses onto the scene of history—most notably, but certainly not limited to, their taking of the Bastille and the October days of 1789 that brought the royal family to Paris from Versailles.[1] Establishing an entirely new government and state apparatus in a country of twenty-five million inhabitants, which quickly came to be the Revolution's mission, however, required institutionalizing political representation. The newly enfranchised citizens would not act themselves; they would authorize others to act in their name because direct democracy, many believed, would mean anarchy. There was, however, a strong and widespread sense among ordinary people that to cede power to representatives was, at least in part, to lose what had been so recently gained. To lend others their newly won authority was to submit themselves to new masters. When the people elect representatives, as Rousseau had warned, they become "nothing."[2] Many people, to the distress of some but not all in government, proved extremely reluctant to renounce their right and capacity to participate directly in political affairs.

Historians have tended to explore the tensions between direct and representative democracy by studying politicians' beliefs about representative politics and about "the people" or by exploring the strains and conflicts between the world of political clubs and the Parisian sections and representative political institutions. By moving outside the traditional binary relation between politicians and the crowd, we can see how a public cultural institution, the theater, could participate in shaping the conception and practices of both political representation and direct democracy. The theater was an alternative space for developing the practices of participation, scrutiny, interpretation, and judgment that newly created citizens would put to use in the sphere of politics, as well as within the theater. It would offer citizens a different structure in which to understand their relation to representation itself and thus to their own new status and identity as citizens.

The tension I am positing between theater and politics diverges from recent attempts to argue that politicians modeled revolutionary politics on theater.[3] Theatrical metaphors are important to revolutionary rhetoric, but they nearly always serve as critiques within revolutionary discourse and usually appear at moments of intense political anxiety.[4] Theatrical metaphors tend to express deep fear on the part of both politicians and ordinary citizens. It was clear to nearly all revolutionaries that the new nation must rely to some degree on representation in its political institutions—but that degree was a matter of deep disagreement. Disputes tended to turn not on the question of whether there should be representation but rather on the problem of how much representation was enough. Theatrical metaphors in political discourse, I suggest, reveal concerns that representation can be perverted and subverted from within. But I am also concerned with theatricality as a complex mode of orientation of self to other and of representation to represented.[5] Theatricality implied the potential failure of political representation to accomplish its mission: to make present the will of the people. For French revolutionaries theatricality in politics signaled politicians' desire and capacity to delude and deceive the represented. In fact, most republican politicians, deeply influenced by Rousseau's antitheatricalism and equally horrified by what they saw as the theatrical machinations of the monarchy, sought to create a politics free of all theatrical taint: a transparent society in which individual essence was immediately perspicuous to all. The new society would be in every way the opposite of the theatricalized world of appearances, dissimulation, and corruption that defined the Old Regime. Moreover, and more startling, the same antitheatrical compulsion so central to revolutionary politics was at the heart of a new revolutionary dramatic aesthetic. For theatricality had a derogatory meaning within the theater as well. Playwrights and actors often opposed what was theatrical to what was dramatic. They associated theatrical effects with a debased, shallow form of the theater that sought to mystify and manipulate its audience. Dramatic effects, on the contrary, served to move and to touch spectators and, in so doing, to make them into sensitive appreciators of art, to bring them into the work of art, to make them moral beings, and to encourage them to enter into a true community with each other.[6] In politics and theater, revolutionaries sought, in very different ways, to create a regime of transparency, a regime in which all hearts and souls communicate perfectly and without obstacle. The threat posed by theatricality was the threat of opacity, the threat that something *in the guise of transparency* had the potential to alienate politicians from those in whose name they spoke and, even worse, to alienate citizens from themselves and from each other.[7]

Modernity began with the French Revolution. With the fall of the Bastille and the creation of the National Assembly in 1789, contemporaries almost instantaneously expressed the belief that they had broken definitively with the past and entered into a new age. From nearly as early a date social critics, philosophers, poets, historians, and artists began to explore what exactly was new about the era initiated by the Revolution and of what exactly modernity consisted. For much of the twentieth century a Marxist interpretation provided the answer: the modernity ushered in by the Revolution was economic; the French Revolution constitutes the originary moment of modernity because it cleared away lingering feudal social and economic structures, established the bourgeoisie as the ruling class, and enshrined the capitalist mode of production. While there is much of value in Marxist studies of the Revolution, by the 1980s the grand Marxist scheme had been largely overturned, and in its place emerged a widespread consensus that the French Revolution was revolutionary because it invented democracy. The French Revolution was a world-historical event, explained François Furet, because "France . . . is the country that invents democratic culture through the Revolution and reveals to the world one of the foundational postures of conscious historical action."[8]

In one view modernity is economic; in another it is political. Both interpretations no doubt express a good deal of truth, but neither interpretation addresses *cultural* modernity. By contrast, T. J. Clark dates modernism in art to the French Revolution—to 1793, to be exact—because it is then, he argues, that art takes on a new consciousness of its relation to history and to its own making. Critics have viewed the revolutionary period, with one astonishing exception, as barren of the sort of great cultural achievements that merit critical attention. That exception, of course, is the art of Jacques-Louis David. Because David is indisputably a great painter, because some of his greatest paintings—above all his *Death of Marat*—are deeply bound to the history of the Revolution, and because David was not only an active revolutionary but also an extremely important one, art historians have been compelled to confront and explore the relation between the aesthetic and political cultures of the Revolution in a way that literary critics have not. Perhaps not surprisingly, while literary critics view the Revolution as a condition that precluded the possibility of real literary creation, art historians view it as the necessary condition for the birth of modern art.

The notion that revolution must make for artistic nullity springs from the belief that true art arises outside of (and above) history and that this very exteriority lends the work of art its status; once art descends into the muck of history, it becomes propaganda. By contrast, T. J. Clark argues that modernism is precisely the art of that muck. David's *Marat* is "made out of" the details of revolutionary politics, Clark writes, and politics "is the form, *par excellence* of that contingency which makes modernism what it is. That is why those who wish modernism had never happened . . . resist to the death the idea that art, at many of its highest moments in the nineteenth and twentieth centuries, took the stuff of politics for its material, and did not transmute it."[9] The rupture brought about by the Revolution, according to Clark, was not between artistic achievement and cultural barbarism. Rather, it demarcates two different types of consciousness about art. Old Regime artists believed that their work was to transmute, to lift the world out of the domain of the material and the quotidian into the separate realm of art and in so doing to create transcendence. David's *Marat,* Clark writes, perhaps despite itself, expresses the consciousness that such transcendence is impossible, that art is made up of its present and its presence.

Whether the French Revolution, for a time, achieved democracy is a matter of sharp debate among historians; but even those who believe that the events of 1789 led inevitably to the Terror, those who attribute to the French Revolution the origin of totalitarianism, and those who emphasize the contradictions between the Revolution's principles and its practices concede that the Revolution initiated the West into modern democratic citizenship. Between June 17, 1789, when the deputies of the third estate proclaimed themselves the National Assembly, and August 26, 1789, when the National Assembly declared the Rights of Man and Citizen, revolutionaries accomplished a monumental shift in power and the conception of power. They disowned the divine right ideology that had made the monarch, by the grace of God, the locus of sovereignty and legitimacy, transferred legitimate authority to the people, and created a new legitimating ideology—popular sovereignty—that transformed subjects into citizens. The metamorphosis of political philosophy and institutions was absolutely bound up with the participation of masses of ordinary people in political action in newly effective ways. Although Ancien Regime France had known many peasant uprisings and urban riots, the events of 1789 were different in their political self-consciousness, in their scale, and in their durability. Spontaneous local actions took on an increasingly organized character and gave birth to new practices, to new self-empowered institutions, and to what Michel Vovelle would call, new "mentalités."[10] Ordinary revolutionary citizens' politics, and the politics of revolutionary politicians, were formed by their participation in and experience of the Revolution.

Tracing theater's part in the invention of modern democracy can help us begin to understand cultural modernity because theater—in terms of both artistic production and reception—defied the very social and political determinism that, until recently, dominated historical and literary studies of the revolutionary period. Revolutionary theater understood its relation to its historical context, to its public, and to art in radically new ways. Although many works from the prerevolutionary canon continued to be performed, new works were often written in reaction to contemporary events. These new works, however, along with their stagings, manifested a complex relation to the historical situation in which they were produced rather than a reflexively simple one. They had to take into account the translation of the revolutionary world into the language and practices of the theater as well as the fact that theatrical representations came into being only in relation to an audience that often considered itself both the maker and the interpreter of meaning. Theater audiences were fluid, ad hoc groups; they formed temporary identities and cohesions in relation to performances, to political events, and to each other.

Before the turn from traditional social accounts of the Revolution to the study of revolutionary political culture, scholars from both the right and the left tended to deduce the meaning of audience actions from the social status of the audience members rather than by examining what those spectators actually said and did. That is, historians and critics have assumed that members of the "lower orders" rebelled against high theater because of their cultural crudity and that they embraced representations of violent attack on symbols of the Ancien Regime.[11] Equally, scholars assumed that the more traditional theatergoing public, the upper middle classes and aristocracy, went to the theater to see affectionate representations of royalty and other signs of the old order. In other words, these scholars largely overlooked the power and effect of culture—in this case theater—on politics. The theater, for them, was merely another convenient locus for the demonstration of predetermined, preformed politico-social allegiances. But the history of the revolutionary theater is a complex story of shifting relations to representation, microcontests over interpretation, struggles over authority, and constructions and deconstructions of political and cultural identities. The theater, as both an artistic and a social institution, set out to remake itself in 1789, but it did so with diverse aesthetic visions and amid competing social and economic interests. The vicissitudes of the revolutionary theater, rather than serving as evidence for the superficiality or triviality of art at times of political upheaval, as the old saw would have it, attest to the centrality of cultural institutions and of art in the production of politics. And the theater, perhaps more than any other cultural institution, illustrates the contingency, rather than the historical necessity or coherence, of the Revolution and of its effects and thus the degree to which its participants were shaped by events even as they shaped them.

By analyzing the relationship between theater and politics during the Revolution, I also explore and broaden the ways in which scholarship conceives political culture, aesthetic culture, and the relationship between the two. The term *political culture* within the field of French Revolution studies sprang to life with the publication of François Furet's *Penser la Révolution Française* (1978).[12] Furet shifted scholarly attention away from the social interpretations of the Revolution—both Marxist and Annaliste—that had dominated the field and back to politics. The Revolution constitutes the break between early modernity and modernity not because it dislodged feudal structures and brought the bourgeoisie to power, argues Furet, but because it invented a new democratic discourse that put a linguistic representation of the people at the center of power. Furet's conception of political culture is sharply limited: it consists exclusively of high political discourse; it was created in 1789 and remained fixed thereafter; it acts as its own agent, circulating among a small group of speakers but owing neither its origin nor its meaning to them; it led ineluctably to the Terror of 1793–1794. Despite these limitations Furet's work is of enormous significance because it brilliantly reminds scholars of an incontestable but nearly forgotten fact: the French Revolution was indeed a political event, and its consequences have been political and social. Moreover, Furet's insistence that power inhered in and was exercised through linguistic representations of power brought representation to the fore as a critical category for studies of the Revolution.

Furet's work sparked a transformation in approaches to the Revolution. Historians moved away from studies of the long-term causes and effects of the Revolution toward studies of political-symbolic practices and representations. Perhaps the two most important works to emerge from the turn toward the political are Mona Ozouf's *La Fête révolutionnaire, 1789–1799* (1976) and Lynn Hunt's *Politics, Culture, and Class in the French Revolution* (1984). The great late-nineteenth- and early-twentieth-century historians Alphonse Aulard and Albert Mathiez both wrote studies of revolutionary festivals and revolutionary religion. But Ozouf returns to what would have seemed to social historians to constitute, at best, an epiphenomenon in order to show that revolutionary festivals were fundamentally important moments in the history of the Revolution. Revolutionary festivals, she shows, sought to restructure time and space—to create new relations among the individual, the community, the state, and the natural world—in order to regenerate citizens, France, and ultimately, humankind. Lynn Hunt significantly expands the range of discourses and practices that could be and should be regarded as political. Inspired by Jean-Jacques Rousseau's intuition that "tout tenait radicalement à la politique (everything depended fundamentally on politics)," Hunt brings her analysis to bear on what might be called the revolutionary cultural imaginary: she investigates revolutionaries' sometimes self-conscious, sometimes unconscious creation of a new repertory of symbols, images, and rhetoric in the wake of the collapse of the sacred monarchy and the entire ordering system, ideological and practical, that had underpinned it.[13] In *The Family Romance of the French Revolution* (1992) Hunt delves deeper into the revolutionary imaginary. Starting from the fact that the monarchy had long explained and legitimated itself by means of an analogy to the family (much to the chagrin of social contract theorists, like John Locke and Rousseau, who insisted that the family was not and could not be the origin of legitimate political authority), Hunt examines the multitude of ways in which the Revolution rethought and redeployed metaphors of the family as it invented a new, fraternal nation.

Recently scholars have pointed out that the works of Furet, Ozouf, and Hunt all concentrate on a rather small group of elite politicians and cultural figures. In *Singing the French Revolution: Popular Culture and Politics, 1789–1799,* Laura Mason, for example, seeks to counter this top-down approach to revolutionary political culture by investigating what she calls "song culture." Because song appealed high and low, was often produced spontaneously on the street, resisted determination by authorities, and was absorbed easily by the uneducated and the educated alike, Mason argues that song can tell us a great deal about how ordinary people participated in, appropriated, and reacted to revolutionary political culture. In an altogether different register Suzanne Desan's *Reclaiming the Sacred: Lay Religion and Popular Politics in Revolutionary France* demonstrates the ways in which common French people reclaimed and reshaped their religious practice in the face of the "enlightened" dechristianization movement coming for the most part from above and from Paris. In their introduction to *Re-Creating Authority in Revolutionary France* Bryant T. Ragan Jr. and Elizabeth A. Williams sum up the ways in which new approaches to political culture distinguish this rising generation of historians from their predecessors. Bryant and Williams argue that, despite the significant differences among them, Furet, Hunt, and Keith Michael Baker all focus on political and social elites. These eminent historians, according to this account, concentrate largely on the production of political culture and neglect its assimilation and consumption. This is a significant gap because reception is a creative process that can escape the intention of the producer. The second-generation studies of revolutionary political culture differ from the first, Ragan and Williams argue, because they turn their attention to "micro-struggles for legitimacy, authority, or power that accompanied but did not always intersect with the central contest for dominance over the state apparatus."[14] But these newer cultural histories, for the most part, share with their predecessors a lack of interest in interpreting the high cultural products—the literature and the art—of the Revolution. In *Revolutionary Acts* I study both the production and the reception of politics and theater, and I focus at once on a central institution of state power, the National Assembly, and a central artistic institution, theater. The term *reception,* however, implies a passivity that is belied by the facts in this case. A better way to express the revolutionary dynamics I study here might be "recursive construction." Theater audiences and citizens of the new representative order were not recipients of meaning created by either politicians or actors; politicians, writers, spectators, actors, militants, and ordinary people brought the beliefs, practices, and structures of the new politics and the new culture into being through a reflexive, reciprocal process.

In *Publishing and Cultural Politics in Revolutionary Paris, 1789–1810,* Carla Hesse argues that the widespread fascination with political culture led scholars to neglect what she calls cultural politics. Hesse demonstrates that culture had its own institutional ambitions, practices, and modes of operation, distinct from those of the political sphere during the revolutionary period. Perhaps what is most significant about *Publishing and Cultural Politics* is that it includes high culture within the domain of culture. Most historians have understood "culture" in an anthropological or sociological sense that, although not of necessity, tends to exclude high culture from its purview. Thus Lynn Hunt defines political culture as "the values, expectations, and implicit rules that expressed and shaped collective intentions and actions."[15] Literary critics have not rushed in to fill the gap; few critics, for example, have studied the ways in which what we typically think of as high literary culture—that is plays, poetry, and prose fictions—contributed to the creation and expression of those revolutionary values, expectations, and rules. The presumption that the Revolution siphoned energies into politics that might otherwise have expressed themselves in literature remains strong if unspoken. Or, put another way, it appears that in times of great political turmoil we must choose between art and society and that during the French Revolution literature entered a period of dormancy.

One notable exception to historians' neglect of revolutionary cultural production is the work of Emmet Kennedy. In his magisterial book *A Cultural History of the French Revolution,* Kennedy gives an overview of nearly every form of cultural life: theater, education, religion, the press, and the visual arts. In recent years Kennedy has done invaluable work gathering data on the life of the revolutionary theater.[16] He has, for example, reconstructed repertories and established statistics on numbers of performances. But Kennedy is less interested in drama as a literary form than in the political allegiances of the theater as an institution. Moreover, the politics of the revolutionary theater are not easily ascertained, and any political account of the theater must be based on a *reading* of the plays, a reading Kennedy does not perform.

I read the plays I discuss in this book, for the most part, in the form of fungus-damaged editions from the 1790s held deep in the belly of the Bibliothèque de l'Arsenal. I read some of them in the less evocative form of microfilm at the Bibliothèque nationale. In other words, many of the works I focus on here belong to the minor culture or popular culture of the past. Such literature typically disappears, both materially and intellectually, from view. Some of the leading playwrights of the revolutionary theater, such as Marie-Joseph Chénier and Fabre d'Eglantine, continued to be thought of as major literary figures well into the first half of the nineteenth century; but even these writers were eventually excluded from the canon, and their works ceased to be reprinted. I seek, however, to understand how contemporaries construed these writers and actors and their theater. This enterprise led me back into the archives, to the newspapers, pamphlets, journals, and government reports of the 1790s.

It is true that there are no Jacques-Louis Davids in the world of revolutionary literature; I have not unearthed any heretofore-unknown literary tours de force. But if I have not found any great writers, I have found a large number of serious and ambitious writers, a cohort of enthusiastic and sincere literary critics, and an abundance of thoughtful, eager theatergoers. Many, if not most, revolutionary playwrights expressed the belief that artistic creation was deeply bound up with the history-making events in which they found themselves and in which they participated. They envisioned a new, central role for theater in the formation of the nation and of its citizens. Several argued explicitly that the Revolution freed them to make art out of the contemporary world and that only such art could attain importance. It becomes critical, therefore, to understand how they perceived their world of constantly shifting and yet momentous meanings, a world cut off from a "usable past." Taking the

Revolution's literary culture and production seriously not only helps us understand the Revolution itself, but it offers new insight into the relationship between eighteenth- and nineteenth-century French literatures, which now appear wholly divided by a revolutionary gulf.

It would have been impossible to conceptualize a study of these minor writers, vaudeville actors, violent theater riots, and long-forgotten revolutionary theater criticism, in short, of the revolutionary theater itself and its relation to French revolutionary politics, without the invention of the new historicism in literary studies. Whereas "old historicism" viewed great works of art and literature as exemplary bearers of the spirit of their age, the new historicism constructed a heterogeneous historical field characterized not by a totalized "spirit" but, as Stephen Greenblatt has explained, by "the unsettling circulation of materials and discourses that is . . . the heart of modern aesthetic practice."[17] The new historicism meant not aestheticizing history, or devaluing masterpieces, but rather refusing either to establish or to recognize a fixed boundary between the literary and the historical. One result is the expansion of the types of objects considered suitable for interpretation: "Major works of art remain centrally important, but they are jostled now by an array of other texts and images. Some of these alternative objects of attention are literary works regarded as too minor to deserve sustained attention and hence marginalized or excluded entirely from the canon. Others are texts that have been regarded as altogether nonliterary, that is, as lacking the aesthetic polish, the self-conscious use of rhetorical figures, the aura of distance from the everyday world, the marked status as fiction that separately or together characterize belles lettres."[18] With the advent of the new historicism, write Catherine Gallagher and Stephen Greenblatt, there has been "a social rebellion in the study of culture" (ibid.). The actors, playwrights, rioters, politicians, drama critics, audiences, and local activists I study in this book are part of that social rebellion in the study of culture, just as they were part of the political, social, and cultural Revolution of their time. This is no rebellion for rebellion's sake: exploring these unlikely characters—their actions and their works—helps us understand literary and cultural production more generally; it illuminates the relations among individual agents and cultural institutions; it reshapes French literary history by reconceiving canonized literature's own literary and historical context.

It would be tempting to propose that this book helps us to hear voices from the past that we have not heard before. But this phrase registers the complexity of such an assertion: how does a book, that is writing, convey a voice?

Books and historical records can and do convey voices, but they do so in mediated, contextualized, "impure" ways. *Writing* and *voice* are important terms for this book because so much important scholarship of the French Enlightenment and the Revolution has been dominated by a Habermasian framework that locates political and social agency solely in print. Habermas first described and analyzed the emergence of a bourgeois public sphere in *The Structural Transformation of the Public Sphere* (German 1962, English 1989). The eighteenth-century bourgeois public sphere, for Habermas, is a virtual place of critical debate and rational consensus outside and over against state authority; it is constituted through writing and the circulation of writing in print. In recent writing Habermas suggests that in modern democratic societies the public sphere is and must be even more "desubstantialized" than was its eighteenth-century ancestor:

> The institutions of public freedom stand on the shifting ground of the political communication of those who, by using them, at the same time interpret and defend them. The public sphere thus reproduces itself *self-referentially,* and in doing so reveals the place to which the expectation of a sovereign self-organization of society has withdrawn. The idea of popular sovereignty is thereby de-substantialized. Even the notion that a network of associations could replace the dismissed "body" of the people—that it could occupy the vacant seat of the sovereign, so to speak—is too concrete.[19]

For Habermas the creation of a rational, democratic public opinion continues to depend on the separation of bodies from ideas. Speech has no place in the public sphere because it is always attached to, and thus infected by, the body from which it issues; only forms of communication that are detached from persons can form the political communication that is the core of sovereignty. Political agency is therefore always mediated by those who possess either the skills or the means to appropriate these technologies of communication. Those who lack these forms of literacy—those who rely on their voices and their bodies—are by necessity excluded from the formation of public opinion and the exercise of sovereignty. The world of the revolutionary theater offers a radically different conception, organization, and exercise of popular sovereignty. For theater is a form of art in which representations are made by bodies and in the presence of a public. The physical, embodied presence of audience members to each other, as well as to theatrical representation, was central to the construction of revolutionary spectators' identities as cultural judges, as members of a public, and as constituent elements of sovereign authority. Studying French revolutionary theater and its relation to politics reveals an alternative conception and practice of the public sphere and thus an alternative vision of democracy.

But why was the theater so important? Why should the theater have enjoyed such a crucial cultural and political position during the Revolution? Part of the answer can be found in theater's historical prestige and part in the relation it established between the aesthetic and the social. Cultural historians have long attributed the creation of a revolutionary public sphere and revolutionary political culture more generally to the explosion of print in 1789.[20] The importance of the phenomenal growth in the production of newspapers and pamphlets with the de facto disappearance of press censorship cannot be overemphasized. But because the sudden and massive development of print culture is so startling, and because it fits so well into Habermas's influential paradigm of the bourgeois public sphere, historians have tended to focus on print to the near exclusion of other forms of communication and expression. Indeed, as we will see in chapter 1, Roger Chartier defines the rational public sphere of letters in opposition to a deceptive, manipulative form of publicity in the theater. But the rapid expansion of print did not displace older, public cultural institutions. And the theater was, for contemporaries, the single most prominent, influential, and prestigious of those institutions. It is easy today to overlook the cultural importance and significance of eighteenth-century and revolutionary theater because theater is relatively marginalized in our own culture: the high price of tickets not only presents a barrier to many, but it also confers an aura that demands a hushed respect from the audience. How many spectators want to hiss or shout in a theater that they paid fifty or sixty dollars to enter? Except for the rare occasions when plays are turned into films, theater is in no way a mass experience.

But in 1789 theater was the closest early modern France came to a mass cultural institution.[21] Major theaters could accommodate eighteen hundred to two thousand spectators, and while prices for the good seats in boxes were no doubt far beyond the means of most people, the pit was much more accessible.[22] Moreover, even before the Revolution brought about an end to the privileged status enjoyed by the Théâtre français, the Comédie-Italienne, and the Opéra, more popular theaters asking lower prices for admission managed to spring up along the Boulevard du Temple.[23] And of course with the end of legal privileges the construction of new theaters was unleashed. The theater was a collective, public experience; as we will see in chapter 1, nearly all contemporary commentators on the theater, those favorable and unfavorable to freedom of the theater, underscored the ways in which theater's effects on the spectator were influenced or even created by the publicness of the theatrical experience, by the reactions and emotions of the other spectators. Theater's meaning was made as much in the pit, among audience members, as on the stage.

The French theater of the Revolution might well be the most vital theater in the history of the West. For despite the seeming incongruity between the gravity and world-historical significance of revolutionary events and the inconsequential pleasure seeking that theatergoing implies, Paris's theaters were singularly productive during the revolutionary period. At least one thousand new plays were written and performed, approximately fifty new theaters opened, and there were roughly twenty-five theatrical performances every day in Paris during the revolutionary decade. Although many theaters experienced economic dry spells at points throughout this period, tough times were caused mainly by the competition produced by rapid growth in the number of theaters. The theater audience did not disappear. Major newspapers such as the *Moniteur,* the *Chronique de Paris,* and the *Journal de Paris* ran daily theater columns; several newspapers were devoted solely to covering the theater and opera; tracts commenting on and offering reforms of the theater abounded.

A surprisingly large number of the Revolution's leading figures were involved in the theater professionally. For example, the Revolution's leading tragic playwright, Marie-Joseph Chénier, belonged to the Paris Jacobin club, was elected to the National Convention, played a major role on the Committee of Public Instruction, conspired in Robespierre's overthrow, and served prominently in the councils of the Directory. Collot d'Herbois, the noted Terrorist, was not only a member of the Committee of Public Safety and responsible for notorious massacres in Lyon, but he was also well-known as an author of comedies and dramas and, before the Revolution, had been the director of the Lyon Theater. The Revolution's most important comic playwright was Fabre d'Eglantine, secretary and confidant of Danton and member of the National Convention. The playwright François de Neufchâteau was compelled to renounce this vocation before the Revolution in order to marry (his in-laws thought the theater was too shameful a profession); during the Revolution he was elected to the Legislative Assembly, wrote a notorious stage adaptation of *Pamela,* and served as minister of the interior from 1797 to 1799. Olympe de Gouges is remembered now primarily as the author of the *Déclaration des droits de la femme et de la citoyenne,* but in her own lifetime she was known as much for her authorship of several plays as for her political activism. A key figure in the revolutionary army, Charles-Philippe Ronsin was also a playwright. This is only a short list of the numerous intersections of revolutionary theater and politics.[24]

Nineteenth- and early-twentieth-century French critics manifested a morbid fascination with the theater of the French Revolution. In essay after essay, in book after book, they expressed shock, horror, and disgust with the subject.[25] What so intrigued and appalled nineteenth-century critics was its alarmingly evident imbrication with the political life of the Revolution. Critical interest in the theater of the Revolution remained more lurid than aesthetic. But the belief in the essential mutual exclusivity of artistic production and mass, revolutionary political upheaval is not the province of reactionary cultural critics alone. No less an intellectual and moral force than Albert Camus commented on the French Revolution's artistic barrenness; ignoring Jacques-Louis David, Camus claimed that "the French Revolution gave birth to no artists, but only to a great journalist, Desmoulins, and to a clandestine writer, Sade."[26] Unlike Camus, however, whose condemnation is moral, philosophical, and humanitarian, earlier critics projected their most dire social fears onto the revolutionary theater: for them it marked the invasion of high culture by the furies, the harpies, and the brutes of the lower orders. The revolutionary theater meant the destruction of France's greatest cultural achievements. The uneducated masses could not appreciate the refinements of classical French theater and so demanded "pièces de circonstances" [timely plays] that would reflect their own cultural and political concerns. Since these concerns were low, they could not produce art. A typical critic insists that "le théâtre . . . vit alors de l'exploitation des instincts les plus bas de la multitude" [the theater lived off of the exploitation of the lowest instincts of the multitude].[27] Revolutionary theater, its critics have claimed, had no artistic value because it was a painfully limpid mirror of the circumstances that produced it and, as Edmond and Jules de Goncourt put it, "l'art est éternel, il n'a pas d'à propos" [art is eternal, it has no circumstances].[28]

Circumstances might have been odious to the Goncourt brothers, but they have been at the heart of literary criticism for the past twenty-five years. Yet even new developments in literary and cultural studies such as new historicism, cultural materialism, and the developing interest in popular culture have done little to alter the critical assessment of or inspire new scholarship about the revolutionary theater.[29] In her pioneering *Rehearsing the Revolution: Staging Marat's Death, 1793–1799,* Marie-Hélène Huet made theater a central concern. Huet's poststructuralist turn embraced the inseparability of politics and theater, history and art, that nineteenth-century critics had condemned. Following the deconstructionist dictum that there is "nothing outside of the text," Huet claims that revolutionary history itself was structured by the same codes that structure language and text.[30] Huet's interest in *Rehearsing the Revolution* is thus less in the theater than in what she sees as the theatricality of revolutionary politics. She argues that revolutionary political practices were in fact modeled on theater and that the theater itself became absorbed and determined by politics. But Huet's interpretation of revolutionary culture largely omits both a reading of the revolutionary plays themselves and an examination of actual practices and conditions in revolutionary theaters. For Huet the real drama of the Revolution was to be found in the National Assembly: the theater is an empty rhetorical figure, and the plays themselves figure little.

Throughout this book I contend that we can understand the revolutionary theater only through a close reading of plays in relation to the conditions of their production and the manner of their reception. For although the theater was indeed deeply connected to revolutionary politics, it was so important and so influential because of its independent operations, not because it passively served a totalized and totalizing political authority. The revolutionary theater, unlike representative political institutions, was a place in which representation and direct participation were entirely compatible. In the theater, spectators retained the right to approve or disapprove, actively and explicitly, of the representations before them. This was a right that revolutionary audiences had to win and to enforce, and the successful battle to establish and maintain audience supremacy in the theater is central to the Revolution's literary, cultural, and political history. Indeed, because the theater structured the relation between the subject and object of representation so differently from representative political institutions, it can be considered a rival to revolutionary government. Throughout the Revolution there were moments of convergence and sympathy between political movements and theater, but even as representative political institutions gained strength, the theater constituted a powerful point of resistance to the totalization of culture by the regime of political representation. Moreover, far from unitary and homogeneous, the theater of the Revolution was itself full of division and difference, movement and mutation.

Our aesthetic values and generic preferences have changed significantly over the course of the last two centuries; as a result, the post-Racinian French theater has, for the most part, disappeared from the canon and failed to find a place in our collective literary frame of reference. Voltaire for us is a great ironist and the virtuoso of the philosophical tale; Voltaire for the eighteenth century was France's greatest tragic playwright. In the late eighteenth century there was still nearly universal agreement that theater was the highest form of literary art. Furthermore, there was still a nearly universal consensus both that the French theater was superior to all others and that the theater demonstrated France's broader cultural supremacy. Thus, for example, the report commissioned by the Commune of Paris in the fall of 1789 on the theaters of the capital asserted proudly that Paris "renferme dans son sein les premiers théâtres de l'Europe, et nous pouvons dire de l'Univers, Paris, dépositaire des chefs-d'œuvre qui servent de modèles aux étrangers" [contains within it the foremost theaters of Europe, and we could say of the Universe, Paris, the guardian of masterpieces that serve as exemplars for foreigners].[31] At the same time, however, *before* the advent of the Revolution this belief that French theater, and by extension French culture, was unparalleled in the world was balanced by an equally widespread sense that the theater had undergone a severe decline. Jean-François Cailhava begins his 1772 tract *Les Causes de la décadence du théâtre, et les moyens de le faire refleurir* (Causes of the Theater's Decline and the Means to Make It Flourish Again) with a boast similar to that of the Commune's report, but his tone quickly changes:

> Le théâtre français, ce théâtre, l'objet de l'admiration et de la jalousie des nations policées; ce théâtre qui contribua si bien à porter la langue française dans tous les pays où l'on sait lire; ce théâtre enfin que les étrangers veulent voir chez eux, ou qu'ils tâchent d'imiter, est aujourd'hui sacrifié au mauvais goût dans le sein de cette même capitale où il a pris naissance.
>
> Nos voisins, corrigés par nos bons modèles et enrichis des traductions ou des imitations de nos meilleures pièces, sont étonnés de nous voir ramasser chez eux les rapsodies, les extravagances que nos anciens chefs-d'œuvre leur apprirent à mépriser.[32]

> [The French theater, that theater, the object of the admiration and the jealousy of civilized nations; the theater that contributed so powerfully in bringing the French language to all literate countries; that theater in short that foreigners want to see in their countries, or that they try to imitate, is sacrificed today to bad taste in the bosom of the very capital in which it was born.
>
> Our neighbors, corrected by our good examples and enriched by translations or imitations of our best plays, are astonished to see us picking up from them the rhapsodies and eccentricities that our former masterpieces taught them to disdain.]

The theater is, in this account, at once the greatest source of national pride and the sign that France's cultural power was waning. Despite the tendency of commentators on the sorry state of French theater to egg their readers on with references to the fact that the barbaric English had two major theaters in London while the French had only one, their concerns are aesthetic and social as well as nationalist.[33] Cailhava was far from alone in his concern about "bad taste"; the only question for many was whether the public's bad taste had caused the theater to degenerate or whether a degenerated theater had corrupted the public's taste.

Because theater was thought to have an overwhelmingly powerful influence on the morals and manners of society, bad theater signaled a more generalized social and moral corruption. It is not surprising, therefore, that in the immediate wake of the Bastille's fall—the signal that the Old Regime had ended and that a new era was to begin—a large number of tracts and reports about the theater quickly appeared. Along with a new edition of Cailhava's treatise and the report of the commissioners came a flood that included *Discours et motions sur les spectacles* (1789); Framéry's *De l'organisation des spectacles à Paris* (1790); Jean-François de La Harpe's *Discours sur la liberté des théâtres* (1790); Aubin-Louis Millin de Grandmaison's *Sur la liberté du théâtre* (1790); Quatremère de Quincy's *Discours prononcé a l'assemblée de la Commune sur la liberté des théâtres* (1790); and Sauvigny's *Du Théâtre sous les rapports de la nouvelle constitution* (1790). The question of the civil status of actors also emerged quickly; under the Old Regime they were considered legally *infâme,* and because they were condemned by the Church, they were unable to marry or receive Christian burial (the only real, available option) unless they had time to renounce their profession before their death.[34] With the advent of liberty, with the opportunity to regenerate France and the French people, came the possibility and the necessity to regenerate French theater—to make it worthy of the new nation and worthy to form its citizens.

At the dawn of the Revolution, then, the theater was in a paradoxical situation: it was both France's most prestigious literary form and most celebrated cultural achievement, yet it was also, according to most contemporary commentators, a grotesque shadow of its former glory. Nearly all writers on the subject believed that the key to revitalizing the theater was freedom: freedom from the monopolies that had kept new theaters from opening; freedom for the writers to retain rights over their own plays and to decide where they would be performed; and freedom for actors to become full members of French society. But the freedom sought by those who worked in the theater was not only legal and entrepreneurial; it was also aesthetic. Actors, authors, and critics wanted freedom from the oppressive rules that had placed so much subject matter beyond their reach. If theater had become trivial, if it had ceased to move the spectator, it was because playwrights could not treat contemporary social and political subjects. The inextricability of theater and politics thus meant something different to contemporaries of the Revolution than it did to later critics. Whereas nineteenth-century critics believed that theater's artistic substance was nullified when it took up political or even modern historical themes and problems, both critics and playwrights of the revolutionary period thought that the theater's undeniable decay in the eighteenth century had resulted from the interdiction on any topical material. The theater could not be a vital cultural institution, they asserted, if it could not treat real cultural concerns. Thus, for example, Millin de Grandmaison explained:

> La tragédie doit enseigner les grandes vérités politiques, et les vertus publiques. Les auteurs tragiques sont donc obligés, s'ils veulent exprimer une idée forte, de tourmenter leur génie pour la couvrir du voile de l'allégorie. . . . Si malgré toutes ces précautions la pièce présente encore des rapprochements trop aisé à faire, des allusions trop faciles à saisir, il est défendu aux comédiens de la jouer, et au public de l'entendre.[35]

> [Tragedy should teach great political truths and public virtues. If they want to express a powerful idea, tragic authors are therefore obliged to torment their genius, to cloak their idea with the veil of allegory. . . . If despite all these precautions the play still presents connections that are too easy to make, or allusions too readily grasped, the actors are forbidden to perform it and the public is forbidden to hear it.]

When the author here expresses the urge to lift the veil, to remove that which obstructs truth and beauty, he is employing a trope that was nearly ubiquitous in revolutionary discourse. That the veil in this case is allegory, a classically approved mode of literary representation, is particularly noteworthy. What had in the past appeared to be art, Millin claims, is in fact the deformation of artistic vision and artistic genius. The more artificial, stiff, or far-fetched the allegory, as perhaps had increasingly been demanded by a nervous state, the less aesthetically valid and affecting the art. Taking up the issues of the day enriched rather than impoverished the theater. Thus, while critics of revolutionary theater have often seen it as an entirely subservient tool of revolutionary government, Millin charges Old Regime theater with that stigma. Under the Old Regime, not the new, Millin claims, "on n'ose y [sur la scène] débiter que des leçons d'une morale usée et commune; la soumission aveugle au despotisme des rois y est réduite en principes et fortifiées par des exemples" [one dares (on the stage) only to mouth the precepts of a used-up and common-place morality; blind submission to the despotism of kings is reduced to principle and fortified by examples].[36] According to Millin the monarchy's desire to forestall all possible criticism led inexorably to a decline in the *quality* of the theater. Millin, along with countless critics and authors, believed that the Revolution would allow them to renew the French theater.

The theatrical world Emmet Kennedy reconstructs would have sorely disappointed Millin.[37] Kennedy suggests that the theater was relatively impervious to real change: many plays from Old Regime repertories continued to be performed, and many plays lacking explicitly revolutionary titles won the favor of audiences. He points out that the Revolution did not produce great formal innovations in the theater: classical models persisted. According to this account the theater should be considered a conservative force that merely provided a diversion from the difficulties and anxieties of revolutionary life. It is certainly true that many classics of the French stage, most notably plays by Molière, continued to enjoy frequent performances, but since Kennedy does not examine how they were received by audiences, we do not know whether or how spectators interpreted these plays in relation to their own experiences. Moreover, the fact that more than one thousand new plays were written during the 1790s must register an effect of the Revolution on the theater. Kennedy is right to note that a great many of these plays do not seem to have explicitly political subjects, although of course many did treat contemporary political and military events.

That Kennedy bases his analysis of theater's revolutionary content on play titles alone begins to suggest how narrowly he defines the political: he seeks to classify plays as either monarchist or republican. But even such a classification would depend on something more than the titles of plays. Revolutionary politics cannot be so strictly circumscribed. The Revolution was a cultural phenomenon; long before transforming France into a republic in 1792, the Revolution had begun a transformation of French culture that is inseparable from its political transformation. Revolutionary plays participated, not necessarily in a programmatic way, in the creation of this new culture and its new values. Thus, for example, a play called *Le Mari coupable* (The Guilty Husband) (1792) explores the problem of marital infidelity, perhaps one of the least historically specific themes available, but it portrays the distress caused by adultery with new social values in mind.[38] Dorfeuil, the "guilty husband," sees the error of his ways not when he recognizes the pain he has caused his virtuous and loving wife but when his daughter refuses to marry her fiancé (despite the fact that she loves him) because she fears that her marriage will inevitably follow the pattern established by her father. Dorfeuil comes to see that he has put the future of the new social order in jeopardy by undermining marriage; his personal transgression has important ramifications for the production of a new French society. Moreover, rather than condemning Adèle, the object of the guilty husband's extramarital amorous adventure who has just become a *fille-mère*, the play stresses the importance of addressing the situation of the wronged girl. The unwed mother must not be marginalized in secrecy and deception but must be brought back into the new society, which draws its strength from the participation of every one of its citizens. When Dorfeuil's friend Dumon learns of the situation, he decides to marry or adopt Adèle depending on her wishes: "Le malheur avilit l'âme; et qui se méprise est bien près de devenir méprisable. Rendons à la société une femme aimable; ne privons point la République d'une mère de famille qui peut lui donner encore de défenseurs" (2.3). [Misfortune abases the soul; and he who has contempt for himself runs the risk of becoming contemptible. Let us return a woman worthy of love to society; let us not deprive the Republic of a mother who can give it more protectors.] And when Dorfeuil, himself the agent of Adèle's disgrace, questions Dumon about the shame attached to marrying a fornicator and an unwed mother, Dumon replies by taking a leaf from Rousseau's *Nouvelle Héloise*: "Des préjugés. Je saurai les combattre. Adèle fille, amante, a pu s'oublier; Adèle épouse et mère saura se respecter" (2.3). [Prejudices. I can combat them. Adèle, the girl and the lover was capable of forgetting herself; Adèle, the wife and mother will know how to respect herself.] *Le Mari coupable* shows that in the new world of the Republic society needs every single one of its members because, unlike a monarchy, a republic is nothing other than its citizens. Thus, for reasons that are both practical (the Republic needs defenders, and Adèle can produce them) and moral (Adèle should not suffer for having been a trusting, too-loving dupe; social regulations that would require such ostracism are barbaric), no one with a good heart is to be excluded.

This play is not political in the narrow sense: it does not advocate a politician, party, or position; it does not recount or comment on current events. Yet it is undoubtedly revolutionary in the sense that it registers and expresses a distinctly revolutionary social sensibility: it portrays a specifically revolutionary conception of marriage and the family and of the relation between the home and the state. The ways in which theaters, plays, and audiences participated in and helped create revolutionary culture cannot be construed within a framework that restricts them to a preestablished dichotomy of political/nonpolitical or republican/monarchist. Even Kennedy's interesting point about the lack of formal innovation in the revolutionary theater should be reconsidered within a less absolute frame of reference. It is true that the rules of the classical theater continued to structure high comedy and tragedy; these plays were still written, mostly if not exclusively, in five acts and in verse. The unities of time, place, and action were not abandoned. Yet the influx of new subject matter, much of which would have been unacceptable according to the *bienséances*—the rules of propriety that governed classical theater and that, for example, forbade the representation of a death or a kiss onstage—could be seen as producing a kind of formal development. The crumbling of the Old Regime's ban on the representation of modern history, similarly, could be seen as more than simply the introduction of a new thematic. As we will see in chapter four, one of the most surprising developments in revolutionary theater was the rapid growth of the *drame* (drama), of plays like *Le Mari coupable.* The drame was the mixed genre, theorized and championed by Diderot at midcentury, that depicted seriously the familial crises of ordinary people; its expansion certainly speeded up formal as well as thematic (and social) change in the theater and led, among other things, to the birth of melodrama.[39] Even when adhering to the system of classical rules, authors could understand themselves to be doing something radically new; thus, as we will see in chapter 2, Fabre d'Eglantine's project was to recreate high comedy by detheatricalizing it. A new antitheatrical comedy, he hoped, would reconfigure the relation between spectator and spectacle and, by way of this aesthetic reformation, would reassert comedy's social mission.

I am not arguing that the theater of the French Revolution was great art and should be valued as such.[40] I do intend, however, to show that it was often ambitious, if aesthetically deficient, art. Playwrights, actors, and audiences of the Revolution were intensely serious about the theater, and despite our often contemptuous treatment of its works, theater was revolutionary France's preeminent cultural form. The Revolution did not take writers, actors, or audiences away from the theater; it threw them more eagerly and excitedly into it. We must take seriously authors' and actors' aesthetic *ambitions* as well as audience desires and expectations if we are to understand the relation between art and politics during the French Revolution.

Whatever the subject matter of the plays—whether explicitly political or far distant from contemporary concerns—the revolutionary theaters remained raucous, activist sites of participation for ordinary people. Indeed, revolutionary audiences bore no resemblance to the silent, pacified, determined gatherings evoked by Huet. On the contrary, early in the Revolution Parisian theater audiences wrested control of the theaters away both from government authorities and from actors, directors, and writers. Audiences frequently violently interrupted and halted performances of plays they did not like and equally insistently demanded the performance of plays that had not been announced. Thus, even when the play demanded by spectators could be seen as antirepublican or antirevolutionary, the audience actions showed that the theater itself was in fact democratic. For the people in the audience decided what would be performed and what would not; to be successful, representation in the theater required the audience members' explicit, active assent. The fundamentally democratic economy of representation in the theater was central to its relation to the newly forming revolutionary political institutions that were based on a very different relation between representative and represented. I argue that the theater and representative political institutions embodied two distinct, often antagonistic, modes of representation. The story of the revolutionary theater therefore illuminates the contested history of what is now the hegemonic organization of modern politics—political representation—at the very moment of its coming into being.

1 Resisting Representation
Theater and Democracy in Revolutionary France

Qu'on juge cependant de l'embarras que causait quelque fois
la foule par ce qui arriva du temps des gracques, où une partie
des citoyens donnait son suffrage de dessus les toits.
Jean-Jacques Rousseau, Du Contrat social, *book 3, chapter 15*

As president of the National Convention during the tense days of Louis XVI's trial, Bertrand Barère faced the unenviable task of quieting the boisterous citizens in the observation galleries: "Je rappelle aux citoyens que c'est ici une sorte de solennité funèbre. Les applaudissements et les murmures sont défendus." [I remind the citizens that there must be a funereal solemnity here. Applause and murmurs are forbidden.] But the citizens were irrepressible, and Barère warned them that the law required their silence: "le règlement, qui est la volonté générale, défend tout signe d'approbation et d'improbation" [the regulation, which is the general will, prohibits all signs of approbation and disapprobation].[1] Barère understood the audience's "applause and murmurs" not merely as breeches of decorum—of "funereal solemnity"—but as significations of judgment, of "approbation" and "disapprobation." Barère's invocation of the general will reminded the citizens in the galleries that because the deputies, not they, embodied the will of the French people, such signs of judgment were illicit. By insistently expressing their own will in the presence of those who claimed the authority to express it for them, the citizens mounted something like a resistance to political representation. In the face of this resistance Barère could only expostulate in vain: "Silence! laissons les applaudisse-ments aux théâtres." [Silence! Leave the applause for the theater.][2]

The codified constraints on gallery participation were continuous with a wider enterprise of institutionalizing a structure of representational relations in which the people, having delegated the exercise of their sovereign power to their representatives, were subsumed by representation. But the gallery's articu-late interference in the Convention's proceedings and the deputies' under-standably anxious reaction reveal that representative politics was far from firmly established. Throughout the Revolution, as the Convention's records amply demonstrate, the encouragements, insults, and threats shouted daily from the galleries effectively ratified, amended, and vetoed the deputies' decisions. Pres-sure from the galleries could bring the legislators to quick decisions. For ex-ample, the unfortunate deputy Pierre Manuel proposed that, in order to ensure all citizens equal access to the Convention galleries, free tickets be distributed in advance. The citizens present, fearful that Manuel was trying to "pack" the galleries, began to chant "à l'Abbaye Manuel, à l'Abbaye l'aristocrate Manuel" [to the Abbaye (prison), to the Abbaye with the aristocrat Manuel].[3] The Con-vention, unsurprisingly, decided not to entertain Manuel's proposal.

Barère's fruitless exchange with the observing public reveals a fundamental struggle over representation at the heart of revolutionary political culture. Al-though recent scholarship has paid a good deal of attention to the develop-ment of the theory and the institutionalization of political representation dur-ing the Revolution, there has been relatively little study of the cultural significance of this development or of the cultural value of the struggle be-tween direct and representative democracy.[4] François Furet has famously claimed that revolutionary culture was defined by the struggle to determine who would occupy the position of representative: "Politics was a matter of es-tablishing just *who* represented the people, or equality, or the nation; victory was in the hands of those who were capable of occupying and keeping that symbolic position."[5] But even Furet seems to operate on the assumption that the practice of representation was unproblematic, that the concept of repre-sentation was, and remains, stable.[6] For revolutionary politicians, playwrights, and citizens, however, the very structure of representation constituted a deeply complex and troubling problem. Revolutionary culture as a whole was signif-icantly shaped by a political and cultural activism that can be understood as resistance to representation or as an attempt to reform and reconfigure the re-lations instituted by representation.

My purpose in this chapter is to recover representation as a central problematic not only in revolutionary politics but in revolutionary culture as a whole. The revolutionary theater was a vital site in the unfolding of that problematic. For Barère's allusion to the theater was intensely motivated: within the theater, audiences developed a distinctly popular conception of the legitimate relationship between the representative and the represented. In the theater, unlike in the National Convention, representation was entirely compatible with direct public participation. Energetic displays of approbation and disapprobation—often taking the form of riots and pitched battles rather than applause and murmurs—demonstrated audiences' determination that they and they alone retain immediate governing authority over representation in the theater. Parisian audiences were often successful: they frequently forced authors and actors to capitulate to their will.

The story of the revolutionary theater illuminates more than theatrical history. The economy of representation audiences institutionalized in the theater posed both a theoretical and a practical challenge to political representation. The bourgeois understanding of political representation, as Albert Soboul has termed it, entailed the effective absence of the represented; by contrast, according to what I am calling the popular conception, representative politics could only be legitimate when, as in the theater, the citizens themselves exercised immediate supervision, regulation, and control over representation.[7] The battle to maintain popular authority in the theater often brought audiences into direct conflict with elected municipal and national officials. Such resistance constituted an attempt to put the popular theory of representation into practice.

My account of revolutionary theatrical culture and its relation to political culture departs radically from two recent influential approaches to the Revolution: the "theatrical interpretation" elaborated by Marie-Hélène Huet and other literary critics and cultural historians, and the Habermasian interpretation developed by Roger Chartier and other historians. Barère's distinction between the theater and the National Convention poses obvious problems for those critics who argue that theatrical representation provided the model for revolutionary politics. Huet's *Rehearsing the Revolution* introduced such an approach by arguing that Louis' trial reveals the homology between theater and revolutionary politics: in the trial, she claims, "we are indeed within the register of the theater" because "the material organization" of the proceedings—"the public, the stage, the loges, the ushers, the galleries"—is identical to the material organization of a theater.[8] Following Huet's lead, other scholars have posited a wholly theatricalized revolution: "the stage was no longer

confined to the theater," according to Scott S. Bryson, "but was found throughout society, at the tribunal, in the National Assembly, on the executioner's
block."[9]

According to the theatricalists, politicians discovered in the theater a model
for forming and controlling the subject: the Revolution made politics into theater, Huet argues, in order to make the people into an audience that could be
disciplined and repressed "by means of the spectacle."[10] At the same time, the
revolutionary government transformed the theaters themselves into "schools
of the revolution," instruments devoted to the dissemination of revolutionary
ideology.[11] But far from conceiving of the theatrical public as a model of de-
sirable passivity, Barère compares the public in the Convention to a theater audience not when it is silent and servile but when it is most riotous and
demanding. Even that comparison, rather than revealing a deep structural
similarity, registers a difference. For Barère bases his distinction between the
two institutions on the different status each assigned to the exercise of popular judgment. In the Convention the expression of popular sentiment was unacceptable, and popular judgments were illegitimate. By contrast, the theater,
Barère implies, was a forum in which spectators might signify their approval
or disapproval of the representations before them.

Barère's construction of the theater as a privileged site for the expression of
public judgment also calls into question the appropriateness of applying Habermas's public sphere model to the study of revolutionary political culture.[12] For
central to that model is a contrast between a "public" that expresses critical
opinions and judgments in writing and a "people" that, incapable of expressing
itself in writing, is excluded from the production of opinion and the expression of judgment.[13] The opposition between "public" and "people" is paral-
leled by one between books and theater: books form the opinions of the literate, critical public; theater seduces and deceives the illiterate, gullible people.

Habermas's privileging of writing reveals a set of values peculiar to eighteenth-
century literary-political discourse. Writing is the constitutive medium of the
Habermasian public sphere because writing allows ideas to be presented inde-
pendently of the persons who authored them. Disjoined from the personal
power of their authors and circulated freely, texts and ideas could be judged
wholly on their own merits. Texts were to be judged by a public whose authority emanated from its literary-critical capacities rather than its social or
political power. In this way the value of ideas would be calibrated neither to
the social status of those who put them forward nor to that of those who

weighed them. If all people were not equal in Old Regime France, at least through the medium of the public sphere, all ideas articulated in print could, in theory, be given equal opportunity. Defined above all by the separation of ideas from persons, Habermas's eighteenth-century public sphere in no way evokes the crowded public forum of the ancients that inspired the antirepresentational Rousseau. Habermas's public sphere makes the mediation of representation the condition of cultural agency: because intervention in the public sphere can be made only through written representations, the public sphere, paradoxically, was composed of readers and writers who characteristically could be found in the semiprivacy of the salon or the isolation of their "cabinets." To be present in the public sphere, one had, in a sense, to be absent from it.

Habermas himself, unlike many of those who have been influenced by him, recognizes that conceiving of the public sphere as constructed by writing necessarily places certain limits on his enterprise: he makes clear that he is tracing the genealogy of a liberal ideology and not an objective history. Thus, Habermas points out that the French Revolution falls outside the limits of his model: "Thus it [*The Structural Transformation*] refers to those features of a historical constellation that attained dominance and leaves aside the *plebeian* public sphere as a variant that in a sense was suppressed in the historical process. In the stage of the French Revolution associated with Robespierre, for just one moment, a public sphere stripped of its literary garb began to function—its subject was no longer the 'educated strata' but the uneducated 'people.' "[14] In this chapter I examine the "plebeian public sphere" that enjoyed such a brief existence but that left so profound a trace. But I do not understand this public sphere to be exactly "stripped of its literary garb"—a figure, by the way, that tellingly evokes the revolutionary language of unveiling I will discuss in chapter 3; instead, I believe that this "variant" public sphere can best be revealed and understood by way of its *relation* to the literary.

Constructing representation *as* agency simultaneously effaces the masses of ordinary people from revolutionary culture and obscures the Revolution's defining struggle between direct and representative democracy. By reducing participation in the public sphere to writing, the Habermasian public-sphere model excludes the people, as it conceives them, from meaningful social agency. By constructing the people as wholly subjected—that is, determined— by theatrical representation, Huet elides the very notion of popular agency. But the very people whose agency is obviated in these two interpretations demanded and secured the freedom of theatrical performance that established the theater—rather than a virtual community of readers and writers—as a crucial institution for the production of revolutionary culture. Throughout the Revolution audiences insisted tenaciously that popular judgment was the supreme authority in the theater. I want to explore two consequences of the people's sovereign authority in the theater, one political, the other dramatic. First, because theatrical representation, unlike political representation, was thoroughly subject to direct popular control, the theater constituted, and was widely perceived as, an embodiment of direct democracy and, hence, an alternative to and potential rival of representative political institutions. Second, the people's central role in the theater is reflected in and helped to shape a distinct genre of revolutionary drama: the drama of popular judgment.

Plays versus Print

From the first heady days of the summer of 1789 through the autumn of 1790, *Charles IX, ou l'École des rois* (Charles IX, or the School for Kings), a tragedy in five acts by Marie-Joseph Chénier, was the focal point of what was perhaps the Revolution's greatest debate over freedom of expression.[15] Playwrights, actors, politicians, and journalists joined the battle on both sides: opponents argued that *Charles IX* posed a grave danger to public order; proponents replied that it would produce only the most salutary effects. This dispute had nothing to do with freedom of the press: Chénier was engaged in a long and bitter campaign not to *publish* his play but to have it *performed.* Many notable foes of *Charles IX* were champions of freedom of the press, but this was a controversy over freedom of the theater, a freedom that many revolutionaries and reformers alike were more chary of granting.

Cultural historians inspired by Habermas—with their overriding commitment to the power of print to create revolutionary culture—have either neglected the struggle over *Charles IX* or misconstrued it as a struggle to secure a free press.[16] But Chénier fought vigorously for *Charles IX* because he believed that the freedom of the French people—that the success of the Revolution—was incomplete even though a free press had been established. In a speech delivered before the new Paris municipal government Chénier argued:

> Le peuple français veut être libre, et vous avouerez qu'il en est digne. Tout homme libre doit pouvoir publier sa pensée, de quelque manière que ce soit. . . . Vainement voudrait-on établir une différence entre la presse et le théâtre. Une pièce de théâtre est un moyen de publier sa pensée. Tout homme libre, je le répète, doit pouvoir publier sa pensée.[17]

[The French people want to be free, and you concede that they are worthy of freedom. Every free man must be able to make his thought public in whatever manner he chooses. . . . Those who want to establish a distinction between the press and the theater do so in vain. A play is a means of making one's thought public. Every free man, I repeat, must be able to make his thought public.]

Elsewhere Chénier insisted that there could be no freedom of thought in a nation that restricted the theater's freedom of expression:

Lorsque cette nation, lasse d'être avilie, veut ressaisir des droits imprescriptibles, elle doit commencer par secouer ces entraves ridicules qu'on donne à l'esprit des citoyens. Alors il devient permis de publier ses pensées, sous toutes les formes possibles. Il ne faut pas s'imaginer qu'on pense librement chez une nation ou le théâtre est encore soumis à des lois arbitraires.[18]

[When this nation, tired of being degraded, wants to reclaim its imprescriptible rights, it must begin by lifting these ridiculous obstacles that have been placed before the minds of its citizens. Therefore, it becomes permissible to make public one's ideas in any possible form. One must not imagine that one thinks freely in a nation where the theater remains subject to arbitrary laws.]

This conjoining of freedom with the uninhibited public circulation of thought might appear entirely consistent with the Habermasian account of publicity, but Chénier was in fact opposing a culturally sanctioned distinction between books and plays that Chartier and other historians reproduce. Chénier did not believe that plays mystified while books enlightened; on the contrary, he understood print and performance to be two different modes of publicity. Different, but not equal: Chénier wanted the freedoms already granted to the press to be extended to the theater because he considered the theater a far more powerful forum for the development of public opinion. Thus Chénier explained that he was moved to write tragedies instead of books by "une persuasion intime que nulle espèce d'ouvrage ne peut avoir autant d'influence sur l'esprit public" (ibid., 145–146) [a deeply felt belief that no other type of literary work can have so great an influence on the public spirit]. By contrast, Chénier placed little faith in the power of books to shape their readers:

Un livre, quelque bon qu'il soit, ne saurait agir sur l'esprit public d'une manière aussi prompte, aussi vigoureuse qu'une belle pièce de théâtre. Des scènes d'un grand sens, des pensées lumineuses, des vérités de sentiment, exprimées en vers harmonieux, se gravent aisément dans la tête de la plupart des spectateurs. . . . Toutes nos idées viennent de nos sens; mais l'homme isolé n'est ému que médiocrement: les hommes rassemblés reçoivent les impressions fortes et durables. (ibid., 15–16)

[A book, no matter how good it is, cannot act on the public spirit in as prompt or vigorous a manner as a beautiful play. Scenes of great meaning, luminous thoughts, true sentiments, expressed in harmonious verses, impress themselves easily on the minds of most spectators. All our ideas come from our senses, but an isolated man is only somewhat moved: when they are assembled men receive strong and lasting impressions.]

Theater, unlike books, acted immediately on the senses; for some critics this meant that theater was inherently a dangerous, deceptive art that appealed to the animal rather than the rational qualities of its spectators. By contrast, Chénier makes use of the well-established, respectable, sensationalist philosophy of his day—a philosophy that understood mental phenomena as having a fundamentally physical origin in the senses—to adduce theater's direct relation to the senses as evidence of its intellectual power.[19] He thus turns on its head one of the traditional accusations made against the theater: the charge that theater is a less elevated form of art because it addresses the senses directly—for if "all our ideas come from our senses," then an art that stimulates the senses will excite the intellect.

The theater's effect on the emotional and sensory experience of the spectator was heightened and deepened by the presence of other audience members—that is, by the fact that theater was experienced in and with a public. Again and again, Chénier emphasized the primal sensibility of human beings and tied this sensibility to theater's moral efficacy:

L'homme est essentiellement sensible. Le poète dramatique, en peignant les passions, dirige celles du spectateur. Un sourire qui nous échappe en écoutant une pièce comique, ou, dans l'éloquente tragédie, les pleurs que nous sentons couler de nos yeux, suffisent pour nous faire *sentir* une *vérité*, que l'auteur d'un traité morale nous aurait longuement démontrée. Ajouté que notre sensibilité, et même nos lumières sont infiniment augmentées par celles de nos semblables qui nous environnent. ("De la liberté du théâtre," 138; emphasis added)

[Man is essentially sensitive. The dramatic poet, by painting passions, directs those of the spectator. The smile that escapes us while we listen to a comedy, or the tears that we feel falling from our eyes in an eloquent tragedy, suffice to make us *feel* a *truth* that the author of a treatise on morality would demonstrate to us at length. Add to this that our sensibility, and even our intellect, are infinitely enlarged by those of our fellow men who surround us.]

On the other hand, books, which are experienced in isolation and act on the senses in a much more mediated fashion, exert far weaker effects:

Un livre dispersé dans les cabinets parvient à faire lentement une multitude d'impressions différentes, mais toujours isolées, mais presque toujours exempts d'enthousiasme. La sensation que fait éprouver à deux mille personnes rassemblées au théâtre-français, la représentation d'un excellent ouvrage dramatique, est rapide, ardente, unanime. (ibid., 138–139)[20]

[A book dispersed in cabinets slowly manages to make a multitude of different impressions, but they are isolated and almost always exempt of enthusiasm. The sensation that an excellent dramatic work can impart to two thousand people assembled at the Théâtre-Français is rapid, ardent, and unanimous.]

Theater was distinct from print culture, then, because it was experienced immediately, emotionally, and collectively. The product of experience in the theater was therefore unanimity, and the sentiments shared were of singular intensity. Theater, according to Chénier, was able to do something print could not; it could forge communities of sentiment. Sentiment, on these terms, as throughout much Enlightenment writing, cannot be seen as opposing rational public opinion; on the contrary, as Luc Boltanski has proposed, sentiment was crucial to the development of the reasoned public discourse that weighed the ethical and political issues of the day.[21] As we will see in chapter 2, sentiment was a key element in the formation of republican moral philosophy.

Because the theater could powerfully move a large assembly, Chénier and his allies believed that it was the single most important institution for the formation of public opinion. The distinguished playwright, critic, and member of the Académie française Jean-François La Harpe, for example, argued that

de tous les lieux ou les hommes se rassemblent, il n'en est aucun ou la communication des sentiments soit plus rapide, plus efficace, plus contagieuse. Comme on n'y va que pour être ému, l'âme toute remplie de ce besoin d'émotions s'ouvre de tout côté pour les recevoir ou pour les répandre; elles s'accroissent en se réunissant; elles s'exaltent, et par leur propre expression, et par celle des autres: on entraîne ou on est entraîné; bientôt toutes les voix ne font qu'un cri, tous les mouvements ne font qu'une impulsion; toutes les affections morales, ou spontanément émues, ou impérieusement assujetties, forment à grand bruit une vaste explosion. C'est là, certes, c'est là que s'élève dans toute sa force la voix dominatrice de l'opinion.[22]

[of all the places where men gather, there is no other in which the communication of sentiments is more rapid, more efficacious, more contagious. Since one goes there expressly to be moved, the soul, full of that need for emotion, opens itself on all sides to receive feelings or to radiate them; they expand as they unite; they are exalted by their own expression and by the expression of others; one leads or one is led. Soon all voices make only one cry, all movements are only one impulse, all moral sentiments, whether spontaneously moved or imperiously subjugated, make a vast explosion. It is there, certainly, it is there that the dominating voice of opinion arises in all its force.]

La Harpe, like Chénier, celebrates the theater's capacity to reshape a multitude of individual spectators into a single public body. And, even more forcefully than Chénier, La Harpe points out that the primary locus of action—of the creation of feeling and opinion—is not the stage but the audience. The theater's capacity to produce unanimity and consensus depends on immediacy and publicness, on the *presence* of the audience members to each other.

Theater, its supporters maintained, would produce more powerfully and more pervasively the very effects attributed to reading by those who insisted on the primacy of print. The respectable man of letters and advocate of freedom of the theater A. L. Millin de Grandmaison offered the relationship between Greek theater and Greek cultural superiority as a case in point:

Pourquoi le peuple d'Athènes, qui n'avait pas la faculté de lire, parce que l'imprimerie n'existait pas, et les copies des manuscrits coûtaient trop chers, était-il le peuple le plus poli et parlait-il un langage si épuré? C'est qu'il se formait aux théâtres, où tous les citoyens sans distinction était admis dans les fêtes publiques, où les grands poètes et les grands historiens récitaient leurs belles compositions, et disputaient les prix; et dans les places publiques où il entendait l'éloquence, tantôt douce, tantôt foudroyante de ses orateurs.[23]

[Why is it that the people of Athens, who could not read because the printing press did not exist and manuscripts cost too much, were the most civilized of peoples and spoke the purest language? It is because they were formed in the theaters, where all citizens, without distinction of rank, were admitted in the public festivals and where the great poets and the great historians recited their beautiful works and competed for prizes, as well as in the public squares where they heard the sometimes gentle, sometimes fulminating eloquence of their orators.]

Because theater held such a central place in Greek society, Millin argues, even illiterate Greeks were more refined and spoke a purer language than did the literate modern French. Hence, there is nothing inherent in print, according to Millin, that promotes the kind of reflection and cultivation claimed for it by its advocates.

Chénier's and La Harpe's accounts of public opinion imply an inversion of the Habermasian hierarchy of print and performance. Precisely those attributes that make reading the essential founding act in the constitution of the bourgeois public sphere for Habermas—that reading is an individual action, that it does not act on the senses, and that it therefore promotes detached judgments—attenuated reading's power for Chénier. Conversely, what makes theater the principal crucible of public opinion for Chénier and La Harpe—that it is a collective experience, that it acts powerfully on the emotions, and that it produces impassioned, immediate conviction—marks the theater as the antithesis of the Habermasian public sphere.

In Roger Chartier's effort to revise our understanding of the relation between the Enlightenment and the Revolution—perhaps the longest-standing problem in revolutionary historiography—he turns to Habermas's model. The benefit of Habermas's analysis, according to Chartier, is that it helps us turn from the question of the Revolution's intellectual origins to a study of its cultural origins.[24] To understand the evolution of the eighteenth century and its revolutionary conclusion, Chartier proposes that we must recognize that the structures and practices of the Enlightenment rather than the content of Enlightenment ideas lent the era its revolutionary potential. The most important cultural innovation of the eighteenth century was the literate public sphere, and its most important practice, indeed its constitutive practice, was reading. Thus Chartier's Habermasian interpretation of revolutionary culture makes writing responsible for the production of the public sphere and the public sphere responsible for the Revolution. In a gentle critique of Chartier, Robert Darnton suggests that despite his new emphasis on culture instead of ideas, Chartier nonetheless attributes the Revolution to "especially the influence of literature on the development of what Jürgen Habermas would call the 'bourgeois public sphere.' "[25]

In a chapter entitled "Do Books Make Revolutions?" Chartier considers the argument that writing "is endowed with such power that it is capable of totally transforming readers and making them into what the texts envisage," an argument he locates in the works of three great historians of the French Revolution—Alexis de Tocqueville, Hippolyte Taine, and Daniel Mornet."[26] Chartier's reconsideration and revision of this view seeks to emphasize the active part taken by *readers* in relation to texts. Thus in the course of studying Tocqueville, Taine, and Mornet he "reserve[s] the right to express a few doubts along the way" (ibid.). Yet Chartier's argument that the eighteenth century witnessed a "reading revolution"—a change in reading practices by which readers wrested the power to read texts critically rather than deferentially—ultimately reaffirms the cultural primacy of print; the difference is that, according to Chartier's account, books are of chief importance because only in relation to books can the reader construct his or her critical capacities.

Thus, Chartier, despite the novelty of his approach, attributes the Revolution to the power of reading and writing, just as did his predecessors. Although Chartier does not exactly agree with his "guides" that "the French of the late eighteenth-century fashioned the Revolution . . . because they had in turn been fashioned by books" (ibid.), ultimately he endows reading with even more power than do his interlocutors. When they argued that books made the Revolution, they meant to attribute the Revolution to the power of the *ideas* disseminated in books. For Chartier, by contrast, it is the practice of reading, rather than the content of reading, that proves so revolutionary. It is only by means of the critical appropriation of texts, through this new disrespectful reading, that revolutionary subjectivity can come into being. Consequently, if by virtue of their "literary inadequacy" the people were necessarily excluded from the public of readers and writers, as Chartier maintains, they must also have been barred from fashioning the Revolution (ibid., 22).[27] Thus the old-fashioned idea-centered interpretation of the Revolution's origins allows the literarily inadequate "people" a far greater potential for participation in revolutionary culture formation since ideas can be created and circulated in modes other than print.[28]

But *why*, finally, is reading, and hence writing, so overwhelmingly powerful? For Chartier the answer is that written expression presupposes the absence of the readerly audience: "printing thus made possible the constitution of a public realm that was unreliant on proximity—a community with no visible presence."[29] By contrast, Chartier argues, the theater was excluded from the public sphere because performance requires the presence of an audience. In the theater, "where the inexpensive places in the pit adjoined the boxes and where everyone had their own interpretation"—where, in other words, the spectators were present to one another—there was no public, only a multitude incompetent to form judgments. And because performance made ideas and emotions present in a physical, sensual form, the theatrical audience was "ensnared, held captive, and manipulated"; thus, for contemporaries these "spectators of the *theatrum mundi* in no way constituted a 'public opinion.'"[30]

Although Chartier excludes the theatrical public and dramatic performances from the public sphere, he includes plays within the ranks of texts. Hippolyte Taine, for example, in a passage Chartier cites, mentions the importance of Voltaire's *Oedipe* and Beaumarchais' *Tarare* to the development of "philosophy" and hence to the Revolution. *Oedipe,* of course, is a play and *Tarare* an opera, yet Chartier assumes that Taine considers them only as *texts* "borne by the printed word" that "conquered people's minds" (ibid., 68).[31] In his own discussion of Beaumarchais' *Marriage of Figaro* Chartier considers the famous monologue in which Figaro relates his struggles to make a literary career for himself—a struggle explicitly articulated as one against theatrical censorship ("et voilà ma comédie flambée" [5.2]), as well as print censorship—as evidence only for Beaumarchais' condemnation of the "obstacles set up by the administrators of the book trade" (ibid., 62).[32] Surely this is an odd reading given Beaumarchais' struggle of several years to have his comedy performed publicly. Chartier, in other words, admits the theater to the public sphere only when it is represented by the printed word.

If Chartier's appraisal of the theater is radically at odds with Chénier's, it is problematically consistent with the antitheatricalism and antipopulism of the critics of *Charles IX* and freedom of performance. The campaign against *Charles IX* and an unregulated theater alluded obsessively to the dangers posed by the presence of the audience. Consider the astronomer Jean-Sylvain Bailly's rejection, in his capacity as Paris's first revolutionary mayor, of the request to perform *Charles IX.* The actors put before the mayor the audience's demand for the play and their own reluctance to perform it. Bailly was not sympathetic to the theater public's view:

Ce matin, les comédiens français vinrent me trouver pour m'instruire que la veille le public avait demandé la représentation de *Charles IX,* tragédie que M. Chénier avait faite, et qui n'avait pas encore été jouée: ils me demandèrent des ordres et ce qu'ils devaient faire. Si j'avais été le maître, je sais bien ce que j'aurais répondu sur-le-champ. . . . Le public dit que la censure était abolie, et qu'il ne fallait pas de permission. J'avais encore sur ce point des principes différents. Je pense que la liberté de la presse est la base de la liberté publique, mais il n'en est pas le même du théâtre. Je crois qu'on doit exclure du spectacle, où beaucoup d'hommes se rassemblent et s'électrisent mutuellement, tout ce qui peut tendre à corrompre les mœurs ou l'esprit du gouvernement.[33]

[That morning the actors of the Comédie-Française came to see me in order to inform me that, the previous night, the public had demanded the performance of *Charles IX,* a tragedy written by M. Chénier which had not yet been performed. They asked me for orders and for what they should do. If I had been master (of the situation?), I know exactly how I would have immediately replied. . . . The public says that censorship was abolished and that permissions were not required. I had different principles on this question. I believe that freedom of the press is the foundation of public freedom, but the same cannot be said for the theater. I believe that one must exclude from the theater, where many men assemble and mutually electrify each other, everything that might tend to corrupt morals or the spirit of government.]

Bailly approved of the free circulation of ideas in print, even of ideas hostile to the government, because the act of reading apparently posed no threat to public order, moral or political. No such liberty could be granted to the theater, however, because the assembling of "many men" into an audience automatically put "the spirit of government" in jeopardy. Bailly thus located the theater's disruptive power less in the content of particular plays than in the "mutual electrification" of the audience members.

The conviction that audiences rather than plays made the theater disruptive and dangerous inspired the playwright and critic Etienne-Nicolas Framéry, an advocate of theatrical censorship, to propose an ingenious solution to the problem the theater posed. Like Bailly, Framéry believed that freedom of expression ended at the theater door because inside the theater a great crowd of people assembled: "[L]a liberté de la presse, doit-elle être indéfinie? En supposant qu'elle le soit, une égale liberté s'étendra-t-elle sur des ouvrages dramatiques destinés à être représentées devant un grand concours du peuple?" [Freedom of the press, must it be without limits? Even supposing that it may be, should an equal liberty be extended to dramatic works which are destined to be performed before a great assembly of people?][34] To the proposal put forward by Quatremère de Quincy that an official panel of "juges du théâtre" pass judgment on plays after their first performance, Framéry objected:

Supposez que l'auteur antipatriote possédait l'art de remuer les cœurs, d'entraîner les esprits, ait eu pour but d'ameuter les citoyens rassemblés contre les lois sacrées de l'état, vous qui connaissez ce que peut le délire du moment, combien il est facile d'égarer la multitude, craignez l'effet de cette première représentation. (ibid., 242)

[Suppose that an antipatriotic author possessed the talent to stir emotions, to carry away spirits, and that his goal was to incite the assembled citizens against the sacred laws of the state. You who understand what the delirium of the moment can bring about and how easy it is to lead the multitude astray, you should fear the effects of that first performance.]

Theater was so powerful, so efficacious, that just one performance might infect an audience and produce irreparable effects. Instead of the trial performance that Quatremère suggested, Framéry argued that plays should be published before being performed so that all the powers of judgment mustered by solitary study in "le silence du cabinet" [the silence of the cabinet] could be brought to bear on them (ibid., 238). Plays, in other words, should be transformed into books in order to make them safe. For what made the theater a menace to order was not the plays themselves but the fact that they were represented before and in the presence of an audience: "[L]es hommes rassemblés apportent des passions plus exaltées, plus irritables. . . . [L]es impressions les plus ardentes se communiquent avec violence et rapidité" (ibid. 238–239). [Assembled men bring more exalted and more irritable passions. . . . The most ardent impressions are communicated violently and rapidly.]

La Critique de la tragédie de Charles IX

Chénier's avowed goal in writing *Charles IX* was to free the theater in a way we have not yet considered: by expanding the subject matter available to it. He sought to create France's first national tragedy: "je dis le premier, car tout le monde doit sentir que des *romans en dialogues* sur des faits très peu importants, ou traités avec l'esprit de la servitude, ne sauraient s'appeler des tragédies nationales." [I say the first because everyone must understand that those *novels written in dialogue,* based on very unimportant stories, or treated in the spirit of servility, cannot properly be called national tragedies.][35] Chénier thus considered *Charles IX* France's first national tragedy for literary as well as political reasons: the Old Regime had placed an interdict on the treatment of subjects of national importance and in so doing had deformed tragedy, forcing it into the realm, if not the form, of the novel. Thus while tragedies ought to be evaluated on literary grounds according to Chénier, political power had prescribed and constrained the very conditions for literary production and literary achievement. The political structure of Old Regime France had impeded the development of a truly national tragic tradition; for Chénier the Revolution, by contrast, made possible the advent of a new national literary tradition for France (which he imagined he would found).

Charles IX tells the story of the Saint Bartholomew's Day massacre of 1572.[36] It shows the weak young king hesitating between the bloodthirsty counsels of his mother, Catherine de Medicis, and her allies the cardinal de Lorraine and his nephew the duc de Guise, on the one hand, and the sage advice of the chancelier de l'Hopital and the Protestant amiral de Coligni on the other. Charles finally assents to the plan to slaughter his Protestant subjects, but he is overcome by remorse after the massacre. And after a stern reproach from Henri de Navarre, the future Henri IV, he realizes that posterity will consider his act and his reign infamous.

The Saint Bartholomew's Day massacre was the best subject on which to build the new national literature because it was the most tragic event in modern history and because "nul autre ne pouvait offrir, peut-être, une aussi forte peinture de la tyrannie jointe au fanatisme" [perhaps no other could offer so powerful a depiction of tyranny combined with fanaticism].[37] In portraying the terrifying effects tyranny and religious fanaticism wrought during the wars of religion, Chénier hoped to attach spectators to the purified and tolerant morality of the new regime. Voltaire inspired this choice of subject; indeed, in several of his numerous defenses of the play Chénier reminds his critics—many of whom objected that the massacre was a wholly inappropriate subject for literature—that Voltaire himself recounted the Saint Bartholomew's Day massacre in the *Henriade*. Chénier cites Voltaire to prove that the great author had looked forward to a time of freedom when the story of what was perhaps the greatest crime in French history could be represented on the stage: "[U]n temps viendra, sans doute, ou nous mettons les papes sur le théâtre, comme les grecs y mettaient les Atrées et les Thiestes qu'ils voulaient rendre odieux. Un temps viendra ou la Saint-Barthélemi sera un sujet de tragédie." [No doubt a time will come when we will have popes on the stage just as the Greeks represented Atreus and Theistes whom they wished to render odious. A time will come when the St. Bartholomew's Day massacre will be the subject of a tragedy.][38]

Chénier needed the imprimatur of Voltaire's authority because *Charles IX* so flagrantly violated rules that had been established for well over a century—indeed since the administration of Richelieu—forbidding the theatrical representation of modern history (which meant essentially French history) and of ecclesiastics.[39] Neither French kings nor clerical garb were to appear on the stage. Thus a play that not only put a king of France on the stage but that represented a king who was, in Chénier's own description, "tout à la fois homicide et parjure, un roi de France qui verse le sang de ses sujets" [at once homicidal and faithless, a king of France who spilled the blood of his subjects] was certain to cause both critical and political outrage.[40] That the play also depicted a prince of the Church advocating a policy of slaughter (for this is how Chénier depicts the cardinal de Lorraine) would naturally rouse the Church and its allies, as well as conservative critics, against the play and its author.

Those hostile to the play argued that the subject of *Charles IX* was both indecent and aesthetically deficient. In a typical critique *L'Année littéraire* claimed that the Saint Bartholomew's Day massacre was "un sujet ingrat, odieux, mal choisi" [an unrewarding, odious, badly chosen subject]; the harmony and order of the state demanded not only that religion be respected, the newspaper asserted, but also that only one religion, Catholicism, be tolerated. However, the newspaper complained, *Charles IX* encouraged the anticlerical feeling that had become a veritable fashion in the Paris of 1789:

> Je ne suis pas surpris que l'ancien gouvernement eût défendu la représentation d'une pareille tragédie. La saine politique ne permet pas qu'on tolère des spectacles propres à rendre la religion de l'état odieuse et méprisable *aux yeux du peuple* qui ne sait pas distinguer la chose d'avec l'abus.[41]

> [I am not surprised that the former government would have forbidden the performance of such a tragedy. Sound policy does not permit us to tolerate plays that tend to render the state religion odious and contemptible in *the eyes of the people* who do not know how to distinguish between the thing itself and its excesses.]

Not only, then, did Chénier's play flatter prevailing passions, but it also played to the lowest common denominator: "le peuple." Although the thoughtful elite could presumably recognize the essential correctness of the Catholic Church's doctrine and practices, even while acknowledging that it had committed some "abus" in the past, fickle, impressionable theatergoers to whose eyes rather than to whose intellects the play appealed—those "people who do not know how to distinguish between the thing itself and its excesses"—could not be so trusted.

Charles IX was not only dangerous from the point of view of the government according to this review; it was also aesthetically worthless. The subject of the Saint Bartholomew's Day massacre could not produce good theater because it required that the characters discuss politics: "Nos maîtres en littérature ont toujours regardé les détails politiques comme très froids sur le théâtre de Melpomène qui doit être le siège des passions grandes et fortes." [Our literary masters have always regarded political detail as very cold on Melpomène's stage which ought to be the seat of strong, great passions.][42] But Chénier takes a diametrically opposed point of view, contending that precisely because the French theater had been arbitrarily cut off from subjects of political, social, and historical importance, it had been deprived of the nourishment it needed to sustain a vibrant, important, literary tradition. In other words, because theater could not take up issues of national importance, it degenerated, and the form this degeneration took was effeminization: "Il faudrait toujours, à ne considérer même que la perfection de l'art, représenter sur la scène ces grands événements tragiques, ces grandes époques de l'histoire, qui intéressent tous les citoyens; et non plus ces intrigues amoureuses, qui n'intéressent que de femmes." [Taking into consideration only the perfection of art, one should always represent those great tragic events, those great epochs in history that are of interest to all citizens, rather than those amorous intrigues that interest only women.][43] It was in the corrupted state's interest to transform theater—which by rights should be the genre that, following the Greeks, formed citizens and bound them to each other and to the state—into novels, the genre that titillated women and distracted pusillanimous men from matters of importance.

Despite the fact that Chénier was no lover of the English political system, in his defense of the theater as a new institution of the nation he took up the juxtaposition between Racine and Shakespeare that Stendhal would so famously study thirty-four years later in order to praise the English dramatist. Racine was indeed the "génie le plus parfait qui ait illustré les arts de l'Europe" [the most perfect genius to have rendered the arts of Europe illustrious], Chénier acknowledges; nevertheless, he goes on to complain, Racine wrote too much for the "petits appartements de Versailles" [private rooms of Versailles] and the "couvent de Saint-Cyr" [Saint-Cyr convent] (ibid.); in other words, Racine wrote for Madame de Maintenon and the other women who sur-

rounded Louis XIV. In seeking to please these female patrons, Racine led theater away from its proper domain—subjects of public importance—and toward the concerns of the novel: "qu'importaient à la France," demands
Chénier, "Esther et Bérénice?" (ibid., 153). [What do Esther and Bérénice matter to France?] (One wonders how Chénier could have read these plays.) Here
conflicts between desire and duty (*Bérénice*), and even conflicts between religion and the state (*Esther*), are gendered female and thus consigned to some
zone outside the province of public or political significance. If, on the other
hand, Racine had used his talents to treat politically relevant manly subjects,
Chénier argues,

> peut-être le conseil de Louis XIV n'aurait pas été animé du même esprit que
> le conseil de Charles IX; peut-être l'industrie des Français n'aurait pas en-
> richi l'étranger de notre ruine; et peut-être le sang des Français n'aurait pas
> coulé sur les échafauds de Languedoc, pour des opinions théologiennes.
> (ibid.)

> [Perhaps Louis XIV's council would not have been animated by the same
> spirit as that of Charles IX; perhaps the industry of Frenchmen would not
> have enriched foreign lands to our ruin; and perhaps the blood of French-
> men would not have flowed on the scaffolds of Languedoc for reasons of
> doctrine.]

If, in other words, the greatest practitioner of the French theater had not
turned to womanish topics, but rather had conceived of theater as a public institution responsible for forming and informing public opinion, then perhaps
Louis XIV would not have been able to revoke the Edict of Nantes, and neither the repression of French Protestants nor their massive emigration to Bel-
gium, Holland, and England would have occurred.

By contrast, Shakespeare, although he lived during what Chénier considers
a barbaric era in relation to his own, managed to create a theater that was vi-
tally concerned with the project of public freedom. The example of Shakespeare demonstrates that theater must treat matters of public importance if it
is to hold its rightfully preeminent place among the arts and reach its highest
incarnation:

> Voyez dans ses pièces nationales, les rois, les princes, les paires du royaume,
> les prêtres, les prélats de l'église romaine et ceux de l'église anglicaine, intro-
> duits sur la scène, et pesés, pour ainsi dire, avec un esprit de liberté que le
> philosophe Hume est loin d'avoir égalé dans son histoire. (ibid.)

[In his national plays you see kings, princes, peers of the realm, priests, prelates of the Roman and the Anglican churches, introduced onto the stage and weighed, so to speak, with a spirit of freedom that the philosopher Hume is far from having equaled in his History.]

Chénier accords Shakespeare what was perhaps the highest form of praise imaginable for an eighteenth-century writer—he calls Shakespeare's plays philosophical and free.

Chénier's view of Shakespeare is idiosyncratic for his time. Men and women of letters in eighteenth-century France routinely referred to Shakespeare as barbaric, graceless, and savage. What distinguishes Chénier from his peers in this respect is his insistence that theater take on subjects permitted only to history and philosophy; those subjects are precisely the ones that affect or comment on public life. Novels and the "novelization" of the theater posed a special danger to the theater, to Chénier's mind, because novels were to represent only the "vraisemblable" and omit the "vrai" on the grounds that the real was often too ugly, too reprehensible, for artistic representation.[44] Many of Chénier's contemporaries—like the writer of the review in *Année littéraire*—and nearly all the critics of the nineteenth century who commented on the theater of the French Revolution believed that art must studiously avoid any contamination by contemporary events or issues if it is to remain art (think, for example, of the Goncourt brothers' dictum that "l'art n'a pas d'à propos" [art has no circumstances]). But some, like Chénier, welcomed the Revolution precisely because it promised to open up a whole new realm of subjects for a theater that appeared, arguably, to have worn out all those available to it. Thus, for example, Millin de Grandmaison claimed that in a tyrannical state, like Old Regime France, the theater could never treat subjects of real importance:

chez un peuple ainsi gouverné, il ne peut donc exister de tragédies vraiment nationales. On n'y peut guère exposer les grandes vérités qui intéressent la nation entière, et l'éclaireraient sur ses droits. On n'ose y débiter que des leçons d'une morale usé et commune; la soumission aveugle aux despotisme des rois y est réduite en principes, et fortifiée par des exemples.[45]

[For a people thus governed, there can exist no truly national tragedies. One can hardly present the great truths that interest the entire nation and that would enlighten it about its rights. One dares only put forth the lessons of a used-up and commonplace morality; blind submission to the despotism of kings is condensed into principle and is fortified by examples.]

Thus while some critics might claim that the Crown's patronage and oversight of the theater had helped it to flourish, Millin makes exactly the opposite claim: under tyrannical rule art functions merely as an ideological prop for power; thus, tyrannical government strangles artistic creativity.

The critic from *L'Année littéraire et politique* complained: "Nos maîtres en littérature ont toujours regardé les détails politiques comme très froids sur le théâtre de Melpomène qui doit être le siège des passions grandes et fortes." [Our literary masters have always regarded political details as very cold on Melpomène's stage which ought to be the seat of great and powerful passions.] Yet like others hostile to the play, this critic appeared disturbed most especially not by any cold or flat parts of the play but rather by what might be seen as *Charles IX*'s most highly dramatic moments: the ringing of the tocsin that calls the murderers to arms and the cardinal's blessing of those arms, soon to be covered with the blood of French Protestants. Even this most unfriendly critic admitted, although bitingly, that "[l]a belle scène, la grande scène, c'est celle du tocsin et la bénédiction des armes" [the beautiful scene, the great scene, is that of the tocsin and the benediction of the daggers].[46] *La Critique de la tragédie de Charles IX* (1790), an anonymous play attributed to Charles Palissot, which represents a salon filled with aristocrats (and one rational man of letters) discussing and condemning *Charles IX*, similarly focuses on the tocsin and the benediction of the arms.[47] Palissot enjoyed a fairly successful career as a man of letters under the Old Regime but was famous, or indeed infamous, for his 1755 play *Les Originaux* and for his 1760 play *Les Philosophes*, both of which mocked d'Alembert, Diderot, and Rousseau. Despite what would seem an inauspicious background for revolutionary literary activity, Palissot enjoyed something of a second wind as mentor and champion of Chénier. And while *La Critique de la tragédie de Charles IX* rehearses criticisms of *Charles IX* only to defend both the play and its author, it does present contemporary charges against *Charles IX* reasonably fairly. The aristocrats of *La Critique de la tragédie de Charles IX* argue, on the one hand, that Chénier's play is cold and dull and, on the other, that it scandalously appeals to the lowest common denominator—"la foule du peuple" [the crowd of the people]—with its grossly sensational ringing of the tocsin in the public theater. Just as *L'Année littéraire*'s critic claimed that "the people" were not qualified to make judgments about what they may see in the theater because they did not possess the requisite powers of discernment, the aristocrats of *La Critique de la tragédie de Charles IX* argue that *Charles IX* has been so successful among "the people" because they lack the real literary sensibility and erudition to make adequate judgments. The people, instead, were galvanized by sensations. So, claims the Vidame de Granson, the hostess of the salon, "j'abandonne ma loge à *mes gens. Il n'y a que ces gens du peuple* qui aient les nerfs assez peu sensibles pour soutenir l'atrocité d'un pareil spectacle" (1.3). [I've given my box over to my people. It is only those people of the lower orders (literally "those people of the people") who have nerves insensitive enough to withstand the atrocity of such a spectacle.] And, indeed, on this score the author of *La Critique de la tragédie de Charles IX* has cleverly had his characters imitate the wicked characters of *Charles IX*. For example, in downplaying the people's affection for the Amiral de Coligni to her son, the king, Catherine de Medicis explains:

> Il subjugue aisément un crédule vulgaire.
> Le peuple aux factions ne fut jamais contraire;
> Et, par un grand éclat se laissant entraîner,
> Il est bientôt soumis dès qu'on peut l'étonner. (2.4)

> [He easily subjugates the credulous herd.
> The people never oppose factions;
> They let themselves be led by a great dazzle,
> They submit as soon as someone astonishes them.]

Chénier's Catherine believes, as do Palissot's Vidame de Granson and the critic for *L'Année littéraire,* that the "people" are attracted to, and led by, spectacular displays—displays that "peut l'étonner" by acting directly on their crude senses. The Vidame believes that Chénier has attracted popular support by using the very means Catherine de Medicis describes.

The aristocratic characters of *La Critique de la tragédie de Charles IX* construct a sustained account of the distinction between what can be shown in the theater and what can be written in books based, in part, on their fear of theater's potential effects on an unrefined, gullible crowd. That account, however, is successfully challenged by Dorimon, the man of letters, and by a sympathetic marquise (the token good aristocrat), who together undertake the defense of Chénier's play and uphold the legitimacy of, and the need for, a new national theater. Thus, for example, the snickering chevalier de Belfort, a salon habitué, claims that the Saint-Barthelemi is an inappropriate subject and that "l'homme pervers qui est allé y chercher un pareil sujet, doit être regardé comme un très mauvais citoyen" (1.3) [the perverse man who sought out such a subject ought to be considered a very bad citizen]. But the marquise reminds him that Voltaire recounted the same events, and she calls into question the differentiation between what can be represented on the stage and what can be read in books: "[E]xpliquez-moi donc comment ce qui nous a tous intéressés dans la *Henriade,* pourrait devenir si criminel au théâtre" (1.3). [Explain to me then how something that interested all of us in the *Henriade* could become so criminal on the stage.] This imperative angers all the others and sets off the following exchange:

> LE CHEVALIER: Ah! Madame, quelle différence d'un récit à une action! Entendez-vous sonner le tocsin dans la *Henriade?*
> LA MARQUISE: Non; mais . . .
> LA VIDAME: Prétendriez-vous sérieusement justifier ce tocsin?
> LA MARQUISE: Je ne dis pas . . .
> LE VICOMTE: Il faut convenir de bonne foi que ce tocsin est révoltant.
> LA MARQUISE: On pourrait, sans se passionner . . .
> LA VIDAME: Je le déclare, il me serait impossible de rester l'amie de quelqu'un qui aurait entendu ce tocsin, sans éprouver des convulsions.
> LA MARQUISE: Ce tocsin est donc bien coupable? Cependant . . .
> LA VIDAME: Il se lie à des souvenirs qui font frissonner d'horreur: tenez, il suffit d'y penser pour que l'imagination se rembrunisse; et, au moment ou je vous parle, il me semble que j'entends bourdonner à mon oreille ce maudit tocsin (elle jette un cri d'effroi). (1.3)

> [CHEVALIER: Ah! Madame, What a difference there is between a narrative and an action! Do you hear the tocsin ring in the *Henriade?*
> MARQUISE: No; but . . .
> VIDAME: Would you seriously claim to justify that tocsin?
> MARQUISE: I do not say . . .
> VICOMTE: You must, in good faith, agree that the tocsin is revolting.
> MARQUISE: One may, without becoming impassioned . . .
> VIDAME: I declare that it would be impossible for me to remain the friend of anyone who could hear that tocsin without going into convulsions.
> MARQUISE: The tocsin is really so guilty? Nonetheless . . .
> VIDAME: It is connected to memories that make one shiver with horror. Listen, it is enough just to think about it for the imagination to darken; and at this very moment that I speak to you it seems that I hear that accursed tocsin ringing in my ears (she screams in fright).]

The ridiculous aristocrats of *La Critique* condemn the ringing of the tocsin in the theater (as opposed to its narration in a book) because it affects the spectators on the level of sensation and because it affects them so strongly that it produces a lasting impression. The ringing of the tocsin in the play recalled the very recent events of 1789—the fall of the Bastille and the march to Versailles that brought the royal family, effectively in captivity, to Paris—that had wrought such momentous changes in the national landscape. These events, too, had been signaled and accompanied by the same call to arms. In other words, Palissot's misguided aristocrats condemn Chénier's play for the very characteristics that, as we have seen, Chénier thought integral to theater's power and mission: its capacity to produce immediate, emotional reaction and its capacity to promote reflection on affairs of national importance. *La Critique* exposes the aristocrats and their views to ridicule; it ironically depicts them as incapable of engaging in a rational, deliberate consideration of the issues. Their stated position is that "the people" lack the capacity for abstract thought (hence the people's supposed interest in the sensational) and therefore the skills necessary for the kind of reasoned, literate debate that, the aristocratic characters claim, characterizes their salon; but as soon as their views are challenged, they interrupt, becoming passionate, childish, and obdurate. One may discuss the issues without becoming impassioned, the marquise tries to suggest to the others. They answer with ultimatums and shrieks. They prove themselves irrational and incompetent to make aesthetic and, consequently, political judgments.

Bailly, Framéry, and the aristocratic characters of *La Critique de la tragédie de Charles IX,* like Chartier, distinguish between a rational reading public to be allowed liberty and an irrational theatergoing people that required policing; but neither Bailly nor Framéry (nor, of course, the fictional aristocrats) imagined themselves to be taking a neutral stance. Theirs was not so much a description as an *ideology* of the public; that same ideology, we will see, was marshaled in the service of protecting the liberal Revolution against a potentially radical popular movement that seemed to be emerging in the theater. The argument for textual representation as the vehicle of publicity and for reading and writing as the only legitimate modes of participation in the public sphere was, it turns out, a partisan position in a debate that raged in 1789 and 1790. The bias in favor of written representation triumphed, which is what has underlain the seeming plausibility of the Habermasian interpretation, but it is to the other term in the struggle—a radically divergent construction of publicity in art and politics—that I now turn.

The Jurisdiction of the Public

The long-neglected debate I have been recovering here suggests, on the one hand, how central theater was to revolutionary culture and, on the other hand, how divided revolutionary culture was over theater's political, cultural, and moral status. Moreover, this debate extended far beyond a literate public sphere composed of journalists, playwrights, and politicians. Indeed, *Charles IX* was performed and freedom of the theater was established because groups of people—rather than their representatives in the political field or the Habermasian public sphere—demanded that the play be performed. The most effective arguments for the power of theater and the legitimacy of audience opinion were made *in* the theater *by* audiences. On August 19, 1789, for example, voices from the pit of the Comédie-Française cried out for the performance of *Charles IX*.[48] When the actors refused to accede to the audience's demand, citing lack of official permission, the audience responded with the shout "no more permissions."[49] With this shout the audience asserted that no permission and no command beyond its own were any longer relevant. The intimidated actors tried to find a way to appease the audience without recognizing the legitimacy of its dictates; they promised to consult the revolutionary municipal government instead of the Gentlemen of the Bedchamber, the appointees of the king, who, traditionally, had governed the theater.

The newly installed municipal government, however, took no more kindly to the audience's demand than did the Gentlemen of the Bedchamber. The theatrical public, in turn, was no more prepared to submit to the newly constituted revolutionary administration than to waning royal prerogative. Fleury, one of the principal actors of the Comédie-Française, understood just how much was at stake in the *Charles IX* affair: "How could we, on the one hand, say to the enraged public, 'this piece is forbidden by order of the court,' or on the other hand, how could we present our weekly repertoire as was our custom, for the approval of the court, with the name of the proscribed piece in the list? This latter mode of proceeding would have been tantamount to telling the king that we were no longer his servants."[50] Fleury saw that to gratify the audience's demand for the play was to acknowledge its authority and to disown that of the king. And once the municipality had taken over the administration of the theater, obedience to the audience meant disobedience to the revolutionary government. Bailly tried to stall the public and the play by passing consideration of the issue on to the municipal council; the council, imitating the courage and decisiveness of the mayor, in turn formed a commission to study *Charles IX*. Only after an unrelenting campaign in the theater, as well as in the newspapers, did the Comédie and the municipality yield. *Charles IX* was finally performed, for the first time, on November 4, 1789. It was an unmitigated success. By pressing their demand for the play in the face of opposition from the Gentlemen of the Bedchamber, the mayor, the new national guard, and (not least of all) the actors, audiences not only displayed their keen interest in France's first national tragedy, but they also successfully established popular jurisdiction over the theater. Indeed, the audience was so deeply involved in *Charles IX* and its fate that it was an audience member who, during the play's second performance, suggested that the play ought to have the subtitle *L'École de rois* (The School for Kings); other audience members agreed, and the subtitle was permanently adopted.

But the struggle over *Charles IX* and audience control of the theater was not over by a long shot.[51] Although *Charles IX* was performed successfully, earned the company excellent receipts, and did not in fact provoke any violence on the part of its "electrified" audiences, the Comédie had essentially removed the play from its repertory by the spring of 1790. Many of the actors' political sympathies lay with the court and they were loath to perform a play that, they believed, encouraged hostility toward the monarchy. Other members of the troupe, however, embraced the Revolution. The theater—like every other corner of France—was riven. By the summer of 1790 the Comédie's refusal to perform *Charles IX* had once again become a Parisian crisis. Many theatergoers expected the theaters to perform what they thought of as patriotic plays during the summer as a way of participating in the fête de la fédération that marked the first anniversary of the fall of the Bastille.

Both Parisians and fédérés (volunteer soldiers) from the provinces demanded again and again that the Comédie perform *Charles IX;* they made their desires known by directly speaking up in the theater and by sending delegations to the theater company. In a pamphlet written and printed sometime in the autumn of 1790, Palissot recounts that the fédérés from Provence were so eager to see the play that when their own attempts to convince the company failed, they turned with no better result to their deputy, the comte de Mirabeau, arguably the most influential politician of the day:

> Les fédérés de Provence principalement, après l'avoir inutilement sollicité, avaient prié M. de Mirabeau, l'aîné, leur député à l'Assemblée nationale de vouloir bien se joindre à leur vœu. Deux fois M. de Mirabeau prit la peine d'en informer les comédiens, même en les avertissant des suites facheuses que leur obstination pourrait entraîner. . . . [L]eur résistance fut inflexible.[52]

[The fédérés from Provence principally, after having requested it in vain, had asked M. de Mirabeau, the elder, their deputy at the National Assembly, to please join them in their request. Twice, M. de Mirabeau went to the trouble of informing the actors of it (the fédérés' desire to see the play), even warning them of the troublesome consequences their obstinacy might produce. . . . They were inflexible in their resistance.]

An anonymous pamphlet entitled "Relation de ce qui s'est passé à la Comédie Française dans la nuit du vendredi 23 au 24 juillet" alleges that the actors' refusal stemmed from orders given by the minister of the royal household (later minister of the interior), the comte de Saint-Priest: "On a su après, par quelques-uns des acteurs mêmes, que c'était Guignard [the pamphleteer's scornful nickname for Saint-Priest] qui donnait des ordres positifs au théâtre. Des ordres citoyens!" [It was made known later, by some of the actors themselves, that it was Guignard who positively gave orders to the theater company. Orders citizens!][53] This writer's anger was provoked not merely by his dislike of the minister or of the actors; rather what produced his expostulation was the idea that a minister would give orders to the theater troupe and that the troupe would accede to these orders when both minister and theater company ought instead to obey the sovereign citizens who were making their will known.

Charles IX was finally performed on July 23, after an extraordinary series of events. Audience demands had become increasingly insistent, and on the evening of the twenty-first the theater public "avait témoigné quelqu'humeur du refus" (ibid., 6) [demonstrated some bad humor at the refusal]. When the curtain rose on that evening's scheduled play, a member of the audience stepped forward and read a demand for *Charles IX*. The actor Jean-Baptiste Naudet replied that the play was still officially banned and that, in any case, the two actors who played the scheming queen, Catherine de Medicis, and the bloodthirsty cardinal were too ill to perform. But Talma, who soon would be recognized as the era's greatest tragic actor, retorted, onstage, that the actors were in fact well enough to perform.[54] Palissot even came forward and volunteered to read one of the parts if necessary. Despite this confusion the audience remained peaceful, and the play on the bill was presented. The next day the theater troupe went to the mayor, asking him to intervene and ban the play. But, perhaps tired of fielding the actors' plaints, Bailly urged the company to perform *Charles IX;* he also took care, however, to ensure an extraordinary show of military force at the theater: on the night of July 23 the pamphleteer notes that "M. Mottier [the marquis de Lafayette, commander of the national guard], réquis par M. Bailly, envoie au théâtre des forces extraordinaires: on y donne *Charles IX* mais le parti était pris de voir dans la foule, quelque perturbateur de l'ordre public." [M. Mottier, ordered by M. Bailly, sent extraordinary forces to the theater: *Charles IX* was performed there but the decision was made to regard the crowd as a disturber of public order.][55] It seems both pro- and anti-*Charles IX* forces came to the theater prepared for violence; troops eventually dispersed the audience, and Danton was arrested for refusing to remove his hat inside the theater.[56]

The July 23 performance of the play clearly did not dispel the public's frustration with the Comédie and with the authorities that seemed to be directing it. The show of force, far from calming spirits, provoked more displeasure: the Cordelier district wrote and circulated a decree demanding that "le pouvoir militaire dans tous les spectacles de la capitale, ne pèse plus sur les citoyens qui assistent aux représentations, mais qu'il se tiennent [*sic*] à l'écart et qu'il soit aux ordres du pouvoir civile qui seul doit présider dans les salles" [military power in all the theaters of the capital no longer weigh upon the citizens who attend performances, but that it remain out of the way and that it be at the command of civil authority which, alone, should preside in the theater].[57] In other words, the Cordeliers perceived the military presence in the theater to constitute a sort of coup against the rightful authority of the audience. And Palissot argued that the presence of soldiers in the theater was inconsistent with real liberty:

> Voyez si les Anglais, qui sont véritablement des hommes libres, laissent introduire ainsi, dans leurs spectacles, des gardes armés. Que serait-ce si ces gardes étaient subordonnés aux comédiens eux-même, et si ces comédiens, non moins audacieux que nos anciens ministres, avaient l'air de croire qu'ils ne sont pas fait pour le peuple, mais que le peuple est fait pour eux?[58]

> [Look and see whether the English, who are truly free men, allow armed guards to be thus introduced into their theaters. What would happen if these soldiers were subordinated to the actors themselves, and if these actors, no less audacious than our former ministers, took it into their heads to believe that they are not constituted for the people, but that the people are constituted for them?]

Because they were so long the servants of the king, Palissot implies, the actors were unable or unwilling to recognize the authority of the theater public. Indeed, the long years of tyranny and servitude had so deformed the actors' understanding (and they had so identified with their masters) that they had strangely construed their relationship to the theater public as parallel to that between the monarch and his subjects: they take the spectators to be the instruments of their pleasure rather than vice versa. Thus the actors' refusal to meet audience demands constituted, to Palissot's mind, a rejection of popular sovereignty.

Talma's act of publicly contradicting his colleagues and allying himself with the theater public only deepened the crisis. The troupe took the unprecedented step of expelling Talma from the company; this expulsion was widely deemed illegal and arbitrary. A campaign on Talma's behalf was unleashed in the newspapers, and night after night the spectators crowding the theater demanded his return.[59] Talma and Mirabeau exchanged public letters. On September 16, 1790, the audience once again demanded both a performance of *Charles IX* and the return of Talma to the company; the actors promised that they would explain their position to the audience the following day. On the evening of September 17 the actor Fleury appeared onstage before the curtain rose to offer the reasons for the troupe's continued unwillingness to readmit Talma into its ranks: "Messieurs, ma société, persuadée que M. Talma a trahi ses intérêts et compromis la tranquillité publique, a décidé à l'unanimité qu'elle n'aurait plus aucun rapport avec lui, jusqu'à ce que l'autorité en eût décidé." [Gentlemen, my company, persuaded that M. Talma has betrayed its interests and compromised the public peace, has unanimously decided that it will no longer have any relationship with him until such time that the authorities might make a decision.][60] Rather than calming spirits, this speech caused an explosion; for Fleury's announcement that the company would await an order from "l'autorité" made it very clear that the company acknowledged neither the public present nor the municipal government as competent authorities since both of these had made their judgments known. "À ces mots" [at these words], write Etienne and Martainville, contemporary historians of the theater, "le désordre et le trouble éclatent de nouveau dans toutes les parties de la salle: les motions se croisent, des orateurs de clubs se disputent la parole" [disorder and trouble burst out again from every corner of the theater: motions crossed each other, club orators competed to have the floor].[61] Events took an even more astonishing turn when, in the midst of this tumult, another actor, Dugazon, burst onto the stage to dispute the account given by his senior colleague Fleury, to demonstrate his solidarity with Talma, and to implore the public's protection. The *Chronique de Paris* describes it this way:

M. Dugazon était dans les coulisses; il s'élance sur la scène et s'écrie: "Messieurs, la Comédie va prendre contre moi la même délibération que contre M. Talma. Je dénonce toute la comédie; il est faux que M. Talma ait trahi sa société et compromis la sûreté publique; tout son crime est d'avoir dit qu'on pouvait jouer *Charles IX* et voilà tout."[62]

[M. Dugazon was in the wings; he threw himself onto the stage and cried out, "Gentlemen, the Comedy is about to take the same step against me that it took against M. Talma. I denounce the Comedy; it is false that M. Talma betrayed the troupe and compromised public safety; his only crime is to have said that *Charles IX* could be performed and that is all."]

The journalist goes on, in a turn of nearly comic understatement, to describe the reaction in the theater: "On sent quelle a dû être la fermentation." [One can feel what the ferment there must have been.][63]

It is clear from several accounts that the audience at the theater that night was particularly galvanized and highly factionalized.[64] Because the company had promised some days in advance that it would explain its actions that evening, those particularly interested in the affair made it a point to attend; those who considered themselves patriots or allies of Chénier, Talma, the Cordeliers, or the fédérés were determined to make their presence known, as were monarchists and advocates of the more conservative actors. According to some accounts, the actors had even distributed large numbers of tickets in advance to their supporters.[65] But no matter what the allegiance, all present made clear their belief that theater was a crucial forum for the expression of public opinion and demonstrated their commitment to audience regulation of the theater; for what followed on Dugazon's extraordinary outburst was raucous debate and deliberation among the audience members.

Two elements of the ensuing debate are particularly relevant. First, it is striking that the next step on the part of the audience was to demand (successfully) that the actors read aloud the minutes of their deliberations concerning Talma and his fate. In other words, the theater public immediately asserted itself as the legitimate judge of the troupe's actions. Second, it is equally striking that the audience's affirmation of its authority to judge provoked at least one monarchist in the audience, François-Louis Suleau, an editor of the antirevolutionary newspaper *Les Actes des Apôtres*, to mock both the audience and the National Assembly:

Sulleau [*sic*], rédacteur d'un journal du matin, s'efforce de ramener le calme, en, parodiant, d'une manière très bouffonne, le président de l'Assemblée nationale, il donne la parole à l'un, s'écrie: à l'ordre, à l'ordre! agite de toute sa force de ses bras une énorme sonnette, et enfin se couvre lorsqu'il voit que tous ses efforts sont inutiles . . . on est obligé d'appeler la force armée, et d'aller avertir le maire de Paris.[66]

[Suleau, the editor of a morning newspaper, tried his best to calm things down by parodying the president of the National Assembly in a very clownish manner. He gave the floor to someone, cried out, "Order, order!," shook an enormous bell with all his force, and finally put his hat on when he saw that all his efforts were futile. It was necessary to call for the national guard and to alert the mayor of Paris.]

By ringing his bell—which, as Camille Desmoulins pointed out at the time, he must have brought expressly for this purpose—and by putting on his hat, Suleau imitated the president of the National Assembly: in cases of disorder these were the official actions prescribed to the president by the Assembly's regulations.[67] The significance of ringing the bell and covering the head was known to all because the Assembly was so very tumultuous; the president frequently had to have recourse to these measures. Suleau clearly meant to indicate his disdain for the Assembly by likening it to what he considered the riotous rabble of the theater public. The rather conservative commentators Etienne and Martainville do something similar when they describe the theater audience's actions in terms of "club orators" and "motions." But Suleau's parody fell flat—"L'apôtre Suleau . . . faisait aller en vain sa sonnette" [the apostle Suleau . . . waved his bell about in vain], relates Desmoulins—because he failed to grasp the meaning of the audience action, as well as its implications for the different ways the theater and the Assembly structured their relation to the publics on which they depended.[68] For in the theater, deliberation and judgment took place in what would be, spatially, the equivalent of the galleries in the Assembly. The theater public exercised precisely those rights and powers the public spectators of the Assembly were forbidden to exercise on the grounds that those rights and powers were being exercised for them. So while Suleau thought to demean the members of the National Assembly by histrionically implying their resemblance to the theater public, he failed to see that the events at the theater that night demonstrated the stark difference between the two institutions. In fact, the deliberations at the theater should be seen as more fully democratic than the "real" deliberations of the Assembly rather than as parodies of them.

The refusal to perform *Charles IX* and the expulsion of Talma—that is the rejection of the audience's will—were seen by some as acts of rebellion against legitimate authority. The newspaper *Révolutions de Paris* lambasted the actors:

Les acteurs du théâtre français, non contents de se qualifier à l'ombre du corps national, du titre vain de comédiens ordinaires du roi; non contents de ne plus représenter *Charles IX* . . . , portent l'impudence au point de ne reconnaître ni la nation, ni ses représentants, dont ils rejettent et méprisent l'autorité.

Ces histrions ont oublié le respect qu'ils doivent au peuple qui les nourrit, jusqu'à oser dire qu'ils reporteront les clefs de son spectacle au roi.[69]

[The actors of the Comédie-Française, not content to call themselves by the vain title of the king's players in the shadow of the National Assembly, not content to no longer perform *Charles IX,* have taken their impudence to the point of no longer recognizing either the nation or its representatives whose authority they reject and hold in contempt.

These actors have forgotten the respect they owe to the people who sustain them; they have gone as far as daring to say that they would bring the keys to the theater to the king.]

And the more moderate *Chronique de Paris* termed the actors' actions "la révolte de la comédie française" [the rebellion of the Comédie-Française].[70] In their accounts both newspapers stress that the actors were rebelling against the theater public and the municipal government. According to the newspapers, the municipal government was legitimate precisely because it was carrying out the wishes of the public—even if, as we have seen, the mayor acted with reluctance and with the sense that he was not, in fact, "le maître." Although the actors of the Comédie insisted for several more days that rather than become the servants of the people they would close the theater and bring the key to the king, continuing public pressure brought demands from the municipal government as well. Bowing to the theater public and to the mayor, who himself acted only because of the theater public's continual pressure, the troupe reintegrated Talma and performed *Charles IX* before a tranquil audience on September 28.[71]

The struggle between audiences and governing authorities over *Charles IX* was paradigmatic for revolutionary theater. In February 1792 the rather conservative *Journal des théâtres* complained that audiences now dictated the orders in the theater: "Il [le peuple] a demandé que l'on bannit les bayonnettes de l'intérieur des spectacles, et il y porte l'arme de son impérieuse volonté, de sa force tumultueuse. Il appelle, il demande, il exige, il veut, il ordonne." [They (the people) demanded that bayonets be banned from the interior of theaters and they bring the weapon of their imperious will, of their tumultuous force there. They call, they demand, they require, they want, they command.][72] At least until 1793–1794 audiences continued to exert extraordinary control over the conditions of theatrical production and performance. Rather than relaxing their vigilance after their victory in the *Charles IX* affair, audiences remained jealous of their authority, which was increasingly understood as a defining sign of revolutionary culture. Thus, Millin de Grandmaison could distinguish monarchic from revolutionary governance by distinguishing between monarchic and revolutionary theatrical cultures. Under tyrannical governments like that of the Old Regime, the audience was passive and silent: "personne ne doit pouvoir élever la voix ni parler au public sauf les acteurs" [no one may raise their voice or speak to the public except the actors], and "des soldats doivent toujours empêcher que les témoignages de contentement ou de désapprobation ne soient publics" [soldiers must always see to it that demonstrations of contentment or disapprobation are not made publicly], for fear that the theatrical crowd would be transformed into a revolutionary assembly.[73] By contrast, Millin suggests, in the new regime power moved from the stage to the pit; under the active jurisdiction of the sovereign people the theater was a crucial site for the direct expression of popular judgment.[74] As the *Chronique de Paris* put it, the public's demand for a play was "une sorte d'élection par acclamation" [a sort of election by acclamation].[75]

The Drama of Popular Judgment

Audiences, having made their judgments, could be unyielding and violent. I want to turn now to a consideration of the tumultuous events surrounding the performance of two plays that provoked particularly intense audience reactions precisely because they thematized the very issue of the people's capacity for judgment and linked it to their capacity for self-government. In the incidents in question audiences resolutely defied political powers, expressed their own judgments, and successfully asserted their own authority. Taken together, the two incidents demonstrate the theatrical public's deep appreciation of the theater, the public's consciousness of its own position as censor, and its determination to discharge the responsibilities of that position.

In February 1792 the journalist Antoine-Joseph Gorsas reports that "le désordre des spectacles" [disorder in the theaters] was "l'ordre du jour" [on the agenda].[76] *L'Auteur d'un moment* (The Author of the Moment), a play now long forgotten, was at the center of the unrest; on February 24 its first performance at the Théâtre du Vaudeville precipitated a riot. News of the play's content had spread rapidly, and the audience on February 25 came to the Vaudeville determined to suppress rather than watch *L'Auteur*. Just as the play was about to begin, spectators insisted that the director of the theater come forward. The actors quickly retired. When the director appeared, a spokesman emerged to pronounce the audience's bidding: "Nous vous sommons . . . de rayer de votre répertoire une pièce qui contient des couplets outrageants pour la Révolution et patriotes." [We summon you . . . to remove from your repertoire a play that contains couplets which outrage the Revolution and patriots.] The director expressed his profound regrets, agreed to obey, promised that the play would not be performed again, and beat a hasty retreat.[77] But the public remained unsatisfied; it demanded that the text of the play be burned. An audience member pointed out that it was against the law to burn the manuscript because it was the property of the theater owner. One of the musicians in the pit resolved the problem by offering the audience his own printed copy of the offending work. The play was burned to the accompaniment of the national song, "Ça ira." The police officers assigned to maintain order in the theater tried to put a halt to the audience action but to no avail.[78]

L'Auteur d'un moment scarcely seems a likely source of disorder. Hastily written by François Léger, an actor in the Vaudeville troupe, it was not an explicitly political play. Rather, it satirized the period's leading tragic playwright and champion of theatrical liberty, Marie-Joseph Chénier; *L'Auteur* responds, in particular, to the enormous success of Chénier's *Caius Gracchus*.[79] Damis, Léger's eponymous protagonist and Chénier's double, is a successful playwright who, encouraged by his aged and sycophantic mentor, Baliveau (a caricature of Chénier's own mentor, Palissot), imagines himself to have surpassed the glory of Corneille. Yet Damis's successes are due entirely to his valet's well-recompensed activities—he keeps Damis's name in constant circulation and packs the theater with a paid "claque"—and to the incompetence of the theatrical public.

L'Auteur figures Damis as a mountebank rather than an artist. After all, theatrical success, Baliveau has taught Damis, depends not on the production of salutary art but on the susceptibility of audiences: "Le crédule public qu'on sait fort bien conduire / Séduit par nos prôneurs, les croit et nous admire." [We know very well how to steer the public so credulous / Seduced by our advance-men, they believe them and admire us.][80] Léger depicts Chénier as a charlatan who, instead of creating faithful representations and inspiring virtuous actions, uses the theater to make himself rich and to fashion for himself a false patriotic identity. *L'Auteur d'un moment* thus impugns not only Chénier's talent but also his sincerity; it disputes, moreover, the competence of revolutionary audiences to discern both truth and aesthetic value.

L'Auteur d'un moment failed miserably as an attack on Chénier. Indeed, the Vaudeville audience's rejection of *L'Auteur* not only ratified but deepened the success of *Caius Gracchus* and Chénier's status as the people's playwright. For whereas Léger figures popular theatrical audiences as incompetent arbiters of social and aesthetic value, Chénier's play valorizes popular judgment and opinion—that is, the very same forces that rejected *L'Auteur* and embraced *Caius Gracchus.*

In Chénier's play tyrannical patricians attempt to discredit the hero, Caius, a "courageux martyr de la cause populaire" [courageous martyr of the popular cause], in order to destroy a popular movement that had seemingly come to maturity.[81] But Caius poses a danger to the patricians not because he speaks for the plebeians but because he champions their capacity to speak and judge for themselves:

> Ce respect filial et cette dépendance,
> Pouvaient servir l'état quand Rome en son enfance
> Croyait dans les Tarquins chasser tous les tyrans:
> .   .   .   .
> Vous n'avez plus besoin de patrons ni de pères.[82]
>
> [This filial respect and this dependency
> Could serve the state when Rome in its infancy
> Believed that with the Tarquins it banished all tyrants:
> .   .   .   .
> You no longer require protectors or fathers.]

The play creates a critical juxtaposition between Caius's faith in a self-sufficient people and the patricians' assumption that the people are incapable of effective action in the absence of leadership. Having assassinated Caius's elder brother and corrupted the tribunate, the senators are certain that only Caius now stands between them and uncontested mastery of Rome and thus conspire to discredit Caius in the eyes of the people.

The patricians' belief in the people's inability to govern and lead themselves is inextricable from their belief in the volatility and fickleness of popular opinion. The corrupt tribune Drusus assures the tyrannical consul Opimius, "Tu sais quelle est la multitude, / Sa faveur qu'on obtient et qu'on perd en un jour" (2.1). [You know what the multitude is, / One gains and loses its favor in a day.] And the people's "favor" is easily manipulated; Drusus confidently predicts, "Le Peuple obéira" (2.1) [The people will obey]:

> Contre tout son parti [Caius's] les Juges et les Prêtres
> Feront parler les lois, les Dieux de nos ancêtres;

Les Dieux, les lois, Consul! C'est par là qu'on séduit;
Et c'est avec des mots que le Peuple est conduit. (3.1)

[Against his party the judges and priests
Will make the laws and the gods of our ancestors speak;
The Gods, the laws, Consul! it is with these that we seduce;
And it is with words that the people are managed.]

Chénier's Roman patricians, then, imagine the people to be just as gullible as revolutionary antitheatricalists imagined theater audiences to be. But the patrician scheme is foiled both by the sublime heroism of Caius, who takes his own life, and by the perspicacity of the people, who, never doubting Caius, avenge his death. Impervious to the patrician machinations, the people show themselves capable of recognizing their true friends and of self-government. The people gain their right to govern themselves precisely because, as a savvy audience, they penetrate the patricians' deceptions.

In the wake of Chénier's successful play, *L'Auteur d'un moment* seeks to produce a rather witty, if nefarious, theatrical effect: Léger's attack on Chénier attempts to replay but *reverse* the denouement of the scenario laid out in *Caius Gracchus*. While Chénier's plebeians reject the plot to discredit their hero Caius, Léger hoped that his audience at the Vaudeville would succumb to the sinister conspiracy against Chénier and join in ridiculing the "écrivain patriote" [patriotic writer] whose only crime according to his supporters "est d'avoir donné des ouvrages propres à fortifier l'esprit public, et qui ont réussi" [is to have offered works suitable for the fortification of the public spirit which have succeeded].[83] But the audience understood the implications of Léger's device: to endorse Léger's mocking of Chénier's success and sincerity would be to confirm Baliveau's assessment of theatrical audiences as fickle and foolish, for they had already approved of and celebrated Chénier. Léger's play, the audience rightly perceived, was above all an attack on their judgment and their authority. For if Chénier were a charlatan, then the people were dupes. The riots against *L'Auteur*, I am suggesting, reaffirm the audience's commitment to Chénier and vindicate his representation of the people as competent judges.

The audience actions at the Vaudeville are momentous, in part, because they effectively asserted precisely those powers Léger's play sought to strip from audiences. For if, as *L'Auteur* insists, the people were not competent to assess the merits of plays, then government authorities should step in and reclaim that function. Léger's satire, then, implied that the people could not be trusted to command in the theater. But if there was a lesson to be learned at the Vaudeville, it was the theater company, not the audience, that was on the receiving end. "Il faut espérer" [It is to be hoped], warned the *Chronique de Paris,* "que les directeurs du théâtre du Vaudeville ne se mêlent plus de lutter contre l'opinion public" [that the directors of the Théâtre du Vaudeville will no longer engage themselves in fighting against public opinion].[84]

Expressing and enforcing their opinions brought theater audiences into conflict not only with theater directors but also with revolutionary government authorities. To elucidate the ways in which these contests for control over theatrical representation were crucially bound up with contradictory notions about the force of public judgment and the proper role of the people in the production of revolutionary politics and culture, I want to turn to Jean-Louis Laya's *L'Ami des lois* (The Friend of the Laws), a play, like *Caius Gracchus,* centrally concerned with the attempts of politicians to manipulate the people. The evil politicians of *L'Ami des lois,* however, are not Roman patricians but overt caricatures of Robespierre, Marat, and other Jacobins. News of the play's inflammatory content circulated for weeks before *L'Ami* opened, and the play was both eagerly and anxiously anticipated in Paris. The anxious acted peremptorily: on January 12, 1793, the municipal government dispatched Nicolas Chambon, the mayor of Paris, to the theater to suppress the play. But the eager proved too eager for Chambon, who had the following letter sent to the National Convention, where it was read aloud to the deputies: "Citoyen Président, je suis retenu au Théâtre-français par le peuple, qui veut que la pièce de *l'Ami des lois* soit jouée." [Citizen President, I am being held at the Théâtre-Français by the people; they want the play *L'Ami des lois* to be performed.] A deputation of citizens would be arriving soon from the theater, the mayor explained, and he begged the legislators to hear its demand for the play.[85]

Laya wrote his comedy, *L'Ami des lois,* especially for the actors of the Comédie-Française. Laya's hero, Forlis, is a moderate ex-aristocrat who, while opposing the extremists in the government, is a friend to the Revolution, the people, and, of course, the laws. The play's revolutionary politicians have perfected a system of advancing their own interests by stirring up popular suspicions against true patriots. Fearing Forlis's probity, these pseudorevolutionaries decide to accuse him of treason and incite popular violence against him. Thus, Duricrâne (Hardhead), a journalist modeled on Marat, assures Nomophage (Eater of the law!), a figure for Robespierre, that they can orchestrate popular action against Forlis despite his reputation for virtue and honesty: "Du diable! un bruit d'enfer! un désordre parfait! / Fiez-vous à mes soins . . . oh! j'ai de la pratique: / Des émeutes à fond je connais la tactique." [The devil! pandemonium! complete disorder! / Put yourself in my hands . . . oh I've experience / I know the stratagems of riots perfectly.][86] These extremists conceive of the people in purely instrumental terms and like the Roman patricians of *Caius Gracchus* believe them fickle, volatile, and gullible.

Forlis, on the other hand, is a true democrat: he has faith in the people's judgment. Tranquil in his innocence, he makes his case calmly to the people, who not only vindicate him but repay his faith in them by embracing him. Together Forlis and the people rejoice in his innocence and their acumen and thus create a truly sentimental tableau that a witness describes to Forlis's loyal friends:

> Oh! monsieur; laissez-le sans contrainte,
> S'entourer de ce peuple et de sa douce étreinte.
> Respectez ces transports d'ivresse et de faveur:
> Ce moment appartient au peuple son sauveur
> Qui de joie en ses bras donne et reçoit des larmes. (5.3)

> [Oh! Monsieur; leave him without constraint,
> To surround himself with the people, in its sweet embrace.
> Respect this exaltation of emotion and attachment:
> This moment belongs to the people, his savior.
> Who take him in their arms and share tears of joy.]

Just as the people correctly perceive Forlis's innocence, they immediately grasp the venal politicians' guilt. Yet even after the people acquit Forlis, Nomophage brazenly asserts his power to seduce them:

> Pensez-vous que ce peuple envers vous si facile
> N'ouvre qu'à vos accents une oreille docile?
> Il est là, dites-vous? J'y vole, il m'entendra:
> Si son courroux me cherche? un mot le contiendra. (5.4)

> [Do you think that the people, so lenient toward you
> Lend a docile ear to your voice alone?
> They are there you say? I fly, they will hear me:
> And if their wrath seeks me? a word will contain it.]

Nomophage's stubborn underestimation of the people's judgment brings about his arrest and downfall at their hands. A witness reports of Nomophage: "De l'intrigant le règne enfin expire. / A séduire le peuple en vain sa bouche aspire" (5.6). [The reign of the intriguer is at last expired. / To seduce the people in vain his mouth aspired.] The play, then, cautions politicians about the hazards of misjudging the people's powers of judgment. Ultimately, the people justify Forlis's faith and show themselves capable of discerning the difference between friends and flatterers.

Ironically, the municipal council had sent the unlucky mayor off to the theater with a decree forbidding the performance of *L'Ami des lois* on the grounds that it made "rapprochements dangereux et tendant à élever des listes de proscription contre des citoyens recommandables par leur patriotisme" [dangerous correspondences which tend toward the proscription of citizens who are commendable for their patriotism].[87] According to the council the play itself constituted a false accusation and an attempt to mislead popular opinion. The council, in other words, feared that *L'Ami des lois* would successfully deceive the people as to the character of their true friends Robespierre and, the friend of the people himself, Marat. Although the play celebrated the people's ability to judge, the municipality acted on the assumption of the people's essential gullibility.

The mayor went to the theater preceded by Santerre, the commander of Paris's national guard, and a detachment of troops and artillery, but, as Fleury recounts the events, "en vain le commandant de la garde nationale, entouré par son état-major, paraît-il en superbe uniforme, on n'écoute rien; on se moque de lui" [the commander of the national guard, in his superb uniform, surrounded by his état-major, appeared in vain; no one listened, no one paid attention]. The crowd, Fleury recalled, continued to shout for the play: "nous voulons la pièce ou la mort" [we want the play or death]![88] The play was performed that night and several more times after the National Convention decided that the municipality lacked the authority to forbid the performance. The mayor was chastised by the municipal council for his ineffectiveness, and he resigned a few weeks later, perhaps because of the "douleurs vives" [sharp pains] he received that night at the hands of his fellow-citizens in the theater (ibid., 136).

Both the play at the Vaudeville and the play at the Comédie-Française were considered, in some sense, counterrevolutionary. Yet in one case the audience insisted that the play be banned, while the authorities insisted that it be performed; in the other case the audience demanded that the play be performed, while the authorities demanded that it be banned. The spectators at the Comédie-Française were no doubt more conservative than those at the Vaudeville. Yet their goal was the same: to retain control over performances in the theater. On both occasions government authorities attempted to discredit the audience in order to denigrate its assertive, autonomous action. In the first case the commanding police officer at the theater grossly exaggerated the audience's destructiveness. He claimed that the audience set fire to the theater, and he branded the spectators wanton anarchists.[89] In the second case politicians maintained that the spectators were traitors and agitators paid by aristocrats, perhaps even by Marie-Antoinette herself, to provoke disorder in the capital.[90]

By attributing unacceptable politics—anarchist and monarchist respectively—to the two audiences, authorities in effect denied that there was any politics particular to audiences *as* audiences. Both accusations amounted to refusing the spectators any independent purposeful agency proper to them in their function as theatrical public. If the spectators were the lackeys of the monarchy, then they carried out the designs of the court, not their own; if they were anarchists, then they acted only to wreak havoc and destroy. Worried authorities, that is, reduced the audience's action to recognizable extratheatrical political positions. In both cases, however, the spectators constructed their own political identity as participants in a theatrical audience. They organized, empowered spokesmen, formed deputations, and defied political and military authority. Indeed, while both audiences were characterized as lawless by government officials, their actions evinced an orderliness and a purposiveness that suggest an inherent sense of law. In effect, these audiences declared their right not to rampage and attack but rather to exercise popular censorship.[91]

Considering themselves the sovereign people, audiences asserted their right and ability to exercise directly their sovereign power. Audiences were neither defending nor opposing freedom of speech; instead, they were insisting that the right and capacity to censor belonged only to them. Popular censorship, moreover, did not mean simply the people's right to subdue and stifle at will. The right to act as censor meant the right to regulate. And this was a right that audiences refused tenaciously to delegate to political representatives. As interpreted by the weekly newspaper *Révolutions de Paris,* the events at the Vaudeville delivered a clear message from the people to their governors: "surtout faisons nous-mêmes et nous seuls la police intérieure de nos salles de spectacles" [above all let us [citizens] and us alone police our theaters].[92]

Because the theater was popularly controlled, it was of particular political significance. *Révolutions de Paris* warned that precisely because the theater was under the jurisdiction of the audience, the court party sought to regain dominion over it:

Ils n'ont donc plus d'autre espoir que dans un événement décisif et calami-
teux. Si le parterre devenait une fois ou deux une arène sanglante, alors
peut-être quelques bons citoyens eux-mêmes se croiraient réduits à rede-
mander les sentinelles qui fourmillaient autrefois dans l'intérieur des salles
de spectacles, au grand scandale de la raison et de la liberté civile; alors, as-
surée des officiers de la garde, comme on l'était au théâtre du Vaudeville, la
cour viendrait peut-être à bout, sous peu de temps, de ne laisser aux spectateurs tout au plus que la licence de tousser; tous battements de mains
seraient sévèrement défendus, et l'esprit public deviendrait ce qu'il pourrait
faute d'aliment, il périrait bientôt; et le patriotisme, sans foyer, sans ressort,
s'éteindrait tout à fait. (ibid.)

[They (aristocrats) have only one hope left, that of a decisive and calamitous
event. If once or twice the pit becomes a bloody arena, then perhaps even
some good citizens will feel themselves forced to ask for the return of the
soldiers who swarmed inside our theaters formerly, to the horror of liberty
and reason: then, assured of the guard, as they were at the Vaudeville theater, the court will shortly arrive at the point where they will not even leave
the spectators the license to cough; all clapping will be severely prohibited,
and the public spirit will become what it may without any nourishment—
it will soon perish; and patriotism, without any shelter, denied any appeal,
will be completely extinguished.]

The court's design to restore tyranny, according to the paper's reckoning, depended on suppressing the theater spectators' signs of approval and disapproval. Once the audience had been stripped of its authority to pass judgment
on a play presented to it, public spirit would languish, and the theater would
cease to be the sanctuary of patriotism. For *Révolutions de Paris* the demise of
the popularly controlled theater and the repression of the citizen-censor meant
the destruction of the Revolution itself.

The implication that revolutionary political institutions were insufficient
for the preservation of liberty and patriotism is unmistakable and remarkable.
For surely one would think that the National Convention could sustain "public spirit" at least as well as the theater. After all, according to elected representatives the Convention was the voice and the agent of the general will; as such
it ought to have been recognized as the sacred center of republican virtue. But
Révolutions de Paris contends that once the forces of tyranny appropriate the
theater, no institution remains to the people. The theater owed its status as a
crucial institution for the Revolution not simply to the content of theatrical
representations: monarchists, in the scenario conjured by *Révolutions de Paris*,

did not seek to substitute plays about heroic kings for plays about heroic republicans. Rather, the theater was deeply revolutionary because the theatrical public exerted continual, exclusive control over those representations. Thus, it was not simply the right but the responsibility of all good citizens to participate in this popular government of the theater: "nous insistons encore . . . ils doivent venir au théâtre pour y exercer le droit de censure qui n'appartient qu'à eux" (ibid.) [we insist again . . . they must go to the theater in order to exercise the right to censor which belongs only to them].

Although the Convention deliberated in the presence of the public, *Révolutions de Paris* made it clear that the public did not wield the same power in relation to its political representatives that it did in relation to theatrical representation. For the newspaper account defines *tyranny* as the prohibition of the public's expression of its judgments, as the interdiction of applause; thus the National Convention—an institution whose very existence, Barère believed, required the suppression of applause—was, at least in theory, the locus of tyranny par excellence.

Political Representation and Theatrical Representation

The theater and the National Convention embodied two antagonistic modes of representation: direct popular participation was not only compatible with theatrical representation but was sustaining of it; political representation, however, displaced the empowering public. According to the prevailing revolutionary theory of representative government, the people of Paris who came to watch the deliberations in the National Assemblies had no right to intervene in debates because they had already delegated their authority to their representatives. The French people, Barère explained, "exerce donc par la Convention sa souveraineté. Le peuple manifeste sa volonté par le vœu de cette Convention. La Convention assemblée est la volonté souveraine qui doit se faire entendre" [exercises its sovereignty through the National Convention. The people manifests its will through the will of this Convention. The Convention assembled is the sovereign will which must make itself heard].[93] Those who filled the observation galleries were simply particular citizens; they did not constitute the sovereign people. Thus, Robespierre could complain with some justice that the Convention had been structured in such a way as to "exclure le public en l'admettant" [exclude the public while admitting it]. Because the public was physically present but barred from carrying out its censoring function, it was effectively absent; it was "absent et présent à la fois" [at once absent and present].[94]

Robespierre's complaint demonstrates that the National Assembly itself was deeply divided over its relation to the empowering people. Many deputies feared the influence the immediate presence of Parisian militants might wield over the Assembly. And while they could be accused of seeking a kind of representative absolutism that ignored the wishes of those who were to be represented, they could legitimately claim in response that the will of the Parisians did not reflect that of their constituents in the provinces, which it was their duty to represent. Some deputies could and did adopt the absolute position, arguing that the representative's duty was to act in what *he* saw to be the best interest of the nation rather than to execute the will of those who elected him.[95] Other deputies, principally those associated with the Jacobins, promoted the authority of the Parisian citizenry both practically, by establishing ties to the political clubs and the sectional assemblies, and theoretically, by espousing a theory of representation that celebrated the virtue and the competency of the mass of the people.

The theory and practice of representative government were put to a practical test when the question of a referendum over the king's fate arose. The history of the "appel au peuple" is especially interesting because it reversed the usual positions in the Assembly and demonstrated the extent to which the Rousseauian language of direct democracy was available to the deputies themselves for a multitude of purposes.[96] While the direct appeal to the people had previously been the province of the Jacobins, the Girondins adopted this position in the case of the king. They argued that only the people themselves could condemn Louis. Some of their Jacobin colleagues accused the Girondins of seeking the referendum in order to stir up the provinces against Paris (on the assumption that those in the provinces retained affection for the king and would reject the Parisian insurrection that had toppled him). Even so, these deputies employed the language of popular sovereignty, and it was to that language that the opponents of the proposed referendum were forced to reply.[97] The debate over the referendum brought to the fore many of the questions at the heart of representative politics: were there inherent limits on the representatives' exercise of sovereign power? Could the people exercise their power directly? What was the relationship between representative and direct democracy?

The answer to the first of these questions was the simplest: in electing representatives, the majority of deputies declared, the people had delegated all of their powers, not just some of them. Second, and this was in a sense the direct response to the Girondins' invocation of popular sovereignty, the Assembly in effect declared that the people could never exercise its will directly because it existed only abstractly. For the people to exist *in fact*, it would have to be capable of meeting as a whole. Thus, the Jacobin Fabre d'Eglantine argued, "il ne peut être émis de majorité réelle et raisonnée, que dans un corps réuni dont la nature et l'organisation soient de former un tout, assemblée dans un seul endroit" [a real and reasoned majority can be produced only from a united body whose nature and organization is to form a whole assembled in one place].[98] Such a gathering into a single body, of course, could never be feasible. It was, after all, precisely this problem that led to the development of representative government. But what is most interesting about this argument is that even its defense of representative government stems from its insistence on *presence,* from the belief that for the real deliberation democracy required to take place, citizens must be assembled in "one place." Fabre conceives democracy as necessarily based on the presence of citizens to each other as individuals and as a whole, but this presence is inherently impossible in a large state; for this reason, according to Fabre's logic, a democratic state must turn to representation. Thus even this absolute conception of representation takes direct democracy for its ideal.

The third argument presented against the referendum was that even if the direct exercise of the popular will were feasible, it would be undesirable because direct democracy and representative democracy were fundamentally incompatible: the practice of direct democracy invalidated political representation. This argument came from an impeccable source: Rousseau's *The Social Contract.* Rousseau argued that "où se trouve le représenté, il n'y a plus de représentant" (139) [in the presence of the represented there is no longer any representation]. By this he meant that when the populace was assembled as the people, sovereignty reverted to it, and any other form of government was temporarily suspended. Once the people took matters into their own hands, representation became illegitimate. Hence, Rousseau concludes, popular assemblies are always deeply distressing for political authorities. Of course, for Rousseau this was not an argument against the presence or participation of the people; on the contrary, it demonstrated representation's lack of legitimacy. The deputies making this case, then, cited Rousseau in support of a position diametrically opposed to his own; after all, in *The Social Contract* Rousseau famously argues that "the idea of representation is a modern one. It comes from feudal government, from that iniquitous and absurd system under which the human race is degraded and which dishonours the name of man. . . . It is remarkable in the case of Rome, where tribunes were so sacred, that no one ever imagined that they might usurp the functions of the people" (141). For Rousseau absolute representation meant the usurpation of the people's sovereignty. But for deputies who either feared the direct intervention of the citizenry or who worried that the provinces could be enlisted against them, the superseding of representative government meant anarchy or civil war.

The defeat of the proposed referendum did not resolve the conflict among those who held different views about the relationship between representatives and the represented. It did not persuade Parisians to refrain from the vociferous expression of their views in the presence of their representatives. Indeed, many revolutionary citizens persistently acted on the belief that representation and the direct expression of popular sentiments could and should coexist.

For many revolutionary citizens popular sovereignty meant direct democracy. But the form of direct democracy that was endorsed by the citizens of Paris was not the incessant participation of all in every aspect of government. Revolutionary citizens believed that delegated authorities should be established to govern, but they also believed that those authorities must submit all their actions to the scrutiny and judgment of the people. Citizens ought to be the censors of their representatives. This meant, essentially, that they ought to have the right to sanction the laws passed in their name, to recall deputies they considered faithless, and to have knowledge of every aspect of their government. The right to elect officials without the right to oversee, to accept, or to reject the actions they undertook would amount to nothing more than "le droit de se donner et de se choisir des maîtres" [the right to give themselves masters of their own choosing]; such officials would constitute an "aristocratie élective" [elective aristocracy], in the words of the Parisian districts.[99] Or, as the *Révolutions de Paris* complained as early as February 1790, a political system in which the participation of the citizenry is limited to voting cannot be called a free one: "élire et payer, payer et élire, voilà à quoi se réduisent les fonctions de citoyens actifs; il reste à savoir si on est libre quand on ne fait que payer et élire" [elect and pay, pay and elect, this is what the function of active citizens is reduced to; it remains to be seen whether one is free when one does nothing other than pay and elect].[100]

Although voting was held to be an important right, it did not by itself make a citizen free; voting did not alone constitute anything like the degree and quality of participation many newly enfranchised citizens sought. In his fascinating and magisterial book *Le Nombre et la raison: La Révolution française et les élections,* Patrice Gueniffey argues that voter turnout declined after 1789 until it swelled again in 1793, when the ratification of a new constitution was put to the people, because, in part, electing representatives, rather than deliberating on issues, was not particularly attractive to many citizens. Thus a significantly greater number turned out for the plebiscite on the Constitution of 1793:

> Pour la première fois depuis 1789, les citoyens n'étaient pas appelés à élire, à choisir ceux qu'ils estimaient les plus dignes de les représenter dans l'exercice de leurs droits, mais à prendre une décision politique. Ils étaient invités à délibérer, puis à désigner des mandataires chargés de porter à Paris le vœu des assemblées. La plébiscite rappelait ainsi le souvenir de pratiques abolies en 1789, et cela d'autant plus que les assemblées privilégièrent—les unes en admettant indistinctement citoyens, femmes, et mineurs, les autres en recourant à l'acclamation collective ou aux différentes variantes du vote public—des procédures qui mettaient en cause le principe du vote individuel.[101]

> [For the first time since 1789, citizens were not called upon to elect, to choose those whom they deemed most worthy to represent them in the exercise of their rights, but rather to make a political decision. They were asked to deliberate and then to designate deputies charged with bringing the decision of the assemblies to Paris. The plebiscite thus recalled the memory of practices that were abolished in 1789, and this was especially the case because the assemblies privileged procedures that put the principal of the individual vote into question—some by admitting women and minors with citizens indiscriminately, others by returning to the practice of collective acclamation or different versions of the public vote.]

The 1793 plebiscite more closely resembled the type of politics practiced in the theaters than that established through political representation. Participation was open to those who were not legally enfranchised; participation meant immediately voicing and debating opinions; opinions could emanate from and be expressed by a group or a collective; and the opinion of the participants was determining.

In his classic work *Les Sans-culottes parisiens en l'an II,* Albert Soboul shows that these practices were at the heart of the political philosophy of the revolutionary Parisian working class and petite bourgeoisie. Over and over again their organizations, the sections and political clubs, insisted that popular sovereignty could be maintained only if citizens retained the power to control and recall their representatives, the right to approve or disapprove of proposed laws, the authority to supervise and be aware of all the activities undertaken by their representatives, and perhaps, most relevantly here, the right to assemble to discuss matters they deemed important to the nation. The foundational principle of popular politics, Soboul argues, was the belief that the people were sovereign: "de ce principe dérive tout le comportement politique des militants populaires, s'agissant là pour eux, non d'une abstraction, mais de la réalité concrète du peuple réuni dans ses assemblées et exerçant la totalité de ses droits" [the entire political comportment of working-class and lower-class militants stems from this principle; for them it was not an abstraction but rather the concrete reality of the people, united in assemblies, exercising all of their rights].[102] On this understanding, representatives were simply those who, as Ross Perot might put it, were hired to work for them. Thus, for example, in November 1792 the Piques section adopted a project for sanctioning all the laws made by the National Convention, explaining that "nous devons seuls dicter nos lois, leur [the representatives'] unique besogne est de nous en proposer" (ibid., 511) [we alone must dictate our laws, their unique task is to propose them to us]. And in the summer of 1793, as some Parisian militants increasingly complained about the Convention, a member of the revolutionary committee of the Contrat-social section of Paris asserted that "la Convention n'était composée que d'hommes payés pour faire les lois qu'on leur demandait" (ibid., 509) [the Convention is composed only of men paid to make the laws we ask them to make].

Recently Maurice Genty has argued that the political aspirations Soboul attributed to the sans-culottes of the year II were in fact present among Parisians from the Revolution's earliest days. Moreover, those who participated in district politics in 1789 were concerned not only with political representation at the national level; they worried that even the representatives each district sent to the municipal government, the Commune, might usurp the political authority of those who sent them. As early as August 1789, for example, a citizen of the Saint-Philippe-du-Roule district, insisted not only on the right to sanction proposed laws but also on the right to participate fully in city administration, for this was a right, he argued, that "les citoyens ne partagent avec personne, qui appartient à eux tous, et nul d'entr-eux en particulier" [citizens do not share with anyone, which belongs to all of them, and to no one of them in particular]."[103]

Revolutionary Parisians wanted to establish a jurisdiction over political representation equivalent to that they exerted over theatrical representation. As early as December 1789, those active in their district assemblies were struggling to maintain the capacity for real self-government that they had won in July. Curiously, the historical precedent the districts cited most often in their case for the legitimacy of direct democracy went back to the days of Charlemagne: "Dans l'origine de notre monarchie, sous Charlemagne, qui respecta tant les droits du peuple, c'était au milieu du Champ de Mars, que les loix étaient proposées. Les applaudissements universels annonçaient leur acceptation; le silence le plus profond était la preuve qu'elles étaient refusées." [At the origin of our monarchy, under Charlemagne, who so respected the rights of the people, laws were proposed in the middle of the Champ de Mars. Universal applause signified their acceptance; profound silence was the proof that they were rejected.][104] Although the gatherings in the Champ de Mars were not theatrical—Charlemagne was not an actor performing a fiction—these mythical legislative sessions do exemplify an economy of power corresponding to that of the theater. Charlemagne did represent the French nation, at least according to the constitutional thinking of the early revolutionary period, yet for the acts of the representative to be legitimate they had to be ratified by the represented. Instead of registering their approval through individual votes, the people ratified the laws in a collective, public, unanimous demonstration that took the form of applause. In most social contract theory the silence of the people signifies tacit acceptance of their government's actions, but many revolutionary Parisians insisted that official actions required their active, explicit assent. The legendary meetings at the Champ de Mars, like the theater, embodied the union of representation with direct popular participation.

Representationalism

The struggle to reconcile political representation with direct participatory democracy, I have been suggesting here, defined revolutionary political and theatrical culture and the relation between the two. That struggle was resolved in the hegemony not only of political representation but of representation per se. And the persistent hegemony of representation in modern culture is reflected in the failure of the theatricalists and the Habermasians to recognize the ideological status of representation—to see that representationalism was a particular position within revolutionary political culture. Indeed, these scholars neglect the historical contradiction between political representation and direct democracy because they fail to detect any meaningful difference between the two.

This tacit conflation of direct and representative democracy reveals the ways that both approaches are inscribed within a representational cultural and political economy—an economy, that is, in which representativeness is the necessary condition for legitimacy and in which being represented is the necessary condition for political and cultural subjectivity. François Furet has elaborated what is perhaps the most complex and self-conscious version of this critical and historical bias for representation: he claims that direct democracy is always already representation. It is the "inevitable paradox of direct democracy," argues Furet, that it produces a politics dominated by representation. When power belongs "only to the people," it belongs to "no one." And that void allows for the creation of a "world where mental representations of power [govern] all actions."[105]

But the new world of representation is not the inevitable product of direct democracy; on the contrary, this version of direct democracy is a product of representational thinking. For "the people" exists only as an idea, only as a "mental representation" of persons, and this is why when power is in the hands of "the people," it is in the hands of no one. Furet thus establishes a false choice: we either believe in "the people" in all its plenitude and ascribe the Revolution to its deeds, or we must acknowledge that revolutionary language, a discourse that could "speak through" political leaders, was the source and site of power (ibid., 59). This is a false choice because it effaces the agency of actual people; it disregards the fact that many people, certainly many more than ever before, did indeed exercise power in previously unknown and unimaginable ways. People in theater audiences did not seek to achieve representative status; they did not understand either power or legitimacy to inhere in representation. Rather, they argued—and acted on the presumption—that since sovereignty resided in the people, each citizen, as a constituent element of the sovereign, had the right to exercise sovereign power in concrete and meaningful ways. Citizens, not representative assemblies and not even "the people," embodied sovereignty. Hence they sought, even while electing representatives, to retain supreme authority over those whose claim to govern derived from them. As we have seen, in the theaters extraordinarily large numbers of ordinary citizens pressed this claim to authority fervently and actively. To neglect the unprecedented effort of revolutionary citizens to participate in, to shape, and to control representation is to miss what made the French Revolution "the most astonishing that has hitherto happened in the world."[106]

2 | *The Comic Revolution*

Molière, Rousseau, Fabre d'Eglantine, and Revolutionary Antitheatricalism

Ce premier sentiment de la violence et de l'injustice est resté si profondément gravé dans mon âme, que toutes les idées qui se rapportent me rendent ma première émotion, et ce sentiment, relatif à moi dans son origine, a pris une telle consistance en lui-même, et s'est tellement détaché de tout intérêt personnel, que mon cœur s'enflamme au spectacle ou au récit de toute action injuste, quel que soit l'objet et en quelque lieu qu'elle se commette, comme si l'effet en retombait sur moi.

Jean-Jacques Rousseau, Les Confessions, *book 1*

In his 1885 essay "Figures oubliées de la Révolution française: Fabre d'Eglantine" (Forgotten Figures of the French Revolution: Fabre d'Eglantine), the indefatigable archivist and pioneering historian François-Alphonse Aulard asked why historians and critics had neglected Fabre d'Eglantine. After all, Aulard reminded his readers, Fabre was the author of the best eighteenth-century French comedy after the *Marriage of Figaro,* and as Danton's right-hand man and a leading member of the Cordelier club he had played a considerable role in revolutionary politics. So why, he asks, "donc y a-t-il quelque chose de douteux et de troublé" [is there something dubious and troubled] about Fabre's reputation?[1] Aulard offered a persuasive answer to his own question: the problem lay precisely in the twofold nature of Fabre's ambitions and activities. Literary critics refused to take Fabre's oeuvre seriously because his political en-

74

deavors seemed to cast suspicion on his literary work: they believed that his plays and poems could only be political propaganda. Conversely, historians refused to attribute any significance to the politics of a sometime actor and playwright. Thus, Fabre's status as a figure of importance for the Revolution had never really been established because "il ne sût mettre ni dans sa vie ni dans sa personne l'unité apparente que l'opinion exige de ses héros" [he did not know how to put in his life or in his person the apparent unity that opinion requires of its heroes].[2]

If for Aulard's contemporaries the propinquity of theater and politics discredited both, recent critics and historians, by contrast, have argued that revolutionary politics and theater were not only compatible but nearly identical. Indeed, Fabre's dual career would seem to offer irresistible proof for one of the claims most frequently asserted by recent literary critics and cultural historians of the revolutionary period: revolutionary political culture was highly theatrical.[3]

Commentators have long used theatrical metaphors to describe the Revolution. Michelet, for example, forged a beautiful theatrical trope to depict the relation between revolutionary orators and the crowds to whom they spoke:

> I have seen that these brilliant, powerful speakers, who gave voice to the thinking of the masses, are wrongly considered to be the only actors. They responded to impulse much more than they imparted it. The leading actor was the people. In order to rediscover it and to restore it to its role, I have had to cut down to size the ambitious marionettes whose strings it pulled, and who were believed to show the secret workings of history.[4]

Michelet's elaborate metaphor seeks to make visible the ways that power and influence moved between "the people" and its leaders, and the way that historians had mistakenly focused only on the leaders who, they wrongly presumed, dictated the course of events.

Recently, however, scholarship of the Revolution has undergone a shift from the use of theatrical metaphors as illuminating descriptions to an understanding of revolutionary politics as, in fact, modeled on theater. What do such critics mean by *theatrical?* In *Rehearsing the Revolution* Marie-Hélène Huet argues that Louis XVI's trial, in particular, reveals the homology between theater and revolutionary politics: "We are indeed within the register of the theater" because "the material organization" of the proceedings—"the public, the stage, the loges, the ushers, the galleries"—is identical to the material organization of a theater (3).[5] In opening the proceedings of the National Assembly to public scrutiny revolutionary politicians transformed them into theater. According to Huet the presence of an observing public makes the *salle du Manège,* a former royal riding hall in which the assembly met, into a theater; recasts the rostrum from which deputies spoke as a stage; and transforms the benches on which observers sat into loges. Daniel Arasse's argument for the theatricality of the guillotine follows the same logic. In *The Guillotine and the Terror* Arasse attributes the powerful fearsomeness of the guillotine not to its function of beheading, but rather to the fact that it was "enthroned centre stage" (1). Executions were theatrical because "backdrop, actors, and a public . . . were present, and the execution was meticulously staged" (88).[6] While it is not quite clear what it means to "stage" an execution (does it mean that executions were ritualized? that they followed a scripted procedure?), it is clear that, on this account, wherever there was a public, there was a theater; thus, because the Revolution was an event of unparalleled mass public participation, it was a wholly theatrical event: "The stage was no longer confined to the theater," argues Scott S. Bryson, "but was found throughout society, at the tribunal, in the National Assembly, on the executioner's block."[7]

By stripping theatrical metaphors of their historical and cultural context, and by treating them as literal rather than figurative, these critics distort the significance of theatricality in revolutionary culture. To be sure, theatricality was an extremely significant concept during the Revolution; when contemporaries labeled the Assembly or an orator theatrical, for example, the term was most often a form of critique—tantamount to calling the participants hypocrites—rather than an analysis of the Assembly's actual operations. The fact that *theatricality* was so often invoked as a term of reprobation demonstrates revolutionaries' ongoing anxiety about the cluster of problems that they associated with theatricality: hypocrisy, opacity, alienation, chicanery. Moreover, to see a theater everywhere there is a public is to conflate publicity and theatricality—an especially grievous error since revolutionaries conceived of publicity as the safeguard of the Republic and sought at every turn to distinguish it and protect it from the nefarious effects of theatricality.

The theatrical interpretation discovers the key to the Revolution in its form and ignores the Revolution's particular political content. For example, in her influential study *Women and the Public Sphere in the Age of the French Revolution,* Joan B. Landes interprets Olympe de Gouges's bid to defend the king at his trial as theatrical ambition and treats the proceedings of the Convention as theatrical performance: "even if Gouges was a royalist, she nonetheless appreciated the dramatic possibilities of the revolutionary stage, for how else are we to understand her (predictably futile) effort to insert herself in such a grand theatrical performance as the trial of the king?"[8] Landes's theatrical interpretation inexplicably nullifies de Gouges's political beliefs—after all, a more plausible reading of de Gouges's actions would have to refer to her very public advocacy of constitutional monarchy—and empties overtly political acts of their political content. But Landes's theatricalization of de Gouges's political actions simultaneously reveals the ways in which the theatricalists ironically empty the theater itself of any real aesthetic or political significance. For although de Gouges was a playwright of some consequence, Landes is concerned only with the theatricality of her political endeavors.[9] This particular neglect is a symptom of a pervasive tendency to assume that political interests appropriated theaters as instruments of propaganda, as "schools of the Revolution." When the National Assemblies become a theater and the events there become plays, the theater itself seems merely a supplemental medium, not only for politics but for drama itself. Thus, the model of the theatrical Revolution, rather than exploring the "textuality of history" or the "historicity of texts," conflates history and text, politics and plays, and in so doing lapses into an inordinately ambitious formalism.[10] As a consequence the literary efforts of serious men and women of letters like Fabre d'Eglantine and Olympe de Gouges remain unexplored.

To recover revolutionary theater as something more than a mere metaphor and revolutionary politics as something other than mere theatricality, I pursue two different critiques of the theatricalist position and elaborate an alternative approach to both theater and politics. Revolutionary culture is remarkable for its profound *anxiety* about theatricality, so much so that a fervent desire to overcome and eradicate theatricality shaped revolutionary political discourse and practice. This same antitheatricalism inspired the development of a novel dramatic aesthetic and an effort to detheatricalize the theater in order to make it a significant and salutary institution for revolutionary culture. Revolutionaries of many different stripes were acutely conscious of Rousseau's radical antitheatricalism—an antitheatricalism that shaped his aesthetics as well as his social and political thought. Thus, Rousseau's critique of theater, and especially of Molière's comedies, inspired Fabre d'Eglantine's elaboration of a distinctly revolutionary comic drama, and his condemnation of the theatricality of social relations deeply influenced Robespierre's political theory and practice.[11]

The particular exigencies of the Revolution made theatricality a central preoccupation and a central peril, for theatricality exemplified representation's hazards and inadequacies at just the moment when the emergence of a new form of political and social organization, modern democratic republicanism, made representation a crucial term in political discourse and practice. Revolutionaries regarded theatricality as an integral element of the old hierarchical, monarchical system that sanctified social and political distinctions and in which rank—that is, identity—depended heavily on successful self-representation. Theatricality belonged to a society ruled by elaborate codes and rituals of politeness that served at least two functions: to exclude those not initiated into "society" and to mask all spontaneous and authentic expression. Revolutionary politicians associated theatricality with the decadent court aristocracy, with femininity, and especially with Marie-Antoinette. They believed that the monarchy used theatrical tricks to dissimulate its real aims and desires on the one hand and to mystify and pacify its people on the other. To establish a new, free, and egalitarian society and politics, the Revolution would have to unmask all those who would use theatrical tricks to disempower the people.

Revolutionaries were committed to the idea of publicity, to opening up all aspects of France's political life to public scrutiny.[12] But theatricality, as a particular mode of publicity, was anathema to revolutionary politics because it aggravated the Revolution's already troubled relationship to political representation. A perfectly transparent relationship between officials and the people was, according to the architects of the new nation, the positive condition for virtue and wisdom in government. And while publicity was necessary to such an endeavor, theatricality threatened rather than secured transparency. For most revolutionaries, publicity meant both the public discovery and display of truth and the participation of citizens in protecting revolutionary governance; theatricality, by contrast, was false representation and concealed truth. For if politicians were theatrical performers, then their true selves were hidden from view; their constituents and fellow citizens could never be certain whether they acted in the public interest or in their own. Historians have rightly argued that revolutionaries were obsessed with the notion of conspiracy; what the revolutionary obsession with conspiracy reveals is a compulsion to unmask, to strip bare, to somehow make the heart transparent and intention itself visible.[13] The desire for transparency became obsessive because the threat of theatricality could never be eliminated.

Like their political counterparts, revolutionary men and women of the theater—playwrights, actors, theatrical entrepreneurs, and, indeed, audiences—associated theatricality with the Old Regime: theatricality was at the heart of the decadent and superficial drama that, according to many critics of the period, had caused the decline of the French stage in the second half of the century. Fabre d'Eglantine believed that he could make a place for theater in revolutionary culture and redeem French drama by developing a new form of theater that would promote the new social order of equality and fraternity. That order required transparency; it required that citizens open their hearts fully to one another; theatricality, by contrast, made citizens opaque to one another by teaching them, or requiring them, to don masks in order to enter society.[14] Moreover, Old Regime theater taught its spectators to think of themselves and others as spectacles. The only way to revolutionize theater, according to Fabre, was to detheatricalize it; thus Fabre hoped to create a genuinely revolutionary theater precisely by refounding it on the basis of Rousseau's devastating critique of theatricality.

Although I have been discussing the intersections of theatrical and political antitheatricalism, I am not suggesting that theater and politics are identical because of their shared antitheatrical investment in transparency. When Fabre became a revolutionary politician, he did not simply transpose his theatrical endeavors to a new arena. For although Fabre was one of Danton's closest friends and associates, he hoped to produce a social revolution not through action in the Assembly but by rewriting Molière's *Misanthrope,* regenerating comic drama, and creating an antitheatrical revolutionary dramatic aesthetic. Fabre and other serious playwrights of the period claimed that the theater's political and social efficacy depended not on its reproduction of revolutionary ideology but on its aesthetics. For Fabre this meant transforming the moribund neoclassical French theater into a theater of sympathy. Such a transformation required not only a revolution in subject matter but also one in the formal construction and the language of plays. For just as theatricality introduced insincerity and deception into politics and corrupted the relationship between the people and political power, so too in the theater it perverted and distorted dramatic representation and corrupted the relationship between the public and the work of art. In the new world that Fabre envisioned, revolutionary political institutions would not shape theater; rather, a regenerated revolutionary theatrical culture would redeem the work of art, generating a new, revolutionary society.

Rather than embracing theatricality both Fabre d'Eglantine and his colleagues in the National Assembly Robespierre believed that overcoming the theatricality of, respectively, Old Regime theater and Old Regime politics was crucial to a successful break with the past. However, they found radically different solutions to defuse the threat of theatricality: Fabre thought that by placing the concept of sympathy at the heart of dramatic aesthetics, theater could be transformed from the training ground for hypocritical, self-interested, aristocratic culture into an institution that promoted transparent, fraternal, republican culture. Robespierre, however, believed that by carrying out the same political function as the people—that of surveillance—he escaped the potential theatricalization of the relationship between the people and the people's representatives. These two strategies were incompatible and resulted in a tragic confrontation: Fabre and Robespierre doubted each other's sincerity. And, as always during the Revolution, when sincerity was at issue, the stakes were very high.

Fabre's Reputation

Philippe-François-Nazaire Fabre d'Eglantine was born in Carcassonne, in the south of France, in 1750. If he is remembered today, it is usually as a close collaborator of Danton and as a suspected embezzler. Although Fabre was executed along with Danton and Camille Desmoulins on April 5, 1794, he is rarely treated with the admiration and sympathy historians often express for his fellow victims. Indeed, Fabre's is one of those extremely rare cases in which historians, with some important exceptions, have been willing to accept as valid charges made in the midst of the Terror. The son of a cloth merchant, Fabre was sent to study with the Doctrinaires at Toulouse, and after completing his education there, he became a lay teacher. But Fabre had literary ambitions and when, at the age of twenty-one, he won the poetry prize of the Académie des Jeux Floreaux, he adopted the name *eglantine* (wild rose) in celebration of this achievement; he called himself Fabre d'Eglantine for the rest of his life. Soon after, perhaps with new confidence from his triumph, Fabre went on the road as a traveling actor. His nomadic existence continued at least through the end of the 1770s, but by 1787 he had settled in Paris, where his first comedy, *Les Gens de lettres, ou le poète provincial,* had its opening at the Comédie-Italienne. The play was a flop, but surely it must be considered a major accomplishment to have had a play accepted by the troupe and performed at one of the three privileged theaters of the capital. Fabre persisted: *Les Gens de lettres* was followed by a tragedy, *Augusta,* which premiered (and did not outlast its premiere) at the Comédie-Française; the comedy *Le Présumptueux* (January 1789), which was withdrawn by the Comédie-Française after the successful playwright Collin d'Harleville accused Fabre of plagiarism, came soon after; Fabre finally found success with another comedy, *Le Collatéral* (May 1789), which ran for twenty-six performances at the Théâtre de Monsieur.[15] In other words, when the Revolution broke out in the summer of 1789, Fabre was just emerging as a productive and potentially important comic playwright.

With the advent of the Revolution Fabre immediately became an active participant in political life. He joined the Cordeliers club—political home to Danton, Camille Desmoulins, and Marat—which met four times each week and quickly became a center for democratic action. Fabre also began to write for the radical weekly newspaper *Les Révolutions de Paris.* When Danton was appointed minister of justice after the fall of the monarchy on August 10, 1792, he invited Fabre to act as his secretary. Eventually Fabre was elected to the National Convention as a representative for the city of Paris. During his time as a deputy Fabre produced his best-known monument: the revolutionary calendar. The National Convention commissioned the calendar from Fabre and adopted it in October 1793. The new calendar remained in use until December 31, 1806. Each of the calendar's ten months drew its name from nature and corresponded to the seasons: for example, Brumaire, which began in late October, was the month of fog; Germinal, which was equivalent to late March through late April, was the month of germination; and Thermidor, since it included parts of what had been July and August, was the month of heat. The calendar, in which seven-day weeks were replaced by ten-day *décades,* in its adherence to nature, was meant to be at once poetic and rational. In the calendar Fabre brought together his political and his literary sensibility.

Fabre, it seems, was never a well-beloved figure. Robespierre always disliked him despite Fabre's early, avowed republicanism. Madame Roland thought him a sinister and unsavory creature, and, after an initial encounter, she sought to avoid him. That he was known to be married to one woman and living with another, an actress, did not improve his profile among the many revolutionaries who believed strongly that the Revolution ought to purify what we now call family values. It seems, indeed, that there was "something dubious and troubled" about Fabre even for his contemporaries.

Perhaps what is most remarkable about Fabre is that throughout the period of his intense political activity his literary output never flagged for an instant. In February 1790 he achieved an unexpected popular and critical triumph with the play *Le Philinte de Molière, ou la suite du misanthrope,* a rewriting of Molière's comedy based on Rousseau's critique in the *Lettre à M. d'Alembert sur les spectacles.* But *Le Philinte de Molière* was only one of a string of successes: in January 1791 *Le Convalescent de qualité,* a sort of inversion of Molière's *Dom Juan* in which an aristocrat who tries to impress servants, women, and creditors with the aura of his rank cannot understand why every effort fails so miserably, was an enormous hit that was performed sixty-one times; the *Intrigue épistolaire,* which opened in June of the same year, was a blockbuster that ran for 146 performances. Fabre's next play, apparently, poked fun at electoral politics: *Le Sot orgueilleux, ou l'École des élections* (March 1792) was a disaster that closed immediately, and the text was subsequently lost. Fabre's next and last success was posthumous: *Les Précepteurs*—based, implausibly enough, on Rousseau's *Emile*—was received with great enthusiasm by both critics and audiences when it was finally performed in 1799.[16] Even the respectable and respected playwright and critic Jean-François La Harpe, who entertained far from friendly feelings for Fabre, conceded that in 1799 Fabre's drama was "celebrated in the newspapers with some sort of adoration since in them the author is called nothing other than the Molière of the century."[17]

Fabre was both a serious politician and a serious writer, and his career may thus slightly unsettle Robert Darnton's account of the Grub Street hack turned resentful revolutionary. Darnton's interpretation sees many prominent revolutionaries as failed writers whose politics stemmed from their anger against an establishment that rejected them and closed the doors of Parnassus on them. While this argument is no doubt often persuasive, the case of Fabre d'Eglantine should remind us of the need to historicize our ideas about writerly success. To have had several plays accepted and performed by the major, privileged theaters of the capital before the Revolution, even though all but one of these plays flopped, should not be seen as either failure or exclusion but rather as the first important steps toward a potentially successful career. Because Fabre is today at best a minor literary figure does not mean that he was so considered in his own time. Indeed, the dual identity that seems to have cost Fabre his place in literary and revolutionary history did not prevent many of his contemporaries from attributing great literary merit to his dramas. Fabre in fact had many admirers who abhorred his politics. Consider, for example, La Harpe, who knew and detested Fabre and who, in an analysis similar to Darnton's, attributed Fabre's ambition to his envy and jealousy of others, rather to any positive aims:

> Envenimé de haine, comme tous les esprits de la même trempe, contre tout ce qui s'appelait homme du monde, contre tout ce qui avait dans la société un rang qu'il n'avait pas et ne devait pas avoir, il eut bien voulu faire croire que toute la société était en effet composé de méchants et de fripons; et cette espèce de haine (on a dû le voir assez dans les événements de nos jours) était bassement envieuse, et pas plus morale que politique. (*Répertoire de la littérature*, 185)
>
> [Venomous and filled with hate, like all the minds of that temper, for all those who were called "homme du monde," for all those who held a rank in

society that he did not and should not have had, he would have had everyone believe that society was in fact made up of malefactors and rogues; and that kind of hate (we must certainly have seen it enough in the events of our times) was despicably envious and no more moral than political.]

But, on the other hand, La Harpe's essay is wildly inconsistent. After pages dripping with loathing and scorn, he goes on to give *Le Philinte de Molière* serious consideration and considerable praise:

> Le plan de la pièce est simple et bien conçu; la marche en est claire est soutenue; et l'action, sans être compliquée, ne languit pas un moment. Toute l'action se rapporte à une seule idée; mais elle est du nombre de celles qu'on appelle, en termes de l'art, idées mères; et il n'en faut qu'une de ce genre pour fournir cinq actes au talent qui sait construire une pièce et disposer les accessoires. Cette idée, très dramatique et très morale, consiste à punir l'egoisme par lui-même. (ibid., 242)

> [The organization of the play is simple and well-conceived; its development is clear and sustained; and the action, without being complicated, never flags for an instant. All the action relates to a single idea but it is one of those ideas that we call in the language of the theater, idées mères, and it requires only one such idea to furnish five acts for a talent who knows how to construct a play and to set out the incidental ideas. The idée mère, very dramatic and very moral, is to punish egoism by egoism.]

La Harpe praises *Le Philinte de Molière* for both its construction and its meaning. When La Harpe describes the play's singleness of purpose, he is not deriding it but emphasizing its adherence to the rules of neoclassical drama: the rule of unity of action demands that all the elements of a play advance a single idea or plot and that no scenes or characters be extraneous to that central idea. Unity of action was considered much more difficult to achieve than the other unities of time and place. For a tragic playwright like La Harpe, working in the shadow of Voltaire, Fabre's successful practice of the unity of action signals his ambition, seriousness, and authorial competence. This is high praise indeed. Moreover, despite La Harpe's low opinion of Fabre's ethics, he agrees with the premises of Fabre's work and believes that Fabre's portrait of Philinte offers a crucial lesson for French society: "On sent qu'un pareil caractère est la mort de toutes les vertus, de tous les sentiments humains et honnêtes" (ibid., 241). [One feels that such a character is the death of all virtues, of all humane and honest sentiments.]

In their 1802 history of the Comédie-Française during the Revolution,

Charles-Guillaume Etienne and Alphonse Martainville similarly consider *Le Philinte de Molière* an important play and Fabre d'Eglantine a major playwright, in spite of the fact that they held political views very unlike Fabre's and, in general, think little of the quality of the theater in this period. Although they find some faults of style in *Le Philinte de Molière,* they insist that "l'auteur attache, intéresse toujours: la pièce est d'ailleurs remplie de pensées fortes et sublimes; c'est un excellent cours de morale" [the author always attracts and interests the spectator: furthermore, the play is filled with powerful and sublime ideas; it is an excellent course in morality].[18] The two critics see politics as Fabre's downfall not because it infected his literary work but simply because it diverted him—ultimately permanently—from his vocation as a playwright:

> Il est fâcheux que la politique ait enlevé Fabre d'Eglantine à la littérature: un ouvrage d'un mérite aussi éminent faisait concevoir les plus grandes espérances, et elles n'eussent point être trompées, car Fabre ne ressemblait pas à ces auteurs qui montrent vingt fois de suite de dispositions qui promettent toujours, et qui ne tiennent jamais. (ibid., 1:85)

> [It is a pity that politics deprived literature of Fabre d'Eglantine: a work of such eminent merit gave reason to form the greatest expectations. And these hopes would not have been disappointed because Fabre did not resemble those authors who display promising dispositions twenty times in a row but who never fulfill their promise.]

Like La Harpe and Etienne and Martainville, Germaine de Stael did not sympathize with Fabre's politics, but she credited *Le Philinte de Molière* with remarkable aesthetic and social importance. Indeed, in *De la Littérature* Stael holds up *Le Philinte de Molière* as the model for a new comedy appropriate to her age: "Je vais rappeler un exemple remarquable des sujets nouveaux que peut traiter la comédie, et du nouveau but qu'elle doit se proposer" (347). [I am going to recall a remarkable example of the new subjects that comedy can treat, and of the new goal that it ought to set for itself.] Stael's brilliant political-sociological account of comedy holds that the comic emerges from the clash between desire and social norms and conventions (think, for example, of *L'Avare*) or from the exposure of a character ignorant of social convention (the obvious example must be *Le Bourgeois gentilhomme*). When social norms and conventions are brought in line with reason and nature—when, for example, there occurs a fundamental change in national culture such as that brought about by the Revolution—the opportunities for such clashes evaporate. Since nature is the baseline for sincerity, comedy depends on a society's insincerity—on the gap between its regulations and those of reason and nature—for its effect. In reasonable societies desire and convention no longer find themselves arrayed against each other; moreover, no one can be ignorant of natural and reasonable manners and morals since these are inherent to all human beings. Briefly put, the more reasonable a society becomes, the less funny it becomes (ibid., 342–347).

Republics still need comedy, however, Stael argues. Since any Republic's success depends on the virtue of its citizens and on their mutual affection and generosity, it is more important than ever to examine the vices of the human heart. This form of comedy, Stael admits, is less funny than the other, but it is infinitely more "philosophical" (ibid., 347). Stael offers Fabre's *Le Philinte de Molière* as the example of philosophical comedy fit for a republic:

> Dans *Le Misanthrope*, c'est Philinte qui est l'homme raisonnable, et c'est d'Alceste qu'on rit. Un auteur moderne, développant ces deux caractères dans la suite de leur vie, nous a fait voir Alceste généreux et dévoué dans l'amitié, et Philinte avide en secret et tyranniquement egoïste. L'auteur a saisi, je crois, dans sa pièce, le point de vue sous lequel il faut présenter désormais la comédie; ce sont les vices pour ainsi dire négatifs, ceux qui se composent de la privation des qualités, qu'il faut maintenant au théâtre. Il faut signaler de certaines formes derrière lesquelles tant d'hommes se retirent pour être personnels en paix, ou perfide avec décence. L'Esprit républicain exige des vertus positives, des vertus connues. Beaucoup d'hommes vicieux n'ont d'autre ambition que d'échapper au ridicule; il faut leur apprendre, il faut avoir le talent de leur prouver que le succès du vice prête plus à la moquerie que la maladresse de la vertu. (ibid., 347)

> [In *Le Misanthrope* it is Philinte who is the reasonable man and Alceste at whom we laugh. A modern author, developing these two characters in the next chapter of their lives, shows us Alceste a generous and devoted friend and Philinte secretly greedy and tyrannically egotistical. In his play the author has grasped, I believe, the point of view from which comedy should be presented from now on; it is the negative vices, so to speak, those which are composed of the privation of qualities, which we now need to see in the theater. It is necessary to point out certain forms behind which so many men retreat in order to be selfish in peace or to be faithless with decency. The republican spirit requires positive virtues, virtues that are known. Many vicious men have no other ambition but that of escaping ridicule; it is necessary to teach them, it is necessary to have the talent to prove to them, that the success of vice leads more surely to mockery than the clumsiness of virtue.]

In a republic, Stael argues, the good man who lacks polished manners—Alceste—is not to be mocked the way he would have been under the Old Regime, which counted its artificial code of comportment above all else. Now he who is lacking in generosity, honesty, and disinterestedness becomes the figure of fun (or, if not exactly fun, ridicule), and that lack becomes the object of comedy. In a sense, then, while deviation from "certain forms" was comedy's topos in the Old Regime, those "certain forms," that is, the conventions of polite behavior themselves, become comedy's target in the new regime.

In this chapter I will focus on *Le Philinte de Molière,* in part, because I believe it was Fabre's most ambitious play and because I agree with Aulard and with Stael that *Le Philinte de Molière,* more than any play that conspicuously intervened in or responded to contemporary political events, was the revolutionary play and, indeed, the revolutionary literary work par excellence.[19] Many revolutionary plays explicitly attacked Old Regime abuses or celebrated revolutionary achievements: among hundreds of plays, one might turn to Sylvain Maréchal's infamous *Le Jugement dernier des rois,* Claude-Michel Carbon de Flins des Oliviers' *Le Réveil d'Epiménide à Paris,* or Jean-Michel Collot-d'Herbois' *La Famille patriote, ou la fédération.* But it is *Le Philinte,* a play that makes no allusions to the Revolution or contemporary events, that most profoundly expresses and attempts to shape a new republican sensibility and that seeks to establish a new republican theater.

Robert Darnton finds this paradox—that *Le Philinte* seems situated in Molière's world of neoclassical comedy rather than the world of the French Revolution, yet it was felt to be so important to the Revolution—particularly interesting and suggestive. Why, he asks, were members of the extreme left so interested in this play "as if it were perfectly natural for the Cordeliers to be concerned with *Le Misanthrope?*"[20] Darnton argues persuasively that revolutionary intellectuals understood that the literary system of Old Regime France was in fact a power system and that it was by means of this literary-power system that the monarchical state functioned. Molière, Darnton argues, occupied the system's "sacred center." To rewrite and revolutionize Molière was to remake literary and political culture.[21] Darnton's sociological interpretation does a good deal to advance our understanding of what would seem to be the peculiarly high level of interest in this most literary mise en abime (Fabre rewriting Rousseau rewriting Molière). Darnton, however, does not offer a literary analysis of Fabre's play, nor does he attend to what is at stake in Fabre's particular conception of *how* Molière should be rewritten for revolutionary society. Focusing exclusively on the act of rewriting rather than the character of the revision leaves some of the most important questions unanswered: why should Molière, and hence comedy, rather than Corneille or Racine, and hence tragedy, come to occupy the sacred center of the Old Regime literary-power system and thus require toppling?[22] After all, comedy was considered the lower of the two classical genres. And if this is indeed the perception of Molière held by revolutionary men and women of letters, how do we account for the extraordinarily deep admiration these writers, including Fabre, routinely express for Molière? And, more important still, why is *Le Misanthrope*, certainly in its time one of Molière's least successful plays, the very play that demands rewriting? What is it precisely about reimagining *Le Misanthrope* that can lead to the creation of a revolutionary theater and a revolutionary culture?

Alceste and Jean-Jacques

In his famous antitheatrical treatise the *Lettre à M. d'Alembert sur les spectacles*, Rousseau argues that *Le Misanthrope* exemplifies the inadequacies of the theater as an aesthetic and social institution. Molière's play was particularly galling to Rousseau, for in Rousseau's view, despite its greatness, *Le Misanthrope* celebrates theatricality as a social practice: the "honnête homme" Philinte's hypocrisy, dissimulation, opacity, and shallowness are entirely successful modes of being in the world. By contrast, his friend and opposite number, Alceste, whose deepest professed desire—"Je veux qu'on soit sincère, et qu'en homme d'honneur / on ne lâche aucun mot qui ne parte de cœur." [I would have them be sincere, and never part / with any word that isn't from the heart.][23]—could be Rousseau's own, is ridiculed for, and gains nothing by, his sincerity and virtue. Thus, Molière, on Rousseau's reading, affirms Philinte's theatrical ethos: "Quand on est du monde, il faut bien que l'on rende / Quelques dehors civils que l'usage demande" (1.1). [It's often best to veil one's emotions. / Wouldn't the social fabric come undone / If we were wholly frank with everyone?]

Rousseau's essay was a contribution to a very long-standing debate, going back at least a century and a half, about the moral status of theater and theater's relation to the moral, ethical, political, and religious health of society. In the seventeenth and eighteenth centuries the antitheatrical position had been expressed, for the most part, by religious intellectuals such as Pierre Nicole and Bossuet; Rousseau's essay was shocking, in part, because it placed the critique of theater in an entirely secular register. But it was also scandalous for the same reason the *Discourse on the Arts and Sciences* had been: because in it the erstwhile philosophe Rousseau attacked the very institution that his former friends and colleagues held to be one of the triumphs and pillars of civilization.[24]

The *Lettre* is an extraordinarily complicated response to Jean le Rond d'Alembert's *Encyclopedia* article entitled "Genève."[25] D'Alembert, encouraged by Voltaire, who was living in exile in nearby Ferney, had suggested that a permanent public theater should be established in Geneva because such an establishment would help polish and perfect the manners and taste of Genevans. Rousseau's central assertion in response is that theater is powerless to improve a society's morals or sentiments; on the contrary, he insists that because theater must please its audience in order to survive, it follows that theater must flatter its audiences' beliefs, customs, prejudices, and fancies. Such flattery affirms and reinforces the society's prevailing passions rather than correcting them:

> La scène, en général, est un tableau des passions humaines, dont l'original est dans tous les cœurs: mais si le peintre n'avait soin de flatter ces passions, les spectateurs seraient bientôt rebutés, et ne voudraient plus se voir sous un aspect qui les fît mépriser d'eux-mêmes. Que s'il donne à quelques-unes des couleurs odieuses, c'est seulement à celles qui ne sont point générales, et qu'on haït naturellement. Ainsi l'Auteur ne fait encore en cela que suivre le sentiment du public. . . . Qu'on n'attribue donc pas au théâtre le pouvoir de changer des sentiments ni des mœurs qu'il ne peut que suivre et embellir. Un auteur qui voudrait heurter le goût général, composerait bientôt pour lui seul.[26]

> [The stage is, in general, a tableau of the human passions, the original of which is in every heart. But if the painter neglected to flatter these passions, the spectators would soon be repelled and would not want to see themselves in a light that made them despise themselves. So that, if he gives an odious coloring to some passions, it is only to those that are not general and are naturally hated. Hence the author, in this respect, only follows public sentiment. . . . Let no one then attribute to the theatre the power to change sentiments or morals [manners], which it can only follow and embellish. An author who would brave the general taste would soon write for himself alone].

Since plays that offered real critiques of social practices would displease their audiences and hence fail, the only place that theater can do any good is in corrupt societies where any diversion from active evildoing—anything, in other words, that gets people off the streets or out of the boudoirs—even flattering plays, is welcome. Of course, for Rousseau Paris qualifies as just that kind of place, while Geneva most certainly does not.[27]

Two branches of Rousseau's argument will be of special concern to us here: first, the claim that even the most moral theater neither inspires its spectators to carry out good actions in the world nor to feel sympathy with suffering humanity outside the walls of the theater. On the contrary, Rousseau argues, the fellow-feeling that theater might inspire is sterile for several reasons: any fellow-feeling that is created is used up completely on fictional characters; theater renders real suffering, which lacks any poetic or aesthetic dimension, unrecognizable; theater teaches spectators that humane actions and humanitarian feelings belong to the world of the theater and only to that world; consequently, when such actions are imaginatively practiced in the theater, the spectator's moral work is done: "En donnant des pleurs à ces fictions, nous avons satisfait à tous les droits de l'humanité, sans avoir plus rien à mettre du nôtre." [In shedding our tears for these fictions, we have satisfied all the claims of humanity, without having to give any more of ourselves.][28] Sympathy and good works, Rousseau argues, are made to seem as foreign to the real world as speaking in verse. "The only theater Rousseau can imagine," David Marshall argues, "stands condemned for the failure of sympathy it institutionalizes. All it can teach (aside from the dissimulation and self-display exhibited by those who show themselves to the eyes of the world) is the false sympathy that allows people to think they have no role to play in the scenes and dramas around them."[29]

The second, related, assertion important for what follows here, and that was particularly incoherent to Rousseau's contemporaries, was his claim that despite the spectators' sense that they go to the theater, among other reasons, to be part of a larger humanity, in fact it is in the theater that individuals are most isolated: "[L]'on croit s'assembler au spectacle, et c'est là que chacun s'isole, c'est là qu'on va oublier ses amis, ses voisins, ses proches." [We believe that we come together in the theater, but it is there that everyone is isolated, it is there that we go to forget our friends, our neighbors, our near and dear.][30] People are isolated in the theater, he argues, because the only lesson the theater really teaches spectators is to conceive of others as objects of their gaze—not as subjects—and to know and understand themselves only as the object of the gaze of others. Spectators foolishly seeking community in the theater are thus in fact doubly alienated: they are alienated from their fellows and from themselves. For Rousseau, to be a theatrical spectator is to live this twofold alienation.[31]

Rousseau's argument in the *Lettre à M. d'Alembert* follows closely from the account he gives of the rise of society in the *Discourse on the Origin and Foundation of Inequality.* In the *Discourse* Rousseau argues that natural man lives only in and for himself: the only spectator to his actions that he can conceive is himself. As society develops, however, people become aware of the regard of others; this gaze is important because Rousseau, like so many of his contemporaries, believed that the desire to be recognized and admired by others was a primal human driving force.[32] In society human beings no longer live within themselves but rather in the gaze and the opinion of others. Thus, for Rousseau, society itself is theatrical: social beings represent themselves to others as they wish to be seen rather than as they really are and, in return, they apprehend others as spectacles. Theater thus stands under a special indictment for Rousseau: theater institutionalizes and celebrates society's theatricality; as Marshall puts it, "theater in its literal manifestation represents or figures the theatrical relations formed between self and others that Rousseau denounces in society."[33]

The case of *Le Misanthrope* occupies a special place in Rousseau's critique both because of its subject and because of its technical prowess. The subject of *Le Misanthrope*, on Rousseau's reading, is precisely society's theatricality: the "perfidious veil" that separates the individual from him- or herself and from other human beings and that is embodied in the codes of politeness that regulate human relations in the salon. Alceste harangues his friend Philinte and his love-object, Célimène, for what he perceives to be their hypocrisy, for the way they warmly embrace those they later profess to dislike or not even to know at all. He condemns a political and judicial system that is based on patronage and therefore on bribery and private connections rather than on merit and justice, for this system is tantamount to forbidding honesty and encouraging flattery. He is most deeply troubled by the ambiguity that this theatrical, polite society inevitably produces: how can he know what anyone really means if everyone is routinely insincere and if such insincerity is rewarded by the society they inhabit? How can he know if his friend is truly his friend, if his beloved genuinely loves him in return? Such uncertainty drives Alceste to greater outbursts, greater rage, and finally retreat.

Many critics have noted Rousseau's emotional identification with Alceste.[34] Like Rousseau, Alceste lives in a world of opacity and longs for transparency. Like Alceste, Rousseau is outraged by what he perceives as the hypocrisy and concomitant injustice of polite society. Like Alceste, Rousseau fears that his outbursts only make him ridiculous in the eyes of that society. Alceste is the virtuous, noble, and sincere character, yet Alceste is the figure of fun both within the fictional world of *Le Misanthrope* and for Molière's audience. This proves beyond any doubt, as far as Rousseau is concerned, that the characters who wrong or humiliate Alceste are corrupt and depraved and that the same must be said of the audience that applauds Alceste's defeat. For Rousseau, *Le Misanthrope* is the sign of theater's structural impotence and its inevitable perversity. *Le Misanthrope* stages social theatricality and finds in its favor precisely because those who make up its audience are *honnêtes gens* (gentlefolk) who hold the same beliefs and live by the same rules as Philinte. Precisely because *Le Misanthrope* is a great play, and because its author was both the greatest comic writer in French and a good man (Rousseau insists that many of Alceste's maxims are, in fact, Molière's own), the play proves that theater, even at its very greatest, can never reform morals.[35]

The *Lettre* provoked a storm of criticism and re-ignited the long-smoldering embers of the debate over the theater; now, however, that debate took Molière and *Le Misanthrope* for its centerpiece.[36] Jean-François Marmontel wrote a series of responses to the *Lettre* for the *Mercure de France* that he later published together in a volume of his *Contes moraux* under the title "Apologie du théâtre, ou analyse de la Lettre de M. Rousseau, citoyen de Genève, à M. d'Alembert au sujet des spectacles." Marmontel agrees with Rousseau that the theater is "a school for politeness and taste," but where Rousseau sees politeness as a "perfidious veil that separates man from himself" and as a sign of man's fall from nature into society, Marmontel argues that politeness is important precisely because it distinguishes human from animal: "Celui qui a regardé les belles-lettres comme une cause de corruption de mœurs; celui qui, pour notre bien, eût voulu nous mener paître, n'a pas dû approuver qu'on envoyât ses concitoyens à une école de politesse et de goût." [He who regards belles-lettres as a cause of corruption of morals; he who, for our own good, would like to lead us out to graze, must not approve of sending his fellow-citizens to a school of politeness and taste.][37]

The dispute between Rousseau and Marmontel over *Le Misanthrope* finally comes down to a conflict between opposing constructions of politeness.[38] Rousseau argues that Molière ridicules virtue when he ridicules Alceste; Marmontel claims that Alceste is ridiculed not for his virtue but for its excessiveness, which, he argues, leads to impoliteness. Alceste is indeed virtuous, Marmontel explains, but "this same probity becomes inflamed, goes beyond its bounds and becomes excessive. The Misanthrope raves and becomes ridiculous, not in his virtuousness, but in the extremes to which it leads." Such excess, Marmontel continues, makes Alceste "unsociable" and "harsh," and it is for these faults that he is held up to the audience's corrective laughter.[39] The very notion that probity could ever be excessive must have seemed criminal to

Rousseau; certainly the idea is wholly foreign to his sensibility. What is at stake for Marmontel is social peace, indeed, the maintenance of society itself. For Rousseau the stakes are the individual's possession of him- or herself, or, put another way, the possibility of authentic identity. Marmontel and Rousseau could never overcome this basic impasse.

Marmontel wants to modify and moderate Alceste so that he can become a member of polite society; indeed, he narrates the reformation of Alceste in his story "Le Misanthrope corrigé." Marmontel's Alceste, while in the country, falls in love with Ursule, the virtuous and beautiful daughter of an upright and virtuous neighbor. Ursule convinces Alceste to live in Paris for part of the year (because change is good); she even secures a promise from him to go to balls with her and to dance. The moral of the story is pronounced by Ursule's father: "'Crois-moi, mon ami,' poursuivit-il, 'sois homme et vis avec les hommes; c'est l'intention de la nature: elle nous a donné des défauts à tous, afin qu'aucun ne soit dispensé d'être indulgents pour les défauts des autres.'" ["Believe me, my friend," he continued, "be a man and live among men; it is nature's intention: she has given everyone faults so that no one may be dispensed from being tolerant of the faults of others."][40] Marmontel argued both that it was human nature to live in society and, by corollary, that the most profound obligation of social beings was to maintain society. Maintenance meant keeping the social peace—formulating, and behaving according to, codes such as those of politeness that would allow individuals to live together without creating hostility and violence: "The first need of a society is to be at peace with itself."[41] Rigorous honesty would inevitably lead to quarrels and ruptures. Rousseau, for his part, held that such a society is irremediably flawed, certainly not worth preserving, and that, if any evidence were needed to prove this fact, Alceste's exile from it constitutes sufficient confirmation.

Modern critics, perhaps surprisingly, have tended to side with Marmontel in his debate with Rousseau. Indeed, they have tended to be even harsher in their criticism of the character of Alceste than was Marmontel. Lionel Gossman, for example, argues eloquently that Alceste is in fact the worst hypocrite of all. Alceste condemns insincerity not out of any ethical superiority but because the ambiguity that insincerity produces torments him.[42] And Jean Starobinski argues that while Alceste wants to be a demystifier, wants to reveal what he correctly sees to be the material interest lurking behind the mask of politeness, he is himself mystified. Although Alceste denounces the vanity and self-imposed illusions of others, it turns out that he is a victim of his own vanity: "That which Alceste attacks is in himself. He claims to have broken free of the illusions of deceitful 'proprieties,' and he falls into the illusion of what Hegel will call 'abstract morality.' "[43] There is a startling gap between eighteenth-century sensibility and our own on this point. For even Marmontel and d'Alembert, while opposing Rousseau, agreed with him that Alceste is a good, noble, and heroic character. The difference would seem to be our own greater tolerance, even embrace, of ambiguity. Eighteenth-century writers and critics were sympathetic to Alceste's struggle for transparency; scholars today assert the inevitability of doubt and uncertainty in human relations and characterize Alceste's unwillingness to accept this ambiguity as a signal failure and a mark of his absolutism.

Rousseau ends his critique of Molière with a suggestion for a morally re-formed version of *Le Misanthrope*:

> De faire un tel changement à son plan que Philinte entrât comme acteur nécessaire dans le noeud de sa pièce, en sorte qu'on pût mettre les actions de Philinte et d'Alceste dans une apparente opposition avec leurs principes, et dans une conformité parfaite avec leurs caractères. Je veux dire qu'il fallait que le misanthrope fut toujours furieux contre les vices publics, et toujours tranquille sur les méchancetés personnelles dont il était la victime. Au contraire le philosophe Philinte devait voir tous les désordres de la société avec une flègme stoïque, et se mettre en fureur au moindre mal qui s'adressait directement à lui.[44]

> [He could have made a change in his plan so that Philinte entered as a necessary actor into the plot of the play, putting his actions and those of Alceste in apparent opposition with their principles and in perfect conformity with their characters. I mean that the Misanthrope should have always been furious against public vices and always tranquil about the personal viciousness of which he was the victim. On the other hand, the philosopher Philinte must view all the afflictions of society with a stoical composure and become enraged over the slightest ill that affected him personally.]

Rousseau imagined a revised *Misanthrope* in which, on the one hand, Alceste's misanthropy would be figured as humane and altruistic, an expression of his hatred not of mankind but of the vices that corrupted it. On the other hand, the new *Misanthrope* would recast Philinte's conventional amiability—practiced in Molière's play in the interest of maintaining social bonds—as a mask for cold-hearted self-interest. Rousseau's prescription would require bringing Philinte forward as one of the play's two main characters: no longer would the play's central pairing be Alceste-Célimène; now it would focus exclusively on the bond of friendship and especially on the relation between Alceste and

Philinte. Philinte is crucial to the revised story because, for Rousseau, Philinte is "one of those decent members of high society";[45] he is one of those respectable gentleman who inhabit Parisian society and who make up the theater audience. Rousseau wants to show that the social codes of such gentlefolk are in fact based strictly on material interest. Philinte is an optimist—that is, he accepts the evils he sees around him and asserts that "tout est bien"—but he has a good reason for doing so; Rousseau asserts that he benefits from the status quo. He is one of those "gentle, moderate people who always find that everything is fine *because it is in their interest that nothing be better.*"[46]

In theory this "new *Misanthrope*" would restore to comedy its classical function of holding a critical mirror up to society. But only in theory. For such a play, Rousseau warned, could never be staged successfully:

> Je ne doute point que, sur l'idée que je viens de proposer, un homme de génie ne pût faire un nouveau *Misanthrope,* non moins vrai, non moins naturel que l'Athénien, égal en mérite à celui de Molière, et sans comparaison plus instructif. Je ne vois qu'un inconvénient à cette nouvelle pièce, c'est qu'il serait impossible qu'elle réussît: car quoi qu'on dise, en choses qui déshonorent, nul ne rit de bon cœur à ses dépens. Nous voilà rentrés dans mes principes.[47]

> [I do not doubt that, on the basis of the idea I have just proposed, a man of genius could compose a new *Misanthrope,* no less true, nor less natural than the Athenian one, equal in merit to that of Molière and incomparably more instructive. I see only one difficulty for this new play, which is that it could not succeed. For whatever one may say, in matters that dishonor, no one laughs with good grace at his own expense. Here we are caught up again in my principles.]

Audiences, Rousseau claims, go to the theater to be flattered, not to be corrected. While a gifted man of letters could produce a reformed *text* of Molière's play, performing a denunciation of Philinte's socially sanctioned insincerity and an affirmation of Alceste's authenticity would be bound to fail. Philinte represents the audience's values and customs; and because audiences demand that the theater endorse their beliefs, a play denouncing Philinte could not be performed. Indeed, Molière's play, on Rousseau's account, remained successful because it embodied and affirmed flattery as social practice and as the very structure of theatrical representation. Just as Philinte flatters Oronte's vanity by praising his bad poetry, Molière flatters rather than reforms his audience by valorizing its proxy, Philinte.

With Rousseau's critique very much on his mind, yet undaunted by his warning, Fabre sought to make himself the "homme de génie" of whom Rousseau wrote: he composed his *Le Philinte de Molière,* first performed in 1790, as a belated but timely response to Rousseau's challenge.[48] Despite Rousseau's warning about the hazards of staging such a play, Fabre's radically different conception of theater and audience convinced him that his play would succeed. In a crucial break with Rousseau Fabre argued that theatricality was the product of specific historical conditions rather than the nature of all theater. Fabre believed that theatricality was inherent not to theater but to aristocracy. In a preface to *Le Philinte* he argued that the controlling interest in the theater exercised by the aristocracy undermined the essential nature of comedy by stripping it of its ancient mission: that of holding up a mirror to expose society's defects. Since aristocracy itself was the root cause of all social and political ills, the aristocracy naturally had an interest in falsifying dramatic representations that might otherwise disclose its tyranny. Old Regime theater avoided realistic and natural effects because these would expose aristocratic vices and the misery they produced; it eschewed deeply affecting subjects and language because these might incite spectators to change the conditions—social, moral, economic, and political—that afflicted so many. Fabre believed that an audience of revolutionary citizens would, by contrast, demand the truth.

Fabre and Philinte

Fabre's faith in revolutionary audiences was fully vindicated: *Le Philinte de Molière* was a critical and commercial success. On February 24, 1790, the *Moniteur*'s theater reviewer raved:

> *Le Philinte de Molière!* Ce titre seul était fait pour inquiéter sur le succès d'un ouvrage dramatique les personnes qui aiment vraiment la littérature et ceux qui en suivent la carrière. . . . C'est dans cette position que nous avons vu, avant-hier, commencer la première représentation du *Philinte de Molière, ou la Suite du Misanthrope.* Notre crainte a été promptement dissipé, et nous avons d'abord pressenti le succès de cet ouvrage.[49]

> [*Le Philinte de Molière!* The title alone was created to make those persons who truly love literature and follow its career nervous about the success of this dramatic work. . . . It was from this position that, the day before yesterday, we watched the start of the premiere of *Le Philinte de Molière, ou la suite du Misanthrope.* Our fear was promptly dissipated, and right away we foresaw the success of this work.]

The *Journal de Paris* and the *Chronique de Paris* agreed with the *Moniteur* that although the play's title provoked some uneasiness—after all, it seemed the height of folly, if not of arrogance, to take on the task of rewriting the supreme master of French comedy—*Le Philinte de Molière* was a deserving hit: "Le titre de *Suite du Misanthrope* avait un peu inquiété sur le succès de la pièce joué avant-hier, pour la première fois, au Théâtre-Français; elle a pourtant pleinement réussie, et a été très applaudie avec justice." [The title, *Suite du Misanthrope,* created some anxiety about the success of the play performed the day before yesterday, for the first time, at the Comédie-Française; the play nevertheless was a thorough success and was very much applauded, and rightly so.][50] All three newspapers lavished praise on the new comedy, and each devoted more than two columns to the discussion. All three remarked on the boldness of undertaking to write a play based on, but departing significantly from, a masterpiece by the founder and greatest practitioner of the French comic tradition. The *Journal de Paris* observed: "Le plus grand nombre des spectateurs, en applaudissant avec la plus grande vivacité, a paru ne se souvenir de la difficulté de cette tentative que pour décerner à l'auteur un triomphe plus éclatant." [The great number of spectators, in applauding with the greatest vivacity, seemed to consider the difficulty of the enterprise only in order to bestow an even more spectacular triumph upon the author.][51] The *Chronique* declared that the play's qualities "annoncent un vrai talent" [announced a true talent].[52]

None of the reviews mentions the relationship between Fabre's play and Rousseau's *Lettre,* but Fabre certainly was making no secret of the source of his inspiration. The play's verse prologue—performed at the premiere—takes the form of a dialogue between Damis, the fictional author of *Le Philinte,* and his friend Acaste. Their subject is the literary genesis of *Le Philinte.* Damis fears that his work does not measure up to that of his master, Molière:

> Content de mon ouvrage? He! Monsieur, puis-je l'être,
> Le serai-je jamais en contemplant mon maître?
> Mon travail à la main et le bien dans le cœur,
> Ce n'est point en rival, mais comme adorateur,
> Que je déposerais cette offrande, amassée,
> Dans ses propres écrits, pleine de sa pensée,
> Aux pieds de ce génie.
>
> [Happy with my creation? Monsieur, how could I be?
> Will I ever be while I contemplate that of my master?

My work in my hand and good in my heart,
It is not as a rival but as a worshiper,
That I place this offering, gathered
From his own writings, filled with his thoughts,
At the feet of this genius.]

Damis then goes on to hail Rousseau as his second master and his authority:

Quand la France renaît, écrasons l'imposture.
Au reste, mon Philinte est peint d'après nature;
Je l'ai vu. De la cour il vint à la Cité.
Me faut-il m'appuyer d'une autre autorité?
C'est JEAN-JACQUES ROUSSEAU
Lisez ce paragraphe;
Voilà son sentiment, et c'est mon épigraphe.[53]

[As France is reborn let us crush imposture
Besides, my Philinte is drawn from nature;
I have seen him. From the court he came to the city.
Must I rely on another authority?
It is JEAN-JACQUES ROUSSEAU
Read this paragraph;
This is his sentiment, and this is my epigraph.]

Acaste goes on to read aloud from the *Lettre à M. d'Alembert* the description of Philinte I have already cited in part above:

Ce Philinte est un de ces honnêtes gens du grand monde dont les maximes ressemblent beaucoup à celles des fripons; de ces gens si doux, si modérés, qui trouvent toujours que tout va bien parce qu'ils ont intérêt que rien n'aille mieux; qui sont toujours contents de tout le monde, parce qu'ils ne soucient de personne; qui, autour d'une bonne table, soutiennent qu'il n'est pas vrai que le peuple ait faim; qui, le gousset bien garni, trouvent fort mauvais qu'on déclame en faveur des pauvres.[54]

[This Philinte is the wise man of the play: one of those decent members of high society whose maxims resemble so much those of knaves, one of those gentle moderate people who always find that everything is fine because it is in their interest that nothing be better, who are always satisfied with everyone because they do not care about anyone; who seated at a good table insist that it is not true that the people are hungry; who, the gusset well-adjusted, think that it is bad form to declaim in favor of the poor.]

Rousseau and Fabre condemn Philinte because they interpret his politeness as imposture and his flexibility, his willingness to accept individual and social flaws, as tantamount to the assertion that "tout va bien," that everything is for the best. It is obvious to Rousseau and to Fabre, on the contrary, that "everything"—that is, social, economic, and political arrangements—are far from the best they might be.

The belief that everything is all for the best (in this best of all possible worlds) is one version of the doctrine of optimism—the version that Voltaire lampooned so brilliantly in *Candide*. What outrages Fabre in particular about this popularized optimistic philosophy is its acceptance of suffering; suffering for writers like Leibniz, Bolingbroke, and Pope must be seen as a necessary, if not fully understood, part of a larger system that is not only good but is necessarily "the best of all possible systems."[55] In the *Lettre* and in *Le Philinte de Molière* Rousseau and Fabre are writing, in part, specifically against this form of optimism and against the quietism it encourages. For if eighteenth-century France were truly the best of all possible worlds, not only was there no need for any reform or any activism, but such attempts at improvement must be seen as springing from nothing other than the folly of human pride. The political and moral attitude one should adopt according to this optimistic creed was explained perhaps most pithily and certainly most famously by Pope in the *Essay on Man:*

> Submit. In this, or any other sphere,
> Secure to be as blest as thou canst bear:
> Safe in the hand of one disposing pow'r,
> Or in the natal, or the mortal hour,
> All nature is but art, unknown to thee;
> All chance, but direction which thou canst not see;
> All discord, harmony not understood;
> All partial evil, universal good.
> And, spite of pride, in erring reason's spite,
> One truth is clear, "Whatever is, is right."

For Fabre, however, it is clear that those who claim that "partial" evil is "universal" good are precisely those who do not suffer the evil. Rousseau's position regarding optimism is more complicated than that of Fabre. Rousseau famously defended Pope and optimism against Voltaire in his *Lettre sur la Providence,* arguing both for God's absolute goodness and for optimism's consoling power.[56] But, at the same time, Rousseau never denies the evils and sufferings of the world; rather, he insists that they are the work of man, not of God, and that most suffering springs from man's abandonment of nature in favor of "civilization." Thus, in a sense, for Rousseau Philinte and the "gentlefolk" he represents are false optimists. Moreover, Rousseau's motivation, at least in part, for writing the *Lettre sur la Providence* seems to be anger at what he takes to be both the cruelty and the hypocrisy of Voltaire's antioptimism position. Voltaire is cruel because he robs the unhappy of beliefs that could bring them solace and comfort, and he is hypocritical because he himself suffers none of the miseries he describes: "l'absurdité de cette doctrine qui saute aux yeux, est surtout révoltante dans un homme comblé des biens de tout espèce, qui, au sein du bonheur, cherche à désespérer ses semblables par l'image affreuse et cruelle de toutes les calamités dont il est exempt." [The self-evident absurdity of this doctrine is especially revolting from a man who is laden with every kind of possession, who, in the midst of good fortune, seeks to drive his fellows to despair with the horrid, cruel image of all the calamities from which he is spared.][57] In other words, Voltaire, the antioptimist, is the equivalent of Philinte and "those gentle moderate people who always find that everything is fine": like them, he is hypocritical and self-interested. Voltaire argues that everything is for the worst, even as he enjoys all of life's pleasures, because it enhances his literary reputation to do so and in spite of the real pain it causes to the truly suffering. Rousseau contemptuously calls the intellectual enterprise that theorizes in this manner "philosophy," and the figure for this type of "philosopher" is the conventionally polite man of the world, Philinte. Thus Rousseau argues that in the rewritten, moral *Misanthrope* he imagines, "the philosopher Philinte must view all the afflictions of society with a stoical composure and become enraged over the slightest ill that affected him personally."

Both Rousseau and Fabre took a further step when they argued that there was a link between optimism as embodied by the "philosophe" Philinte and those he represents and self-interest—when, that is, they argued that those who "stoically" accept a measure of human suffering do so not because they believed that "all discord" was truly "harmony not understood" but because they, in fact, benefited from the prevailing state of affairs. When Rousseau and Fabre observed suffering and misery around them, they understood the existence of such unhappiness not in relation to a divine system but in relation to the happiness of the few.[58] In other words, they assumed a theory of power that connected the privileged with the suffering and saw the happiness of the few as predicated on the misery of the many. The optimists—or for Rousseau, the false optimists—had an interest in a system of social arrangements that necessarily caused some part of humanity to suffer. And this being the case, these optimists were not true philosophers but hypocrites. They had a stake in human suffering and in perpetuating that suffering; their philosophy was simply an elaborate mask to hide suffering and to disguise their part in it. Because they could never avow their interest in the status quo, they were forced, by their own investment, into imposture and insincerity. So while Marmontel, for example, believes that codes of politeness serve to keep the social peace, Rousseau and Fabre believe that they serve to conceal the material interests of those who dictate them. Codes of politeness, ritual dissimulation, and social theatricality become necessary and central to a society that cannot acknowledge the brutal truth of its organization. Thus Rousseau, and Fabre in his wake, discovered a conjunction between theatricality and suffering.

Suffering is only one theme among many in Rousseau's *Lettre à M. d'Alembert* but it becomes the central focus of Fabre's rewriting. Fabre's fury is aroused by the self-satisfaction of a highly theatrical society that expends all its energy on projecting pleasing surfaces that mask real iniquities. The chevalier de Méré describes the work involved in the creation and maintenance of this society:

> C'est un talent fort rare que d'être bon acteur dans la vie, il faut de l'esprit et de la justesse pour en trouver la perfection. . . . De faire toujours ce qu'il faut, tant par l'action que par le ton de la voix, et de s'en acquitter d'une manière si juste, que la chose produise l'effect qu'elle doit, cela me paraît un chef-d'œuvre. . . . Je suis persuadé qu'en beaucoup d'occasions il n'est pas inutile de regarder ce qu'on fait comme une Comédie, et de s'imaginer qu'on joue un personnage du théâtre.[59]

> [It is a very rare talent to be a good actor in life. It takes a good deal of wit and accuracy to achieve perfection. . . . Always to do what must be done both in action and in tone of voice, and to perform so accurately as to produce the required effect—that, it seems to me, is the work of a master. . . . I am convinced that there are many occasions when it is not a bad idea to look upon what one does as a Comedy, and to imagine that one is playing a character on the stage.]

The point of all human interactions was to produce effects, and as Méré explained, achieving the desired effects required tremendous discipline from the members of this society. Discipline and self-control are worthwhile for the participants because the comedy they perform is for themselves as much as it is for others. Such a society operates according to a tacit contract, the terms of which require each member to accept and perpetuate pleasant surfaces. As

Starobinski argues, the society's object is not to fool outsiders but to maintain an illusion for its own members; the codes of politeness create and sustain the individual's and the society's vanity: "La relation réciproque . . . devient une transaction où des perfections fictives s'autorisent mutuellement, en vue de maintenir pour chacun un niveau égal de satisfaction narcissique." [Reciprocity . . . becomes a transaction in which mythical perfections justify one another so as to sustain an equal level of narcissistic satisfaction in all.][60]

Society's theatricality helped mask the suffering it either generated or tolerated, and theater had an important role in producing social theatricality according to Rousseau's critique. If social theatricality is an elaborate form of group hypocrisy, theater is, essentially, a hyperdistillation of that hypocrisy that society requires to reflect and reassure itself. This, in any case, is Fabre's accusation against the successful comedy of his own time. And although Fabre was deeply indebted to Rousseau for the principles of his play, his immediate motivation came from elsewhere. The contemporary context for *Le Philinte de Molière* is not the *Lettre à M. d'Alembert* but rather an extremely successful 1788 comedy called *L'Optimiste* by one of the era's most respectable and flourishing playwrights, Jean-François Collin d'Harleville.[61] In the preface to *Le Philinte,* published with the play in 1791, Fabre explains that he wrote his play to combat *L'Optimiste:*

> Je l'avouerai, jamais je n'ai pu, sans indignation, entendre *L'Optimiste* de M. Collin. Je n'ai point eu du repos que le théâtre n'ait pas été armé d'une morale specialement contraire aux principes de cet ouvrage. C'est pour les retorquer et en diminuer l'influence autant qu'il était en moi, que j'ai composé *Le Philinte de Molière, ou La Suite du Misanthrope.*[62]

> [I will confess it. Never could I listen to Mr. Collin's *Optimist* without indignation. I have had no peace over the fact that the theater was not armed with a lesson formed especially to contradict the principles of that work. It is in order to reply to those principles and to diminish their influence to the best of my ability that I composed *Le Philinte de Molière, ou la suite du Misanthrope.*]

Fabre objected so strongly to *L'Optimiste* because it seemed to embody very precisely all the evils that Rousseau linked to the theater and to the theatricalization of society: *L'Optimiste*'s principle theme was that everything was all for the best when, as even Louis XVI had to admit in 1788, France was not exactly the best of all possible worlds; it employed the language of sweetness and false sentiment, "sensiblerie," that attenuated the possibility of any profound dramatic effects; by means of its plot and language *L'Optimiste* both flattered and reassured the powerful and privileged who made up its audience.

Fabre begins his critique of Collin by describing the France of 1788, the France in which *L'Optimiste* premiered, as far from perfect:

> La France, cette belle partie du globe, cette belle surface de trente mille lieues, l'amour du ciel, le chef-d'œuvre des éléments, la protectrice de l'humanité, le triomphe de la civilisation, était dégradée, désolée, dévorée par un petit nombre d'êtres malfaisants, revêtus de la figure humaine. De l'une à l'autre extrémité de cette vaste région, la nature éperdue, la tête courbée sous un joug de plomb, les yeux épuisées de larmes, les mamelles désechées, les bras chargés de fers, le bâillon à la bouche, la nature errait sans asyle, procédée de la crainte et de la terreur, ridiculisée par la dépravation, trahie par la lâcheté, méprisée par la sottise, trafiquée par l'avarice, persécutée enfin par l'orgueil, par la cruauté, par le mensonge, et par tous les vices ensemble.[63]

> [France, that beautiful territory of thirty thousand leagues, beloved of heaven, masterpiece of the elements, protectress of humanity, triumph of civilization, had been degraded, desolated, devoured by a small number of malevolent creatures assuming human form. From one extreme of this vast country to another, Nature overcome, head bent beneath a leaden yoke, eyes worn out with crying, breasts desiccated, her arms loaded with chains, her mouth gagged, Nature wandered without shelter, proceeded by fear and terror, mocked by deprivation, betrayed by cowardice, scorned by stupidity, sold by avarice, and finally, persecuted by pride, by cruelty, by duplicity, and by all the vices combined.]

In an indignant tone Fabre denounces the Old Regime and, employing a sustained personification, figures its victims as a wretched woman, oppressed, physically tortured and afflicted, humiliated, without any succor. Against this poor peasant woman Fabre arrays all those who have the power to inspire fear—those who profit from her exploitation, those who take pleasure in her misery, those who are so unnatural, so inhumane, that they can only be imagined as brutal creatures who wear the mask of men. The wretched woman is nature and all the simple people who live close to nature; her tormentor is the artificial society of the Old Regime's elite. France, in other words, had reached its lowest ebb; vice and corruption had utterly defeated nature and innocence according to Fabre. And just as conditions became so terrible that the political and social order could no longer be preserved, Collin's play announced that everything was all for the best: "C'est du centre de cette dépravation, c'est l'année avant la Révolution, qu'un homme s'élève pour nous assurer 'que nos maux se réduisent à rien! Et qu'il est grand sujet de dire: tout est bien.'" [It is from the center of this depravity—it is the year before the Revolution—that a man rises to assure us that "our troubles amount to nothing! And there is every reason to say: everything is for the best."][64]

Collin's play, according to Fabre, succeeded in reducing theater to ideology; this theater was nothing other than an attempt to rationalize and naturalize the prevailing order—it formulated an imaginary relation to the conditions and practices of production that reassured those who benefited from the status quo. Or, put another way, it flattered them:

> L'ésprit de la comédie de M. Collin est de flatter la cour, les grands, les riches, les heureux du grand monde, et d'invétérer leur perversité en leur présentant le mal comme nul, en cherchant à leur persuader que leur cupidité, leur tyrannie et leurs malversations ont tout laisser dans le meilleur ordre de choses.[65]

> [The spirit of Mr. Collin's play is to flatter the court, the great, the rich, the happy of high society, and to confirm their perversity by representing evil as unimportant, by seeking to persuade them that their cupidity, their tyranny, and their thievery have left everything in the best possible order.]

Indeed, *L'Optimiste* is a startlingly bald apology for the status quo; Collin even begins his preface by heaping praise and thanks on his censor.[66] The optimistic hero of the play, Plinville, with whom Collin identified himself—"Que je suis heureux! Que j'ai bien sujet de m'écrier avec mon optimiste, tout est bien!" [How happy I am! What good reason I have to cry out with my optimist, everything is good!][67]—makes mind-boggling speeches about the felicity with which society is constructed:

> On est vraiment heureux d'être né dans l'aisance.
> Je suis émerveillé de cette Providence,
> Qui fît naître le riche auprès de l'indigent:
> L'un a besoin de bras, l'autre a besoin d'argent;
> Ainsi tout est si bien arrangé dans la vie.
> Que la moitié du monde est par l'autre servie.

> [We are very lucky to be born in comfort.
> I am amazed by Providence,
> That arranges for the rich to be born next to the poor:
> One needs labor, the other needs money;

> Thus everything is so well arranged in life
> That half of the world is served by the other half.][68]

Plinville's speech reaches nearly Panglossian heights: "Observe that noses were meant to wear spectacles; and so we have spectacles. Legs were visibly instituted to be breeched, and we have breeches," explains Candide's tutor.[69] But it would be a mistake to assume that Collin means to expose Plinville to the audience's derision: Plinville, after all, is the triumphant hero of the play, and Collin does nothing to discourage the audience from embracing a Providence that constructs the universe so wisely that poor people are placed near rich people so that the rich have no servant problems.

Fabre was infuriated by this sentiment of self-satisfaction, this sense that human suffering is part of Providence's divine plan and that the current arrangements made everyone as happy as possible. For this sentiment discouraged pity and sympathy with the unhappy (who, according to Plinville's account, ought simply to tell themselves to be happy: he tells a complaining old servant "sois content de ton sort ainsi que moi du mien" [be happy with your lot as I am with mine]). Pity, Fabre argues, is the basis for all morals because it binds men together in their essential humanity and is the indispensable basis for all true, free human society:

> Je me suis élevé avec force contre la doctrine répandue dans la comédie de *L'Optimiste,* parce qu'elle attaque les droits de l'homme et la dignité de son être; parce qu'elle tend à rompre les liens de la société en étouffant ce fondement de la morale, la pitié, la base de toutes les vertus; parce que j'ai vu dans cet ouvrage les principes cachés du fatalisme qui n'a jamais fait que des esclaves.[70]

> [I rose up forcefully against the doctrine that fills *L'Optimiste* because it attacks the rights of man and the dignity of his being; because it aims to break the bonds of society by stifling the basis for all morality: pity, the basis for all virtues; because I saw in that work the hidden principles of fatalism which have never created anything but slaves.]

Fabre rises up against Collin's doctrines, not in his capacity as a politician but as a playwright, because he believed that theater's great power and great responsibility is to awaken and strengthen its spectators' capacity for pity and thus to reaffirm the bonds among human beings. By stifling this instinctive human faculty, Collin's theater separates man from man and thus undermines the very foundation of humane society.

Fabre does not imagine that theater can produce the experience of pity through clumsy didacticism; having characters declaim the principles of pity would be easy enough but would leave the audience cold. To achieve his goals Fabre would have to remake *the very ways in which* theater represented emotion. In particular, Fabre believed that dramatic language itself had to be transformed and that the tableau had to be the central organizing principle of dramaturgy. *L'Optimiste*'s lack of salutary dramatic effects was due to the absence of tableaux. Denis Diderot, the great theorist of the tableau in theater and painting, argues in the *Entretiens sur le fils naturel* that the tableau was the means by which theater could produce truly dramatic effects on its spectators. Diderot attributes the tableau's effect, in part, to the illusion of naturalness it creates and opposes this to the manifest artificiality of the coup de théâtre:

> J'aimerais mieux des tableaux sur la scène où il y en a si peu, et où ils produiraient un effet si agréable et si sûr, que ces coups de théâtre qu'on amène d'une manière si forcée, et qui sont fondés sur tant de suppositions singulières, que, pour une de ces combinaisons d'événements qui soit heureuse et naturelle, il y en a mille qui doivent déplaire à un homme de goût.[71]

> [I would rather see tableaux on the stage where there are so few and where they would produce so certain and so pleasurable an effect, than to see these coups de théâtre that many writers stage in so forced a manner and that are based on so many unlikely suppositions that for one of these combinations of events that appears felicitous and natural, there are a thousand that a man of taste must find disagreeable.]

The tableau, like a good painting, assembles characters on the stage in a striking moment of absorption in their own story: "Une disposition de ces personnages sur la scène, si naturelle et si vraie, que, rendue fidèlement par un peintre, elle me plairait sur la toile, est un tableau." [An arrangement of those characters on the stage, so natural and so true to life, that, faithfully rendered by a painter, it would please me on canvas, is a tableau.][72] The subjects of the tableau were by preference sentimental: the return of the prodigal son; the poor but virtuous family gathered around the hearth; the death of a beloved, white-haired parent. Unlike the coup de théâtre, the raison d'être of the tableau was not to make a surprising revelation to the audience; the purpose of the tableau was to penetrate the audience with emotion. Diderot, Michael Fried argues, believed that a tableau was "capable of moving an audience to the depths of its collective being."[73] Diderot favored the tableau, Fried argues, because he considered it a highly dramatic, rather than theatrical, form of composition. For the figures or characters assembled in the tableau are arranged so naturally and are so absorbed by the subject of their scene that, paradoxically, the tableau creates the illusion that it exists for itself and in itself; in other words, it creates the illusion that the audience does not exist. Hence the figures on the stage (or in the painting) do not address themselves to a spectator. Collin avoided tableaux, Fabre claimed, precisely because he was catering to an audience that wanted to avoid pity:

> J'observe que M. Collin semble s'être appliqué à affaiblir toutes les sensations fortes qui, j'en conviens, sont désagréables pour les délicats du grand monde; mais dont la nature se sert pour émouvoir la pitié. Je parle de ces tableaux frappants et douloureux que la vertu rappelle quelquefois à la mémoire de ceux qui l'abandonnent, pour en obtenir quelqu'accès de résipiscence en faveur de l'humanité. S'il est une souvenance impérieuse, une émotion irrésistible qui puissent attendrir une âme émoussée par les jouissances du monde et endurcie de plaisir, c'est sans doute le tableau des misères et des douleurs de l'infortune.[74]

> [I observe that Mr. Collin seems to have applied himself to weakening all those strong sensations that are, I agree, disagreeable for the delicate folk of high society; but which nature makes use of to stir pity. I speak of those striking and distressing tableaux that virtue sometimes recalls to the memory of those who have forsaken it to obtain some bout of remorse in favor of humanity. If there is an imperious recollection, an irresistible emotion that can touch a soul made blasé with pleasures and hardened by dissipation, it is without a doubt the tableau of the miseries and pains of misfortune.]

In *L'Optimiste* Collin attenuated theater's potential force in order to shield his audience from strong emotion. This was an audience that did not want to experience pity, according to Fabre, because it did not want to take the actions that pity would demand. But Fabre believed that even this audience, despite its hardness and indifference, could be touched if theater were allowed to develop its potential. Following in the footsteps of Diderot, Fabre argued that the heartrending tableau—the tableau of the miseries and sorrows of misfortune—was the key to regenerating theater.

The second obstacle to pity in Collin's play was its affected language of false sensibility. Collin attempts to put a soft finish (*velouter*) on the fundamental coldness of his characters by giving their language a "sensibilité doucereuse" (sickly sweet sensibility).[75] Indeed, Fabre complains, all of Old Regime theater has been infected by this honeyed language, the purpose of which is to conceal rather than convey truth, to flatter rather than reveal; this "affectation de douceur et de sensibilité" [affectation of sweetness and sensibility] is essentially a form of hypocrisy, a "puerile tartufferie," that those in power have adopted in order to hide from others and from themselves the miseries that surround them. The hypocritical language of Old Regime society has, Fabre argues, "overcome the theater."[76] By adopting this language, theater becomes complicit in a political project of concealing oppression and injustice. Moreover, in so doing, theater not only abdicates its moral mission, but it abdicates its aesthetic mission as well and thus is doubly corrupted. For the affected language of false sensibility leaves the spectators of the theater untouched and unmoved; it protects them from the strong feelings, especially those of compassion and pity, that theater in Fabre's view was meant to foster.

Fabre's conception of pity was, no doubt, greatly influenced by Rousseau. Rousseau argued that pity for and commiseration with other "sentient beings" and the instinct for self-preservation were the two human principles that came before all others.[77] Pity was an innate faculty of the mind, universal to all humans and even present in animals. According to Rousseau natural law emerges from the combination of our innate sense of our connectedness to and commiseration with others and our sense of self-preservation. Only when human beings leave nature and live in society is the faculty of pity weakened or silenced. Fabre's preface demonstrates that his moral and political thinking was shaped by what Hannah Arendt calls "a politics of pity," a politics that reached its most important expression in Rousseau. The politics of pity is urgently concerned with a vision of suffering humanity and divides humanity into two classes: those who suffer (the unhappy) and those who do not (the happy).[78] In an important reconsideration of Arendt, Luc Boltanski argues that for the politics of pity it is morally unacceptable not to experience emotion when faced with suffering; a "that's the way it is" attitude, he explains, simply demonstrates that witness's inhumanity. For this is a politics that understands morality and emotion as inextricably linked and as elements of a single mental faculty. Moreover, "with the entry of pity into politics two kinds of emotions are freed which specify and extend the states of feeling pity," Boltanski argues; these two kinds of emotion are tenderheartedness and indignation, which correspond to two literary modes: the sentimental and the accusatory.[79] *Le Philinte de Molière* owes its singular tone to its mixture of both these modes.

Just as Rousseau suggests a plan for rewriting the *Misanthrope,* in the preface to *Le Philinte de Molière* Fabre offers a scenario for a rewritten *Optimiste*— an *Optimiste* that would be filled with tenderheartedness and indignation and that would, in turn, communicate these states to its audience. If he wanted to show the French as they really are, if he wanted to portray a tender and sensitive father, Collin should have composed a quite different play:

> Ce Plinville a une fille jeune, jolie, spirituelle, et vièrge; que n'a-t-il fait convoiter cette fraîche enfant par un duc, par un intendant, par un factotum de commis d'où vient qu'à la résistance de la fille, qu'à l'indignation du père, il n'arrive pas une lettre de cachet qui, dispersant la famille, pour la surêté accoutumé de l'état, jette le père dans le fonds d'un château fort et la fille dans un dédale de séductions d'où elle sort flétrie, corrompue et dénaturée?[80]

> [This Plinville has a young daughter: pretty, clever, and a virgin. Why not have a duke, an intendant, a factotum of a clerk, lust after this sweet child with the result that, due to the resistance of the daughter and the indignation of the father, a *lettre de cachet* arrives—for the security of the state—which disperses the family, throws the father into the bowels of a fortress and the daughter into a web of seduction from which she emerges disgraced, corrupted, and depraved?]

The play Fabre imagines here would certainly not be a comedy. It would belong to that new, mixed genre of *drame* whose goal was to provoke the sympathetic tears of an audience. It is easy to imagine the troubling tableaux to which this story line could give rise: the dignified, worthy parent torn from the arms of his family and then thrown in a dank dungeon; the innocent daughter alone at the mercy of the debauched villain; a final reunion of a now devastated father and his ruined daughter. Surely this play would heighten its audience's sense of pity and produce rage against a constituted order that could cause such crimes. Why, then, did Fabre himself not write a reformed *Optimiste?* Fabre's *Optimiste* would have included particular, affecting scenes of suffering, but Fabre's ambition was more sweeping: in *Le Philinte de Molière* Fabre treats instead the very conditions of pity. Rather than trying to interest the sympathy of spectators in one particular case, Fabre chose to write a play that was a meditation on sympathetic spectatorship itself. Fabre's ambition explains his choice of the *Misanthrope;* no other neoclassical masterpiece would have allowed for as comprehensive a consideration of the fundamental ties that bind people together and of the role of theater, theatricality, and pity in the formation of a just and humane society.

Fabre and Sympathy

Fabre's great alteration to Rousseau's plan for a revised *Misanthrope* was to place sympathy at the center of the play; and in this he was completely original, for neither Marmontel's sequel, *Le Misanthrope corrigé,* nor the play that it inspired, *Alceste à la campagne, ou Le Misanthrope corrigé* (1790), took up the question of sympathy in their considerations of the proper relation between the individual and society. In Fabre's play the *homme du monde* Philinte, identified by Rousseau as an optimist, is a cold egoist, and the outsider Alceste is a heroic protagonist whose undiplomatic outbursts always arise out of his selfless commitment to help others. The sincere Eliante of Molière's play, now married to Philinte, is horrified by her husband's lack of sympathy and engages herself in Alceste's altruistic adventures. The plot of *Le Philinte de Molière* turns on Philinte's optimism, on his lack of sympathy, and on his "philosophical" indifference to the hardships and reversals of others.

When the play begins, we learn that through some influence at the court Philinte has recently received a noble title—he is now the comte de Valances. This new identity has two immediate consequences: because he now has a new name, his old friend Alceste, on a visit to Paris, cannot find him, and they only meet by chance; and because he is now a count instead of a simple gentleman, Philinte believes that he must change his style of life—a count must have all the trappings that befit his station—and he condemns Eliante for wishing to live a plainer existence. For Philinte, we gather quickly, identity depends on appearances, and appearances are mutable. Moreover, Philinte is so blind to his wife's character that he believes her desire to live simply springs from an ulterior motive—the will to dominate the household:

> Mais il vous faut, Madame, un empire absolu.
> Ce qu'une femme veut, ce qu'elle a résolu,
> Ne peut souffrir d'obstacle; et quand la circonstance
> Lui fournit les moyens d'établir sa puissance,
> Il ne faut douter de sa précaution
> A dominer partout avec prétention. (1.1)

> [But Madame, you require an absolute empire.
> That which a woman wants, that which she has resolved,
> May brook no obstacle; and when circumstance
> Furnishes her the means to establish her power,
> One must not doubt her disposition
> To dominate pretentiously everywhere.]

Philinte's icy tone—calling his wife Madame, for example, instead of one of the many sentimental appellations that abound in other plays of the period—reveals his distance from his fellow human beings; for indeed, if he is so cold with his wife, then surely he has little sentiment for anyone but himself. It thus also reveals his adherence to an Old Regime aristocratic conception of marriage, which was very much at odds with the bourgeois, sentimental idea of companionate conjugality that, as we will see in chapter 4, was expressed in the popular drama of the period. Philinte is utterly wrong in his belief that his wife seeks to rule the household. He makes this mistake because he projects onto Eliante his own feelings and desires. In fact, according to one contemporary reviewer, Philinte "commande à sa femme en maître absolu" [commands his wife as an absolute master]; Philinte, not Eliante, wants to establish his mastery over others. Philinte fails to understand Eliante because he fails to recognize others as full subjects. This failure stems from Philinte's coldness: on the understanding that Fabre inherits from Rousseau and from the eighteenth century more generally, only emotion, and specifically sympathy—the recognition of the primordial humanity of the other and thus the primordial connection among all human beings—allows for what Boltanski calls "the recognition of self by self."[81]

Fabre's Philinte is practiced in the art of acting, and his failure to enter into Eliante's feelings and understand her motivations is based, in part, on his belief that everyone else is an actor, too. When, for example, Eliante continues to implore her husband to come to Alceste's aid after Philinte has announced that he has no intention of helping, Philinte can only imagine that Eliante is acting the part of sympathetic friend out for some reason of her own: "Je le vois, votre esprit indocile / Feint de ne pas sentir ma solide raison. . . . Cette feinte est sans doute une nouvelle addresse / Pour me contrarier et vous rendre maîtresse." [I see that your defiant spirit / Pretends not to understand my solid reason. . . . This feint is, doubtless, a new attempt / To oppose me and to make yourself mistress.] Philinte's own act goes into full swing when he hears that Alceste is in Paris and in trouble. Privately, Philinte expresses his annoyance, mocks Alceste's eccentricity, and expresses his disinclination to get involved. But when Alceste appears in the very next scene, Philinte throws his arms around him and exclaims:

> Alceste, embrassons-nous! que j'aime
> ce souvenir touchant! Qu'en malheur extrême,
> Vous avez pris le soin de venir, de voler
> Vers vos plus chers amis, prompts à vous consoler. (1.4)

[Alceste, let us embrace! I am so pleased
By this touching remembrance! That in extreme unhappiness,
You have thought of coming, of flying,
To your dearest friends who are ready to console you.]

Alceste sees through Philinte's hypocrisy, and he clearly identifies Philinte's exaggerated behavior and language with theatrical performance. Eventually, exasperated with Philinte's warm words accompanied by refusals of help, Alceste exclaims against his friend's dissimulation:

Et pensez-vous, monsieur, que sottement que je croie?
A tous ces faux semblants de la sensibilité?
Non, non, elle n'a point ce langage apprêté.
Quittez ou démentez ces grimaces frivoles,
Mais par des actions, et non par des paroles. (3.8)

[And do you stupidly think, Monsieur, that I believe
In all these false signs of sensibility?
No, no, sympathy does not use this borrowed language.
Leave aside those frivolous grimaces,
Or disprove them by actions, not by words.]

Here Alceste describes Philinte's comportment in terms almost identical to those Fabre employed in his condemnation of Old Regime comedy; like the corrupt theater of the Old Regime, Philinte is emotionally empty and puts on a show of sensibility. In the prologue to his play Fabre urges spectators to reject the old theatrical ways, the artificial declamation and mannerisms epitomized by the *grimace:* "Messieurs, pour un instant, oubliez donc de grâce / De mille faux portraits à la coquette grimace. C'est mal, à qui les peint, de déguiser nos mœurs." [Messieurs, please forget for an instant / The thousand insincere portraits with coquettish grimaces. It is wrong of those who paint them to disguise our manners] (*Le Philinte de Molière,* lxiv–lxvii). The grimace was associated with falseness not only in the theater but also in painting and even in society. For Diderot, according to Michael Fried, the grimace meant "the mannered working up of physical gesture and facial expression." Diderot detested the grimace, Fried explains, precisely because he associated it with theatricality and hypocrisy; thus, Fried cites a passage in which Diderot writes of a painting: "Ne voyez-vous pas que la douleur de cette femme est fausse, hypocrite, qu'elle fait tout ce qu'elle peut pour pleurer et qu'elle ne fait que grimacer?" [Can you not see that this woman's grief is insincere, hypocritical, that she does her best to cry but manages only to grimace?][82] Indeed, Diderot and d'Alembert's *Encyclopédie* even contains an article entitled "Grimace," authored by Watelet, that treats the problem of the grimace and its relation to hypocrisy in painting:

> Artistes qui voulez plaire et toucher, soyez donc persuadés que les figures qui grimacent, soit pour paraître avoir des grâces, soit pour jouer l'expression, sont aussi rebutantes dans vos ouvrages aux yeux équitables d'un spectateur instruit, que les caractères faux sont dans la société pour les honnêtes gens.[83]

> [Artists, you who seek to please and to touch, understand that figures that grimace, either in order to appear to have charms, or to appear expressive, are as repulsive in your works in the eye of the educated beholder, as are hypocritical characters in society in the eyes of decent people.]

The grimacing figure in art is like, and as odious as, the hypocritical person in society. But things are more complicated than that simple comparison would imply because the grimace is not limited to the sphere of art: there are plenty of figures in the real world who grimace as they try to act a part in society. "Je sais," Watelet concedes, "que vous pouvez m'objecter que presque toutes les expressions que vous envisagez autour de vous sont ou chargées, ou feintes, que presque tout ce qu'on appelle grâce est affectation et grimace: ce sont-là des obstacles qui s'opposent au progrès de l'art" (ibid.). [I know that you can reply that nearly all the expressions that you see around you are either overelaborate or feigned, and that practically everything which we call grace is affectation and grimace: these are obstacles that confront the progress of art.] Here Watelet laments the ubiquity of hypocrisy in society as an aesthetic problem— how is the artist to represent real emotion when all he or she sees is false, when, in other words, falsity is the reality of the artist's society? Philinte is a figure for both these forms of falsity: he is the representative of those "hypocritical characters" that abounded in Old Regime French society, and he is also a figure for the "figures who grimace" in painting and theater.

Philinte's theatricality is signaled not only by his grimace, but also by Alceste's exhortation that he demonstrate his sentiments with actions instead of false words. Alceste thus echoes Fabre's complaints about the theater's reliance on the affected language—the "affectation de douceur et sensibilité" [affectation of sweetness and sensibility]—that he associated with aristocratic discourse and with the corrupt theater of Collin d'Harleville and his peers. Philinte's theatricality—his willingness to perform—ultimately empties him of genuine identity even as it alienates him from others. For like the actor, in

Rousseau's estimation, "displaying sentiments other than his own," always playing a role, Philinte "annihilates himself, as it were, and is lost."[84] Philinte, then, in his coldness, his insensitivity, his lack of connection with his fellows, and his hypocrisy stands for both Old Regime society and Old Regime comedy.

Alceste is Philinte's opposite in every way: Alceste is all authenticity, and his relation to others is characterized wholly by sympathetic identification and resulting activism. Indeed, the plot of the play is driven by Alceste's sympathies: he comes to Paris because he has taken up the cause of a neighbor, a poor peasant whose land is being stolen by a greedy Parisian. Alceste has been so effective in his defense of the peasant that the Parisian is now suing him, and he must defend himself. Alceste, in other words, has so fully identified himself with the peasant that the peasant's affairs have literally become Alceste's own.

But soon after arriving in Paris, Alceste lets his attention wander from what is now his own legal plight—wander precisely because it is now his plight rather than another's—to the plight of a new other. On arriving in Paris, Alceste sends his servant, Dubois, to the Palais de Justice to find a lawyer. He instructs Dubois to find a lawyer with an honest countenance rather than a big reputation. Dubois brings back a man who is dressed poorly but who is eloquent and virtuous. Aulard suggests plausibly that Robespierre was the original for Alceste's honest lawyer: "The poor suit and the awkward bearing, is this not a figure we have already seen? Is it not, feature for feature, the lawyer from Arras, the incorruptible Robespierre in the first flush of his career as a deputy?"[85] The lawyer, however, is too occupied with another affair to take Alceste's case; he has stumbled across a terrible fraud: a man has unwittingly signed a note conveying his entire fortune to a conman. The lawyer knows that the note is false, but since the signature is genuine, and since the victim has not been located, the case is extremely tricky. When Alceste hears this tale of crime and deception, he is outraged, and he quite literally forgets his own troubles in his haste to enter into those of the anonymous victim: "[c]ar sur votre récit je me sens en courroux, / et je prends à l'affaire intérêt comme vous" (2.4) [because upon hearing your tale I am enraged / and I take the same interest in this affair that you do]. The lawyer's narrative provokes a double identification for Alceste; he feels indignation on the part of the victim, and he identifies himself with the lawyer in his quest for justice and probity.

Two factors are needed, it seems, to create the type of identification that Alceste experiences and that propels him into action: first, there must be a compelling narrative of injustice or suffering; and, second, the listener must be capable of feeling sympathy, capable, that is, of representing to him- or herself the sentiments of another. Everything that follows in *Le Philinte de Molière* consists of Alceste's and Eliante's attempts to teach Philinte to sympathize with his fellow human beings and Philinte's rejection of sympathy in favor of his philosophy of optimism. After hearing the lawyer's story, Alceste promises his own help and that of Philinte, who has some influence in high circles. Alceste is shocked to learn that Philinte refuses to become involved:

> ALCESTE: Vous vous en chargerez, j'en ai fait la promesse.
> PHILINTE: J'en suis fâché pour vous: mais je promets bien, moi,
> De ne pas m'en mêler. Alceste, en bonne foi,
> N'est-il donc pas étrange et même ridicule,
> Jusqu'à cet excès pousser le scrupule?
> Et que vous regardiez comme un devoir formé;
> Ce zèle impatient et plus que fraternel,
> Qui vous fait, sans réserve, avec tant d'imprudence,
> Offrir à tout venant votre prompte assistance. (2.9)
> [ALCESTE: You will take the matter up, I promised it.
> PHILINTE: I am sorry for you, but I too promise
> Not to get mixed up in it. Alceste, in good faith,
> Isn't it strange and even ridiculous,
> To push scruples to such an excess?
> And that you regard as a firm duty
> This impatient and overly fraternal zeal
> That compels you to offer your instant aid
> Without reservation, with such imprudence
> To anyone who comes along.]

Philinte employs the language of prudence to condemn Alceste's interventionism as ridiculous and more than fraternal. But for Alceste fraternity can never be excessive; his actions are required by and are the foundation of humanity. Alceste thus takes Philinte's prudence as a sign not just of his selfishness but also of his inhumanity:

> Et quel êtes-vous donc, si ce que j'en ai dit,
> Si l'horreur du forfait dont j'ai fait le récit,
> Si le péril touchant de l'homme qu'on friponne,
> Toute étrangère enfin que nous soit sa personne,
> Ne vous émeuvent point, vous laissent endurci,
> Jusqu'à refuser le peu qu'il faut ici? (2.9)

[And what are you then if what I have told you,
If the story of the horrible crime that I have recounted,
If the pathetic peril of the man whom they rob,
No matter how much a stranger to us he may be,
Does not move you, leaves you cold,
To the extent that you refuse the little required here?]

What calls Philinte's fundamental humanity into question—"Et quel êtes-vous donc?"—is his insusceptibility to the power of narrative to move and to touch. How is it possible, Alceste demands, that on hearing the same story that brings Eliante and him to tears, Philinte remains unmoved? The answer is to be found in Philinte's profound alienation from self and others, an alienation that he masks with his optimistic philosophy.

Philinte's response to Alceste is Fabre's sarcastic caricature of Mandeville and laissez-faire more broadly. The victim in the case, Philinte argues, merits his loss because of his carelessness; moreover, no one else is hurt by the crime. In fact, Philinte claims, society gains because the money will circulate among more people: "Eh bien! C'est un trésor qui change de bourse" [So what? It's money that changes hands]. Alceste recognizes this account as optimism and condemns it as the worst sort of sophistry:

Tout est bien, dites-vous? Et vous n'établissez
Ce système accablant, que vous embellissez
Des seuls effets du crime, et des couleurs du vice;
Que pour vous dispenser de rendre un bon office. (2.9)

[Everything is fine, you say. You propose
This damning system, that you embellish
With criminal effects and with the colors of vice,
In order to avoid doing a good deed.]

Optimism, for Alceste, is a hypocritical "system" that lays claim to reason only to indulge the self-interest of its adherents.

But, what is even worse, optimism works to squelch and contain the sympathy that is the natural human response to suffering:

Eh! Quoi! si tout est bien, à ce cri désastreux,
Que va-t-il donc rester à tant de malheureux,
Si vous leur ravissez jusques à l'espérance?
Vous endurcissez l'homme à sa propre souffrance?
Il allait s'attendrir, vous lui séchez le cœur? (2.9)

[And so, if everything is fine, at the sound of this slogan
What will become of so many unfortunates
If you take from them everything, even hope?
You harden man to his own suffering?
He was about to feel pity, you harden his heart?]

Optimism gives the self-interested an aura of legitimacy; combined with the Mandevillian belief that the pursuit of individual interest brings the greatest possible benefit to society as a whole, it encourages the individual to think that he or she is doing good even as he or she retreats into what Robespierre called the "abjection du moi personnel" [abjection of the personal self].[86] Or, as Philinte puts it: "Je pense et vois le monde, et dis, de vous à moi, / Qu'il faut, pour vivre heureux, se replier sur soi" (3.1). [I think and I see the world and I say, between you and me, / that in order to live happily one must withdraw into oneself.]

Philinte's ideology shrivels his heart, disguises his self-interest, and separates him from his fellow human beings. Philinte lacks the faculty of sympathy. Thus, despite Alceste's and Eliante's exhortations he continues to think only of himself. In his efforts to save the victim (who is ultimately revealed to be Philinte himself), Alceste is arrested. And even when his friend loses his liberty trying to help him, Philinte fails to think of Alceste:

EL: Vous rentrez seulement, et vous venez de faire
Une assez longue absence . . .
PH: Eh oui! pour mon affaire.
EL: Et je vois que pour nous inquiet, empressé,
A ce sincère ami vous n'avez pas pensé
Ah! Philinte . . . (5.1)

[ELIANTE: You are only now returning, and you have been out
A long while.
PHILINTE: Yes, for my case.
ELIANTE: And I see that for us you are worried and busy
But you have not even thought of our sincere friend
Oh, Philinte . . .]

For adherents to a sentimental moral philosophy—a philosophy that held that a harmonious society could be achieved only through a correspondence of sentiment—emotion was of paramount importance to moral life.[87] As Boltanski argues, it became crucial to distinguish between authentic feelings, "going back directly to the roots of the heart," from "purely external, imitated, or depicted emotions with no internal reference."[88] Whereas Alceste and Eliante experience the former, Philinte performs the latter. In the new, fraternal society of revolutionary France, emotion as performance was intolerable since it made knowledge of true feelings and beliefs impossible—since, in other words, it posed an insuperable obstacle to transparency. But equally important was the fact that the individual whose emotions were nothing more than conventional signs could not partake of the delights of the opening and sharing of hearts—that is, of the fraternity—that revolutionaries so desired and that was the aim of the transparency they sought.

Alceste and Eliante share precisely this sort of transparent communication of hearts. Each enters into the feelings of others and, in the phrase of Adam Smith, "brings them home to himself."[89] Alceste and Eliante, in other words, both possess the faculty of sympathy. It is this faculty that allows them to detect virtue and vice instantly: Alceste recognizes the probity of the honest lawyer at first sight; Alceste and Eliante instantly perceive the importance of the fraud case. Sympathy, as Alceste explains it to Philinte, springs from our primal sense of self: "L'homme sent qu'il est homme; et tant qu'il sentira / Que les malheurs d'autrui peuvent un jour l'atteindre, / Il prendra part aux maux qu'il a raison de craindre" (2.9). [Man feels that he is a human being, and so long as he feels / that the misfortunes of others can touch him one day, / he will enter into the ills he has a reason to fear.] Man feels his own humanity and recognizes that others are his fellows. Once the individual understands his or her essential commonality with others, he or she inevitably shares the misfortunes of others since these can always be brought home to oneself.

Eliante exemplifies the sympathetic morality Alceste describes. At precisely the same moment that Alceste's arrest fails to move Philinte, Eliante, despite her own troubles, worries only for Alceste and his sufferings:

Ah! tout ce que j'apprends me frappe et m'attendrit;
Alceste, Alceste seul préoccupe mon esprit.
Oubliez-vous sitôt sa peine et ses services?
Avez-vous donc, pour lui, d'assez grands sacrifices?

. . . .

Et savez-vous quel sort lui menace à présent?
Ce qu'on a fait de lui? Ce qu'il fait? Ce qu'il sent?
Ce dont il a besoin? . . . qu'il réclame peut-être?
He! devant lui, du moins, hâtons-nous de paraître. (5.1)

[O, everything that I hear affects me and touches me;
Alceste, only Alceste occupies my mind.

Have you already forgotten his efforts and his trouble
Have you made sufficient sacrifices for him?
. . . .
And do you know what fate now menaces him?
And what they have done with him? And what he is doing? And
what he is feeling?
What he needs . . . what he is asking for perhaps?
Let us at least hurry and go to him.]

Eliante tries to imagine Alceste's experience; rather than being faced with the spectacle of his suffering, she represents this suffering to herself and is amazed that Philinte does not do likewise. For in Fabre's play sympathy does not indicate romantic love but rather fraternal virtue. It might appear from my account here that the play's real interest is in the mismatch between Philinte and Eliante and the lost opportunity of a marriage between Eliante and Alceste. In fact, one outstanding feature of Fabre's play—a feature that distinguishes it sharply from Marmontel's rewriting of the *Misanthrope*—is the absence of any romantic plot or language. The play never suggests that Eliante should leave Philinte and join Alceste in his wilderness; instead, Eliante's capacity for sympathy shows that she is worthy of inclusion in the fraternal, transparent social order, and this inclusion is registered by her friendship with Alceste, which persists even when, at the play's end, Alceste cuts all ties to Philinte. Moreover, the new bond ("noeud") formed at the end of the play is not between Alceste and Eliante but between Alceste and his honest lawyer. They retire together to Alceste's country home to live virtuously and improve each others' characters. The new order is explicitly a masculine one, and the bonds it establishes are *called* friendship or fraternity rather than love. Eliante's role in the play, however, demonstrates the potential inclusion of women in this new order at the same time that her marriage to Philinte—at the end of the play still undissolved and apparently permanent—indicates the limits on her freedom of action and choice.

Just as Eliante is always moved by picturing to herself the suffering of others, Alceste's activism always begins with imagined tableaux of misfortune or injustice. Imagining the scene of his own persecution brought on by his good deeds spurs him to action:

Que j'éprouverai toujours leur noire violence,
Dans le moment précis d'un trait de bienfaisance.
Il sera beau me voir, sauvant un inconnu,
Par la main des méchants dans les fers détenus. (3.3)

[Let me face their malevolent violence,
At exactly the moment I am doing a good deed.
It will be beautiful to see me, while saving a stranger,
Put in chains by the hands of villains.]

He finds the tableau of his own unjust suffering so beautiful that he cannot resist its call to action. It is important to notice sympathy's aesthetic dimension: it is aesthetic representation—images and narratives, albeit often virtual ones—that nourishes sympathy within these two characters. These images and narratives owe their force, at least in part, to their beauty. Narratives that paint pictures of suffering always provoke a sympathetic reaction from Alceste. When there is no one to evoke a scene of suffering for Alceste, he conjures one up in his mind's eye. Thus, for example, alone in prison, Alceste forgets his own suffering and imaginatively considers Eliante's plight; as he later tells her, "[v]otre douleur, sans cesse était devant mes yeux" (5.3) [your sorrow was constantly before my eyes]. And when Eliante greets Alceste on his release from prison, taking his hands "with sentiment" according to Fabre's stage instruction, Alceste tells her that he felt her pain much more deeply than his own: "J'ai plaint votre embarras. J'ai senti vos douleurs bien plus que mon outrage" (5.3). [I lamented your situation. I felt your sorrows infinitely more than the outrage done to me.]

The representational strategies of Fabre's play mimic Alceste's internalization of sympathetic tableaux. Again and again Alceste moves himself through the scenes he hears about or imagines, despite the fact that he is never directly presented with any examples of pain. Similarly, the play's spectators never confront scenes of suffering. For the play does not include a single scene of misery or affliction; instead, it represents scenes of pure sympathizing: scenes in which Alceste and Eliante sympathize with absent victims and with each other, scenes in which they conjure up touching images in an attempt to awaken Philinte's faculty of sympathy. The play, in other words, does not simply try to teach spectators how to react to the pain of others but to summon forth affecting scenes for themselves. For once the spectators develop the imaginative capacity for sympathy, instead of simply shedding tears over the sorrows of the particular theatrical character with whom they have been presented (the situation that so worried Rousseau), they will be able to extend their sympathetic regard infinitely. Thus, the play does not turn suffering into spectacle; suffering is constructed as always already imagined, seen only within the heart and thus invulnerable to the deceptions practiced by spectacle. Fabre not only prefers the tableau to theatrical spectacle; the tableaux he chooses to stage are tableaux in which characters are absorbed in their efforts to imagine tableaux of other characters suffering.

Philinte's insensibility to tableaux and narratives ultimately reveals more than the absence of the faculty of sympathy and thus the absence of any real relation to his fellow human beings; it also reveals his profound alienation from himself. As Boltanski argues, adherents of sentimental moral philosophy construct emotion as not only crucially decisive in one's relation to others but also "the summum of presence to self."[90] Philinte is like those actors Rousseau describes who lose themselves because they play the part of others. Fabre makes Philinte's self-alienation the cause of his own ironic fate. For Philinte is himself the "unknown victim" of the fraud plot and never recognizes himself in the woeful tale he hears recounted so often: the honest lawyer, Alceste, and Eliante all tell Philinte of the victim's plight. It is significant, too, that the signature on the document is in fact authentic—Philinte has indeed signed the bill. He was, however, so distant from his own actions that he has affixed his signature to a fraudulent note. While Eliante and Alceste feel themselves in others when they hear their stories or picture their sufferings, Philinte does not even feel himself in himself. He cannot open his heart to others because he has no access to it himself.

Fabre thus establishes sympathy as central to a new kind of citizenship proper to the fraternal revolution: one protects one's own interests by protecting everyone's interests, by collapsing the difference between one's own interests and the interests of others. But Alceste and Eliante are meant to exemplify not only model citizenship but also a model for a new form of spectatorship; indeed, their good citizenship is inextricable from their imaginative, sympathetic spectatorship. For these two representation does not distance or objectify—on the contrary, representation enables them to deepen their connection to others. Fabre's Alceste and Eliante articulate, exemplify, and inculcate sympathetic spectatorship. *Le Philinte de Molière*, I am suggesting, is a reflection on the theater as much as it is a reflection on society: Alceste and Eliante are models for both revolutionary citizenship and revolutionary spectatorship. For in Fabre's rewriting, the emphasis is less on the individual as actor (and hence inauthentic)—although this remains an important element of the meditation on theatricality—and more on the individual as spectator. Put another way, Fabre ties authenticity and altruism to a particular model of spectatorship. Furthermore, Fabre's relentless critique of Philinte's Old Regime social values is bound up with a critique of the Old Regime theater that endorsed those values. Fabre's Philinte stands not just for the conventional sociability of prerev-

olutionary polite society but also, as Fabre's reinterpretation of Collin's optimist, for the highly theatrical conventions of Old Regime comedy itself. Thus,
Philinte's insensibility and Alceste's passionate sympathy describe both two
different characters and two different visions of dramatic representation.

Fabre's play presents his conception of a sympathy that could undo the theatricality Rousseau saw as inherent in spectatorship. In the *Lettre à M. d'Alembert* Rousseau claims that theater teaches spectators to think of themselves and
others as spectacles; spectatorship thus establishes a distance between beholder
and beheld and estranges the spectator from the object of viewing and from
him- or herself. The difference between Fabre and Rousseau on this score
arises from the different weight each assigns to the imagination. For Rousseau
sympathy is nothing other than an instantaneous identification between individuals, from a communication of souls; it is what Boltanski calls "transmis-
sion from sentiment to sentiment, from interiority to interiority."[91] Fabre, on
the other hand, demonstrates in his play that imagination is crucial for nourishing the faculty of sympathy. Fabre believed that sympathy was "le fonde-
ment de la morale" [the foundation of morality] and "la base de tous les vertus" [the basis for all virtue], but he also believed that the capacity for
sympathy could be nurtured and heightened. This explains why Fabre would
write a play based on Rousseau's explicitly antitheatrical theories. For theater,
Fabre believed, if it abandoned theatrical language and plots and hewed to
touching tableaux and exemplars of sympathy—if, in a sense, it could detheatricalize itself—was the most powerful site possible for the cultivation of
sympathy. Recreating the French theater as a theater of sympathy would thus
establish the theater as a central institution for revolutionary culture. The theater, as Fabre imagined it—regenerated because detheatricalized—would, paradoxically, play a primary role in the creation of a fraternal, transparent society.

Robespierre

As I will argue in chapter 3, Robespierre shared Fabre's desire to establish transparent representational and social relations. As Lionel Trilling has remarked,
Robespierre, following Rousseau, saw himself in a sense as Alceste's third
avatar, as a seeker of virtue, sincerity, and transparency.[92] But Fabre and Robespierre did not understand themselves to be engaged in the same enterprise, at
least not after divisions—especially divisions between those who sided with
Danton's rejection of the Terror and those who argued that the country was in
such great danger that the Terror was still necessary—roiled the Jacobins.

Fabre, a Dantonist, believed that Robespierre resembled more nearly a treacherous Tartuffe, whose very sincerity was performance, than the authentic Alceste.[93] Fabre demonstrated his skepticism while he observed Robespierre at the podium of the Jacobin club:

> Fabre écoutait et regardait Robespierre à la tribune avec une curiosité qui n'avait rien de respect béat. L'ancien acteur se donnait des attitudes et des jouissances de spectateur. Aux Jacobins, à la Convention, assis comme dans une stalle, il maniait sans cesse une lorgnette de théâtre avec laquelle il fixait l'avocat d'Arras.[94]

> [Fabre listened and watched Robespierre at the podium with a curiosity that had no beatific respect. The former actor gave himself the attitudes and pleasures of a spectator. At the Jacobins, at the Convention, sitting as if in the stalls, he manipulated his opera glasses constantly and used them to stare at the lawyer from Arras.]

Fabre played the part of a theatrical spectator to signal his belief that Robespierre's oratory was a theatrical performance; and when he played the part of a spectator, Fabre made Robespierre into an actor. By fixing Robespierre with his opera glasses, Fabre reestablished the very distance between Robespierre and his audience that the orator, as we will see below, tried so hard to eliminate. For his part, Fabre watched Robespierre with all the detached irony he hoped to banish from the theater itself. Playing with the opera glasses was no idle gesture; Fabre reminded Robespierre that the spectator governed the representation—when the spectator was displeased, he could let his glasses drop and dismiss the performer.

Robespierre was infuriated by Fabre's antics. On 19 Nivôse, Year II (January 8, 1794), Robespierre lashed out at Fabre from the podium at the Jacobin club: "[E]t je demande que cet homme, qu'on ne voit jamais qu'une lorgnette à la main, et qui sait si bien exposer les intrigues au théâtre, veuille bien s'expliquer ici; nous verrions comment il sortira de celle-ci." [And I demand that that man, whom one never sees without his opera-glasses in his hand, and who knows how to conduct a plot so well on the stage, please explain himself here; we shall see how he gets out of this one.][95] Robespierre was fully able to turn the tables on Fabre; whether he was a hypocrite or not, he was most certainly an astute politician.[96] His politics were not theatrical, he maintained; rather it was Fabre who sought, for his own self-interested motives, to import theatrical techniques into the political sphere and make the National Assembly into a theater. In a written report found among Robespierre's papers after his death, Robespierre prepared his case against Fabre:

> . . . habile dans l'art de peindre les hommes, beaucoup plus habile dans l'art de les tromper, [Fabre] ne les avait peut-être observés que pour les exposer avec succès sur la scène dramatique; il voulait les mettre en jeu, pour son profit particulier, sur le théâtre de la Révolution. . . . Ce grand maître s'était même donné la peine de composer lui-même le beau discours que Bourdon avait lu à la tribune . . . car tel est le genre de sa politique, qu'il aime mieux mettre les autres en action que d'agir lui-même. Fabre est peut-être l'homme de la République qui connaît le mieux le ressort qu'il faut toucher, pour imprimer tel mouvement. . . . Personne ne connût mieux l'art de donner aux autres ses propres sentiments.[97]

> [. . . skillful in the art of portraying men, even more skillful in the art of deceiving them, (Fabre) perhaps only observed them in order to better expose them on the stage; he wanted to put them in play, for his own personal profit, in the theater of the Revolution. . . . This great master even went to the pain of himself composing the beautiful speech Bourdon read at the podium . . . because that is the genre of his politics, he prefers to put others into action rather than to act himself. Fabre is perhaps the man of the Republic who knows best which mechanism to put into action in order to produce a specific reaction. No one knew better the art of giving others his own feelings.]

Robespierre accuses Fabre not of being an actor himself but of making other representatives into actors. By having other deputies speak his words and express his sentiments, and by directing their actions, Fabre shaped politics into a dramatic production of which he was the author. Behind the scenes of politics Fabre pulled all the strings; he transformed deputies into puppets of whom he was the master, Robespierre claimed, and thus controlled the politicians whose simulated debates duped naive spectators.

In his report on Fabre, Saint-Just followed the same line of argument: Fabre was guilty of conspiracy because he practiced politics as though it were a theater: "Il y a un autre parti qui se joua de tous les autres. . . . Ce parti, comme tous les autres, dénué de courage, conduisit la Révolution comme une intrigue de théâtre; Fabre d'Eglantine fût à la tête de ce parti." [There is another faction that made use of all the others. . . . This faction, like all the others, lacking courage, conducted the Revolution as if it were the plot of a play; Fabre d'Eglantine was at the head of this party.][98] Ironically, in light of his deepest aesthetic ambitions, Fabre's erstwhile allies' chief count against him would be his theatrical skill.

But why did Fabre's enemies find this accusation so important, so telling, so damning? That theatricality should bear a taint not only criminal but also moral makes sense only in a political culture whose very core is threatened by theatricality; to have accused an enemy of theatricality in the Old Regime, by contrast, would have been the height of incoherence. Fabre's pantomime with his opera glasses menaced Robespierre because it charged him with the only crime that was inexcusable. Fabre's actions demonstrated his belief, not that revolutionary politics was theatrical but rather that Robespierre was. The critique had particular force because Robespierre himself was committed to purging politics of dissimulation and making it a place of transparency and because, as will see in chapter 3, anxiety about theatricality pervaded his entire conception of republican politics. If for revolutionaries politics had been simply theater with higher stakes, then Robespierre's analysis of Fabre's politics would have been an homage instead of a denunciation. But theatricality was not only always a charge to be leveled at an enemy; it was perhaps the only charge that was indefensible. Indeed, it is possible that one's skill in defending against it only proved the depth of one's guilt. Fabre's actions were understood as an indictment of Robespierre; Robespierre's speech against Fabre was a death sentence. Fabre was executed on April 5, 1794. For in revolutionary political culture theatricality was not identical to politics; it was synonymous with the antithesis of politics: conspiracy.

3 ∎ *Robespierre's Eye*

Revolutionary Surveillance and the Modern Republican Subject

> *Dans l'entreprise que j'ai faite de me montrer tout entier au public, il faut que rien de moi ne lui reste obscur ou caché; il faut que je me tienne incessamment sous ses yeux; qu'il me suive dans tous les égarements de mon cœur, dans tous les recoins de ma vie; qu'il ne me perde de vue un seul instant, de peur que, trouvant dan mon récit la moindre lacune, le moindre vide, et se demandant: Qu'a-t-il fait durant ce temps-là? qu'il ne m'accuse de n'avoir pas voulu tout dire.*
> Jean-Jacques Rousseau, Les Confessions, *book 2*

As Rousseau reflects self-consciously on the ambition of his autobiographical project in the *Confessions,* he demonstrates at once his compulsion to solicit the unwavering scrutiny of the public and his anxiety about just what that readerly surveillance might construe.[1] He reveals his desire for total revelation to his reader, yet at the same time he discloses his suspicion of the reader, or rather his suspicion that he, Jean-Jacques, despite his vaunted sincerity, could himself become suspect by failing to subject himself absolutely and exhaustively to the (obviously suspicious) reader.

Rousseau's expression of a longing for surveillance—a surveillance conceived as the means by which the authenticity and goodness of the self can be constituted, recognized, and affirmed, as the relation by which a bond of true sentiment between self and other can be formed—resonates deeply in revolutionary culture. But so too does his fear, implied if not fully confessed, that surveillance may ultimately fail in its efforts to create a transparent relation to the self and to the other. For if there is some small "gap" or "void," no matter how minute, in one's account of oneself, the surveilling reader is bound to think not exactly that there is something hidden from him or her but, more important and more damning, that the entire project of transparency and sincerity is a sham, that sincerity itself is a disguise, that from the beginning one did not really want to say or show everything. And how can anyone hope to accomplish this total disclosure and discovery?

The Rousseauian problematic of surveillance was paradigmatic for revolutionary culture.[2] Over and over again in revolutionary political discourse, from high to low, we see the expression of a willingness to be the object of surveillance, along with an eagerness to be its agent. We see the Rousseauian faith in surveillance as a guarantor of individual virtue, communal bonds, social well-being, and political freedom paired with suspicion of those who seem to prefer obscurity to this transparency. At the same time, however, we see most starkly the inevitable fallibility, indeed the impossibility, of the utopian practice of surveillance. Surveillance's ultimate failure during the Revolution—its metamorphosis into terror—has shrouded its Rousseauian, idealistic origin.

The Rousseauian vision of surveillance, as it came into being during the Revolution, constitutes a lost chapter in the story of the shift from a regime of spectacle to a regime of surveillance, the shift from monarchic states ruled by powerful princes to liberal industrial nations dominated (at least according to the French literary imagination) by bankers and other capitalists. It is, of course, Michel Foucault who has placed the transformation of the gaze at the heart of the passage from early modernity to modernity in his crucial and seminal work *Discipline and Punish*. Foucault argues that the Old Regime deployed and depended on a politics of spectacle. Thus, for example, the king's power inhered in his person, and the spectacular display of his person constituted one of the most significant weapons in his political arsenal.[3] But sometime between the eighteenth century and the nineteenth, power, once located in the object of the gaze (the king), came to be exercised by the subject of the gaze: the prison warden, the doctor, the factory manager, the expert, and so on. Under the Old Regime of spectacle, power inhered in the object of the gaze, the king, in large measure because of his radical singularity; the spectacular organization of power created, on the one hand, a singular sacred center and, on the other, an undifferentiated mass of subjected witnesses to that authority. By contrast, the panoptic surveillance that came to characterize the nineteenth century atomized and isolated its object—transformed the mass into a series of individuals—the better to order it, contain it, and extract profit from it. Both these models, in contrast to Rousseau's, assume the nonreciprocity of the gaze; in neither model does the gaze establish anything like mutual recognition. In *Discipline and Punish* Foucault does not attempt to explain *how* the shift in the character and operation of the gaze took place; indeed, although he shows that on one side of the divide lies a regime of spectacle and on the other a regime of discipline, he argues that the same politics, tyrannical statism, informs both regimes of power. But surely such a momentous development was not wrought at once; surely surveillance must have taken on a variety of forms before it came to constitute the heart of the disciplinary machinery of the nineteenth century; surely all forms of surveillance are not alike.[4]

Foucault himself recognizes that the historical character of surveillance means that it cannot be always and everywhere the same. In an interview entitled "The Eye of Power" Foucault explains that Jeremy Bentham's panopticon and the mode of power it incarnates are both "the complement" and "the opposite" of the revolutionary conception of surveillance:

> What in fact was the Rousseauist dream that motivated many of the revolutionaries? It was the dream of there no longer existing any zones of darkness, zones established by the privileges of royal power or the prerogatives of some corporation, zones of disorder. It was the dream that each individual, whatever position he occupied, might be able to see the whole of society, that men's hearts should *communicate,* their vision be unobstructed by obstacles. . . . Bentham is both that and the opposite. He poses the problem of visibility organized around a dominating, overseeing gaze. He effects the project of a universal visibility which exists to *serve a rigourous meticulous power.*[5]

Although both these "dreams" or visions strive for a total visibility, the characters and aspirations of that visibility are very different. Benthamite visibility seeks to discipline its object in the service of a "dominating" center of power that remains invisible. Revolutionary visibility, by contrast, is dreamed of as a kind of reciprocity of the gaze—as a communication of hearts and souls that have been laid bare—that works to create a community of equal individuals. Whereas Benthamite surveillance requires a center, the revolutionary dream imagines a form of surveillance that is disseminated throughout society and imagines that each individual, each citizen, is that center.

Perhaps because Foucault's account of the rise of "disciplinary society" in *Discipline and Punish* is so compelling, or perhaps because, as Foucault argued, we live in the "panoptic machine" today, the historicity of surveillance—the fact that surveillance could take different forms, have different ends, and be experienced differently from its triumphant panoptic form—has received scant attention from scholars and cultural critics. Despite Foucault's own awareness that panoptic, disciplinary surveillance is only one model of surveillance, surveillance is almost always understood by cultural critics today as an oppressive, disciplinary tool of a stable, hegemonic power. In this chapter I want to retrieve the lost variant of surveillance that was first articulated by Rousseau and recalled to life by the French revolutionaries. The French Revolution, especially its radical republican phase, was a crucial and highly particular moment in the development of surveillance. For the French Revolution is precisely what happened in that "sometime" between the eighteenth century and the nineteenth, that time that seems to belong to both centuries and to neither. I will examine the ways that what Foucault calls the "Rousseauist dream" was expressed by revolutionaries and the ways that it came to be practiced. Revolutionary surveillance as it was conceived, and sometimes even as it was practiced, was highly democratic; therefore, revolutionary surveillance was very different, not simply in degree but essentially in kind, from its nineteenth-century successor.

It is always dangerous to establish sharp period distinctions. It would certainly be possible to find some prerevolutionary movement toward constructing panoptic techniques or institutions of surveillance. In fact, Foucault discusses both the mid-eighteenth century dormitories of the Paris École militaire and Claude Ledoux's saltworks at Arc-et-Senans as precursors to Bentham's panopticon.[6] One could also, doubtless, discover some nineteenth-century uses of spectacular power. It nevertheless remains worth pointing out how distinct revolutionary surveillance seems from its panoptic cousin. In its democratic ubiquity and its self-consciousness revolutionary surveillance belongs to a world inspired by two related but separate strains of thought. On the one hand, revolutionary surveillance sprang from the popular insistence that popular sovereignty have a concrete, practical meaning, from the same spirit we saw expressed in chapter 1 that demanded that the people must exercise continual supervision over those to whom they delegated power. In other words, the idea of popular surveillance emerged in large measure from the widespread distrust of representation. On the other hand, revolutionary surveillance owed its idealism, its affective side, what Foucault called its "lyrical note," to the

Rousseauian longing for transparency, authenticity, and community.[7] Moreover, revolutionary surveillance differed from its successor in that it came into being in a world that was fundamentally dominated by politics and in which politics was understood as essential and integral to all aspects of life. It emerged from and helped shape a culture that believed, as Rousseau wrote, "that everything depended fundamentally on politics, and that, no matter how one looked at it, no people could ever be anything but what the nature of its government made it."[8] Revolutionary surveillance was thus critically different from the nineteenth-century surveillance that flourished in a culture that sought to separate the social from the political, for revolutionary surveillance was an important means by which politics became enmeshed in daily life.

The power to surveil was thought to be shared by all citizens and was considered by many the single most important means to protect the Republic from counterrevolutionaries and would-be usurpers. But surveillance on Foucault's account is not simply a disciplinary tool; it is also an important mode of subjecting those who are its object. If this is the case, as many following Foucault's lead have argued convincingly, then surely the revolutionary experience of being the *subject* of surveillance and, in fact, of being at once its subject and object, will form a different kind of subject than that shaped by the surveillance of modern, liberal states. This chapter will attempt to delineate this modern republican subjectivity.

We have seen how a perceived need to detheatricalize the theater was at the heart of ambitious efforts to regenerate both the theater and republican society. The same will to detheatricalize sustains and helps to explain the political history of the revolutionary period. Indeed, a fervent desire to overcome and eradicate theatricality shaped revolutionary political discourse. Just as Rousseau's antitheatrical theory influenced Fabre d'Eglantine's project of reforming the theater, the same antitheatricalism equally informed the political theory and practice of many important revolutionaries, most notably that of Maximilien Robespierre. The particular exigencies of the Revolution made theatricality a central preoccupation and a central peril; for theatricality exemplified representation's hazards at just the moment when the emergence of a new form of political and social organization, modern democratic republicanism, made representation crucial to political discourse and practice. The task facing revolutionary republicans, Robespierre believed, was to create representative institutions that would be free of all taint of theatricality. For revolutionaries theatricality characterized the old hierarchical, monarchical regime that sanctified social and political differences and in which rank—tantamount to identity in the Old Regime—depended on successful self-representation, on assimilation of the complex codes of behavior that scripted human interactions, on the kind of dissimulation Rousseau and Fabre saw condemned in Molière's *Le Misanthrope*. These revolutionaries were not wrong to link theatricality with monarchy: many scholars have shown how Louis XIV masterfully deployed theater in his successful project of building absolutism. They have demonstrated how he transformed Versailles into a stage on which he appeared before all the kingdom and all Europe, how he remade the court into an intricately coded and rigorously maintained sequence of ritual performances and scripted speech.[9] And although Louis XVI was no Sun king, although he himself, strangely and sadly, had more taste for the new sentimental values of home and family, the monarchy at the end of the eighteenth century still practiced and depended on the theatrical power Louis the Last's great predecessor had honed.[10] It is not surprising that revolutionary republicans associated theatricality with absolute monarchy, with decadent court aristocracy, with effeminization and servility, and perhaps most especially, with Marie-Antoinette. Following Rousseau, they viewed Old Regime society as wholly and hopelessly theatricalized, and just as Fabre linked the theatricalization of society to suffering, injustice, and inhumanity, other revolutionaries linked that theatricalization to corruption, oppression, and tyranny.

But if absolute monarchy was now widely recognized as intolerable, many citizens believed that representative democracy posed its own share of problems. Perhaps foremost among these was the very novelty of imagining that representation and democracy could be compatible since theretofore democracy had always meant direct rule of the *demos*.[11] And just as this problem was at work in the theaters, it was equally present in the domain of high politics. One important solution to this problem of reconciling democracy and representation, and perhaps the one that gained the widest support, was publicity. Publicity could, at its best, restore to the sovereign people the power they gave up when they authorized representatives. Publicity could be conceived in any number of ways and could thus redistribute, so to speak, varying degrees of agency and authority to the people. The people could be imagined, as Marcel Gauchet has explained, as tribunal, as censor, and even as surveillant.[12] Thus, for example, Robespierre exhorted his colleagues to build as much publicity as possible into the new constitution: "Qu'on délibère à haute voix: la publicité est l'appui de la vertu, la sauvegarde de la vérité, le fléau de l'intrigue. Laissez les ténèbres et le scrutin secret aux criminels et aux esclaves. Les hommes libres veulent avoir le peuple pour témoin de leurs pensées." [Let us deliberate out loud: Publicity is the mainstay of virtue, the safeguard of truth, the scourge of intrigue. Leave the shadows and the secret ballot to criminals and slaves. Free men want to have the people witness their thoughts.][13]

But for Robespierre publicity itself posed a set of problems. The puzzle presented by a system of representative democracy supplemented by publicity was this: how could the Republic create and sustain the maximal publicity that he, along with many others, believed necessary to the protection of liberty and democracy while ensuring that that very publicity not be perverted into a species of theatricality? How could the Revolution open up all aspects of France's political life to public scrutiny without creating a theatrical relation—a relation that could mislead, mystify, or otherwise introduce opacity—between those who watch and those who are watched? Publicity corrupted, publicity degenerated, threatened to widen, rather than mitigate, the gap between represented and representative. Publicity was truly a dangerous supplement: while it was necessary to lend representative democracy its democratic character, it risked transforming the represented into spectators and their representatives into actors.[14] And if representatives assumed the position of actors vis-à-vis their constituents—if they assumed roles and masks—how could the sovereign people ever really know what was in their hearts? How could they effectively judge them? Publicity, meant to assure the transparency of politics, could, if it were not practiced correctly, cause a veil to fall between the people and their deputies.

The strategy that Robespierre devised might seem a strange one: the best tool to defeat theatricality, he would argue, was surveillance. But in his seemingly paradoxical recourse to surveillance Robespierre was deeply Rousseauian; as David Marshall has persuasively argued, Rousseau, too, turns to surveillance to ensure the innocence and openness of society. The ball for the "jeunes personnes à marier" Rousseau describes at the end of the *Lettre à M. d'Alembert* successfully promotes the constitution, recognition, and celebration of the community only because it is thoroughly subjected to surveillance.[15] Whereas nearly all commentators on the *Lettre* take the famous outdoor, communal *fête* to constitute Rousseau's answer to both the theater and theatricalized society, Marshall shows that it is the radically supervised ball that allows for a recuperation of sociability and publicness. For Marshall Rousseauian surveillance is not opposed to theatricality but rather is an extreme form of it. The surveillance form of theatrical exposure works according to the structure identified by Jean Starobinski as the "remède dans le mal": Rousseau must turn to a kind of theater in order to inoculate against theater. In a small city like Geneva (as opposed to Paris) everyone is constantly under the scrutiny of a neighbor—

surveillance is coextensive with society—and this continual surveillance produces good behavior. So, Marshall argues, "[w]e witness in the ball a carefully staged display of the everyday surveillance with which Genevans play spectator and censor to each other" (163). Marshall argues that Rousseau, the famous "citoyen de Genève," perhaps as a sign and an assertion of his citizenship, seeks to identify himself with the surveilling function of the state (ibid., 166).

Like Rousseau, Robespierre conceived of surveillance as an antitheatrical tool, and again like Rousseau, he conceived himself in the position of surveillant. This chapter will follow the revolutionary career of surveillance from its beginnings as a defense against theatricality and monarchy, to its importance as a means of direct participatory democracy, to its demise as a democratic tool and the rise of disciplinary surveillance with the fall of the radical Republic. Recovering this story should prompt us to rethink some of the most important accounts of subjectivity and subjection that prevail today.

Theatricality

Just as Fabre d'Eglantine sought to eliminate the theatricalizing distance between the subject and the object of the gaze in the theater, Robespierre sought to detheatricalize the relation between the representative and the represented and, in so doing, close the gap between them. Indeed, purging theatricality from politics was Robespierre's central preoccupation. Consider, for example, the debates surrounding the trial of Louis XVI. Recent critics typically construct Louis' trial as one of the foundational dramas of the theatrical Revolution. Although Marie-Hélène Huet, in describing the king's trial, explains that "this theater was not theater" because it was in fact the unfolding of history, she also insists on its theatrical character: "January 16, 1793, at the theater of the Tuileries. The auditorium is packed; the representation about to unfold is the conclusion of a trial that has gone on just short of two months."[16] Despite the acknowledgment that this theater was not one, Huet concludes, "The condemnation of Louis XVI: a theatrical manifestation nearly perfect despite its length" (5). But Robespierre—the central figure of Jacobinism—was opposed to trying the king at all. Robespierre's part in that trial has been largely misunderstood. Scholars typically take Robespierre's objection to putting the king on trial as a sign of his bloodthirstiness and as an omen of the Terror to come.[17] In fact, I suggest, Robespierre objected to a trial for the king on the grounds that such a trial would inevitably be theatrical and, hence, would degrade the Republic's new political representatives. In other words, what Huet sees as the trial's object—the staging of justice—Robespierre saw as the Revolution's antithesis.

Robespierre's argument against a trial rests on a set of Lockean assumptions about the relations between people and their rulers. In the *Second Treatise of Government* Locke argues that no earthly judge can adjudicate a case between a people and their ruler. Thus, when the people consider their government to be tyrannical, they must submit themselves to heavenly judgment by means of a trial by arms.[18] The *journée* of August 10, 1792, the day when the people of Paris, by invading the Tuileries and defeating the king's military forces, demonstrated that they would be ruled no longer by the monarchy, was, Robespierre declared, just such a trial of arms: "Louis dénonçait le peuple français comme rebelle; il a appelé, pour le châtier, les armées des tyrans, ses confrères; la victoire et le peuple ont décidé que lui seul était rebelle." [Louis denounced the French people as rebels; he appealed to the armies of tyrants, his brothers, to chastise them; victory and the people have decided that he alone is a rebel.][19] Robespierre drew a simple and logical conclusion from this argument: "Louis ne peut donc être jugé; il est déjà jugé." [Louis cannot be judged; he has already been judged.][20] The king had been tried and judged by the people—an authority greater than the Convention—and he had been tried according to the law of nature, a law superior to that of the Republic: "Le droit de punir le tyran, et celui de le détrôner, c'est la même chose. . . . Le procès du tyran, c'est l'insurrection; son jugement, c'est la chute de sa puissance." [The right to punish a tyrant, and the right to dethrone him are one and the same. . . . The tyrant's trial is the insurrection; his judgment is his fall from power.][21]

On this logic, if the Convention were to try the king, it would simply be repeating the process the people had already carried out. But how can a trial be repeated? Trials, as Robespierre reminded his colleagues, required the presumption of innocence and an undetermined outcome: "En effet, si Louis peut être encore l'objet d'un procès, Louis peut être absous; il peut être innocent. Que dis-je? Il est présumé l'être jusqu'à ce qu'il soit jugé." [Indeed, if Louis can still be the object of a trial, Louis can still be acquitted; he could be innocent. What am I saying? He is presumed innocent until he is judged.][22] But since the people had already overthrown the monarchy and established the Republic, the king's guilt was already proven, and the trial's verdict was already announced. To entertain the possibility of the king's innocence—let alone to presume it, as a fair trial must—was to assert the possible illegitimacy not only of the Republic but also of the people's actions in overthrowing the monarchy. Since it was unthinkable to even consider these propositions, the king's trial would necessarily be a pre-scripted show trial in which all the participants, like actors, would know the conclusion from the outset yet would continue to play their roles. "Vous ne donneriez à l'univers," Robespierre warned his colleagues, "qu'une ridicule comédie" (ibid., 124). [You would do nothing but perform a ridiculous comedy before the universe.] Since the people whom the representatives represented had already judged Louis, to try him in the representative assembly would be to render the representatives mere impersonators, rather than agents, of the people, and to render the acts of the representative body merely parodic of the primary and foundational act that took place beyond its confines.

Show trials, Robespierre argues, are unworthy of a republic. They are the tools of tyrants and usurpers rather than of a free people. Neither the trial of Mary, Queen of Scots, nor that of Charles I should be considered precedents for the actions of the French Republic:

> Que Cromwell ait fait juger Charles Ier par un tribunal dont il disposait; qu'Elisabeth ait fait condamner Marie d'Écosse de la même manière, il est naturel que des tyrans qui immolent leurs pareils, non au peuple, mais à leur ambition, cherchent à tromper l'opinion du vulgaire par des formes illusoires. Il n'est question là ni de principes, ni de liberté, mais de fourberie et d'intrigues. (ibid., 123)

> [So Cromwell had Charles I judged by a tribunal under his control; so Elizabeth had Mary Queen of Scots condemned in the same way. It is natural that tyrants who put their peers to death, not for the sake of the people, but for that of their ambition, should try to beguile common opinion by means of illusions. It is a question in those cases neither of principles nor of freedom, but of deceit and intrigue.]

These rigged trials, Robespierre argues, do not offer models of justice. Rather, they were extensions of the tyrannical policies of dissimulation and corruption, which they simply perpetuated under another name. It is noteworthy that Robespierre employs the terms *fourberie* and *intrigues* to describe these tyrannical show trials; both are terms associated with the theater. *Intrigue*, of course, means plot in the theater, and *fourberie* inevitably recalls Molière's farce *Les Fourberies de Scapin*. Robespierre thus fought so hard against trying the king because he knew that no matter what form the trial took, it would be a farce that would demean the newly assembled Convention and inaugurate the Republic under the sign of theatricality.

The problem of theatricality, however, was not peculiar to the king's trial; rather, it was inherent to institutionalized political representation. Representative government, Robespierre argued incessantly, required publicity; publicity was the safeguard of liberty. The public must be allowed to witness the proceedings of the National Assembly. But the presence of the people in the galleries inevitably threatened to theatricalize the Assembly. For the very difference between the citizens in the galleries and the delegates—the difference that both enables and is instituted by representation—inevitably established the citizens as audience and the representatives as performers. Where there is a theatrical distance between subject and object, audience and performance, Robespierre warned, there is always deception and abuse. This problem was immediate and pressing, according to Robespierre, because the topography of the hall in which the Assembly met exacerbated the distance or obstacle between the deputies and the observers in the galleries:

> On a observé, avec raison, que ses abus tenaient en partie à la disposition du local où l'assemblée représentative est renfermée. J'avoue que si quelque chose prouve à quel point nous sommes inconséquents dans notre conduite et mesquins dans nos institutions, c'est l'indifférence avec laquelle nous avons souffert que le Manège des Tuileries fut si longtemps le temple de la législation. On ne s'est même aperçu que la nature de ce local était incompatible avec la publicité, que nous semblions regarder comme la sauve-garde de la liberté. On ne peut pas dire que les représentants de vingt-cinq millions d'hommes délibèrent publiquement, lorsqu'ils ne peuvent être vus ou entendus que de trois ou quatre cents hommes entassés dans des cages étroites et incommodes. (ibid., 5:129)

> [It has been rightly observed that these abuses sprang in part from the disposition of the space in which the representative assembly is enclosed. I confess that if there is something that proves how thoughtless we are in our conduct and how petty we are in our institutions, it is the indifference with which we have allowed the Manège of the Tuileries to remain so long the temple of legislation. It has not even been perceived that this location's characteristics are incompatible with publicity, which we pretend to regard as liberty's safeguard. We cannot say that the representatives of twenty-five million men deliberate publicly when they can only be seen and heard by three or four hundred men crammed into narrow, uncomfortable cages.]

Robespierre's description of the disposition of the salle du Manège, in which the Convention met, inevitably recalls not the revolutionary theaters of the capital but Rousseau's characterization of theaters as places that "renferment tristement un petit nombre de gens dans un antre obscur; qui les tiennent craintifs et immobiles dans le silence et l'inaction" [dismally enclose a small number of people in a dark den and keep them fearful and immobile in silence and inactivity].[23] For Rousseau, as we have seen, the theater's oppressive structure isolated, misled, and alienated the spectator. The National Assembly should, by rights, constitute the very opposite of the theater; it should be the place that brings what Starobinski calls the "solar myth of the Revolution," the idea of total enlightenment, total visibility, and, consequently, total truth, to the practice of politics.[24] Instead, it makes room for only a small number of spectators, a number whose puny size (three or four hundred) is emphasized by its relation to the twenty-five million who are to be represented. It is especially interesting that Robespierre does not here attempt to figure the appropriate numerical relation between represented and *representatives;* the shame and the crime are not to be found in the small number of deputies but in the small number of those who *watch over* the deputies. And the condemning allusion to the Assembly's defective meeting place as a theater actually further underscores the Manège's relative lack of publicness, for while the salle du Manège might make room for three hundred to four hundred observers, Parisian theaters on average had between eighteen hundred and two thousand places.

According to Robespierre the Revolution's enemies, not true revolutionary patriots, sought to make the National Assembly into a theater in order to subvert and pervert the publicity necessary to safeguard republican liberty. The conspirators, he claimed, hoped to create a theatrical setting for the Convention in order to trick the eyes and the ears of its observers:

> Tous les observateurs se sont aperçus qu'elle [la salle] a été disposé avec beaucoup d'intelligence, par le même esprit d'intrigue . . . pour retrancher les mandataires contre les regards du peuple. . . . On a enfin trouvé le secret, recherché depuis si longtemps, d'exclure le public en l'admettant; qu'il puisse assister aux séances, mais qu'il ne puisse entendre. . . . [Q]u'il soit absent et présent à la fois.[25]

> [All observers have noticed that it (the hall) has been designed with a great deal of intelligence by the same spirit of intrigue . . . in order to shield the deputies from the gaze of the people. . . . They have at last discovered the secret means, sought for so long, to exclude the people while admitting them;

they may attend the sessions, but they may not hear. . . . They are absent and present at the same time.]

In Robespierre's striking formulation, being spectator to a contrived spectacle is to be absent and present at once. This perversion of publicity made a pretence of admitting public scrutiny only to nullify the public's authority by making it witness to a pantomime—sometimes the citizens can see, sometimes they can hear. Because their senses and thus their perception are so manipulated by the theatrical Convention, the people had only an ersatz presence. The means by which the people are flummoxed is itself a special "secret," even a trade secret, devised by those who are meant to act on their behalf. Perhaps, Robespierre implies, this is the only kind of presence ordinary citizens can ever attain in a system of what at that time was called "absolute representation." In other words, the threat of theatricalization served to point out an essential truth of political representation: even if they were physically present at the scene of politics, citizens were rendered effectively absent by representation. To function legitimately, Robespierre observed, political representation had to be supplemented.

Theatricality, Robespierre claimed, was pervasive outside of the Convention, as well as inside it. For Robespierre and the revolutionary citizens who supported him, the ubiquity of theatricality required a general mobilization of popular surveillance because spies, conspirators, and counterrevolutionaries— whether inside or outside the Convention—were nothing but actors. These enemies infested every shadowy corner of the Republic, including the Convention itself: "si tous les cœurs ne sont pas changés, combien de visages sont masqués! combien de traîtres ne se mêlent de nos affaires pour les ruiner" (ibid., 10:361) [if all hearts are not changed, how many faces are masked! how many traitors interfere in our affairs in order to ruin them]. One sign of this generalized fear was the frequent recurrence of the figure of the mask. Masked counterrevolutionaries were everywhere; indeed, when faced with patriots the aristocratic party simply dissimulated: "à l'approche des hommes libres, le despotisme a tremblé; et il s'est hâté de recouvrir son visage hideux de ce masque grossier du patriotisme qu'il avait déposé" (ibid., 4:257) [at the approach of free men, despotism trembled, and it hastened to cover its hideous face once again with the crude mask of patriotism it had put aside].

Attacking Brissot and his associates, Robespierre conjured a scenario of political betrayal, carried out by the Girondins, made possible by masking:

> Lorsque ces hommes concluent avec la cour le traité qui lui livre le bonheur de la nation, et l'espérance de tous les peuples et des siècles futurs, il est stipulé qu'ils garderont, le plus longtemps que possible, le masque de patriotisme qu'ils lui vendent. (ibid., 4:79)

> [When these men conclude the treaty with the court that will hand over to it the happiness of the nation and the hope of all peoples and of posterity, it is agreed that they will maintain, for as long as possible, the mask of patriotism that they are selling.]

And after the Girondins had been dispensed with and other "factions" arose in their place, Robespierre declared that "a few skilled stage-hands are hidden in the wings operating the machinery silently behind the scenes. At base it is the same faction as that of the Gironde, except with different actors. Or, rather, it is always the same actors but they are now wearing different masks. But it's the same stage, and always the same drama."[26] And Robespierre warned of an even more generalized masquerade of conspirators who "conspirent dans les ténèbres et sous le masque de patriotisme. Hier, ils assassinaient les défenseurs de la liberté, aujourd'hui ils se mêlent   eurs pompes funèbres, et demandant pour eux des honneurs divins, épiant l occasion d'égorger leurs pareils" [conspire in the shadows, concealed beneath the mask of patriotism. Yesterday, they assassinated liberty's defenders, today they insinuate themselves into their obsequies and, while demanding divine honors for those they have killed, look for the opportunity to slaughter their comrades].[27] Here it seems that counterrevolutionary success depended on extraordinary theatrical skill and on the mass nature of revolutionary Parisian political culture; that large masses of citizens participated in the new regime allowed conspirators to "se mêlent" in political affairs and in communal affairs—themselves perhaps indistinguishable. More complicated still, Robespierre urged his readers to recognize that the unmasked—the counterrevolutionary who declares himself such—is not the Revolution's true menace: "Ce ne sont point ceux qui ne se cachent pas qu'il s'agit de démasquer; ce sont ceux qui sont encore à *demi-cachés* sous le voile du patriotisme." [It is not those who do not hide that we must unmask; it is those who are still partly hidden beneath the veil of patriotism.][28] The most effective mask of all was a sort of demi-mask, the mask of moderation, for that was precisely the one that was most convincing.

Theatricality and masquerade were the hallmarks of counterrevolution. James H. Johnson has written eloquently about the status of the mask during the Revolution. From the Revolution's very early days, he argues, revolutionary culture displayed anxiety about masks; only six months after the fall of the Bastille, following a proposal made, significantly, by a neighborhood council, the city of Paris decreed an official ban on all masks. But, as Johnson points out, "[m]asks were banished from the street only to resurface as a central rhetorical figure in speeches, in print, and in the characterizations of conspirators both real and imagined."[29] Acknowledging the degree to which the revolutionary fear of masks spiraled into a paranoid fantasy of invisible, ubiquitous enemies, Johnson points out that this fear was expressed first by local, grassroots associations; that is, it emerged from the bottom, not the top, of political society. There was, he argues, a real, material origin for this fear, which sprang from a dual source: the culturally widespread beliefs about the theatricality of the court aristocracy and the real use of disguises on the part of emigrating nobles. Massive anxiety about masks and inauthenticity emerged out of "long entrenched associations with courtly dissimulation that predated the Revolution and was fed by popular responses to actual masks and disguises. . . . Brought to popular consciousness by the flight of aristocrats, the figure of the mask gradually shifted from describing actual disguise to denouncing all enemies, real and imagined, as *dissemblers* and *deceivers,* that is 'aristocrats'" (ibid., 97–98; my emphasis).

When Robespierre inveighed against the mask, the parade of patriotism, the disguised enemy, he expressed and responded to a fear of falseness and a compulsion for transparency that resonated widely. The problem of dissimulation was urgent; it required immediate action. If citizens did not quickly discern and denounce the theatrical enemy, Robespierre warned, a wholesale inversion of all republican values would follow swiftly: "[L]es traîtres cachés jusqu'ici sous des dehors hypocrites jetteront le masque; les conspirateurs accuseront leurs accusateurs." [The traitors hidden until now beneath hypocritical facades will throw down their masks and the conspirators will accuse their accusers.][30] But of what precisely will these true patriots be accused? Of demanding transparency and denouncing opacity. For even if these hypocrites were to remove their masks and reveal themselves, what would be revealed other than their hypocrisy? For Robespierre, frighteningly, the danger to the Republic lies less in evil actions theatrically obscured—less, that is, in what theatricality hides—than in theatricality itself. Here again we see Robespierre's deep Rousseauianism. As Derrida famously argues, Rousseau's animus against the theater is not directed primarily at the messages or morals of particular plays but at the possibility of playing: "what Rousseau criticizes . . . is not the content of the spectacle, the sense *represented* by it, although that *too* he criticizes: it is re-presentation itself." Similarly, for Robespierre it is what Derrida calls the "rift between represented and representer,"[31] the difference or gap between the authentic soul and the adopted role, that constitutes the crime and that must be extirpated: "[L]a loi pénale doit nécessairement avoir quelque chose de vague, parce que, le caractère actuel des conspirateurs étant la dissimulation et l'hypocrisie, il faut que la justice puisse les saisir sous toutes les formes." [The penal law must, necessarily, be somewhat vague because the character of conspirators today, being dissimulation and hypocrisy, justice must be able to seize them in all their forms.][32] Hypocrisy and dissimulation, affecting to be what one is not: this is not just the form but the very character of conspiracy and counterrevolution since dissimulation and hypocrisy were the defining features of the Old Regime.

Surveillance

In the spring of 1794 Maximilien Robespierre entered into an open battle with his fellow Jacobin and fellow deputy to the National Convention Joseph Fouché, future minister of police under Napoleon and Louis XVIII, future inventor of the modern police, and the original for Balzac's diabolical police chiefs. Ultimately, this turned out to be a battle between two opposing views of surveillance: Robespierre believed that the Revolution could succeed only if the people watched over those who governed; Fouché believed that order could be maintained only if the governors watched over the people. Robespierre sought to have Fouché expelled from the Jacobin club—a move that boded ill for Fouché's future. Robespierre disliked both Fouché's excessive violence—Fouché, along with Collot d'Herbois, organized the gruesome mass executions in Lyon—and his radical atheism. It was Fouché who penned the infamous declaration that "la mort est un sommeil éternel" [death is an eternal sleep], whereas Robespierre insisted, on the contrary, that belief in the immortality of the soul was republican and that atheism was aristocratic.[33]

Hostility had been brewing between these two for a long time before it burst into the open with Robespierre's denunciation. What is particularly interesting, however, is the way Robespierre attacked his enemy. Consider the taunting accusation Robespierre cast against Fouché:

> Craint-il les oreilles du peuple? Craint-il ses yeux. . . . Craint-il que sa triste figure ne présente visiblement le crime? Que six mille regards fixés sur lui ne découvre dans ses yeux son âme tout entière, et qu'en dépit de la nature, on n'y lise ses pensées?[34]

[Does he fear the ears of the people? Does he fear their eyes. . . . Does he fear that his dismal countenance will present his crime visibly? That six thousand gazes fixed upon him will uncover his whole soul in his eyes, and that, in spite of nature, the people will be able to read his thoughts?]

Robespierre identifies Fouché as someone who unnaturally, or rather suspiciously, tries to retreat from the people's scrutiny; indeed, his effort to escape the people's eyes is the telling sign of Fouché's crime.[35] Furthermore, Robespierre's accusation, made in the midst of the crowded club, put into motion the very operation Fouché sought to avoid; for surely the denunciation drew all eyes in the club to Fouché, and despite his undoubted political prowess, it must have been nearly impossible for Fouché's face not to betray *something*— anxiety, fear, hatred, or perhaps even the truth, that Fouché was in fact plotting against Robespierre—that could be read as suspicious. Here, in Robespierre's imagining, the hypothetical object of the gaze (Fouché) wields no power over those who look (the people, his fellow Jacobins). Fouché's appearance has no effect on its viewers; on the contrary, Robespierre ascribes extraordinary force and authority to the subject of the gaze—to the six thousand ordinary citizen-observers. The power of the multiplied gaze of the people has something supernatural about it. It resembles what Martin Jay calls "inspired vision"; it is a kind of sight that transcends physiological ocularity and attains the power to read the soul, to expose intention "in spite of nature"—that is in spite of materiality itself.[36] Robespierre was not alone in this conception of the power of the people's gaze. The Girondin sympathizer Nicholas de Bonneville, editor of the newspaper *La Bouche de fer,* also celebrated the citizen's gaze: "his penetrating vision pierces masks and sees into hearts; they may shut the door but he sees through doors into the folds of their soul."[37]

The power that Robespierre believed to inhere in the people's scrutiny became central to his conception of the Republic. Precisely because Robespierre attributed such enormous force to the citizenry's gaze, he sought to ensure that citizens would have ample opportunity to observe. Robespierre complained that the salle du Manège, the hall in which the National Convention met, was not sufficiently public; it offered only the illusion of publicity. As we have already seen, it only made room for three or four hundred observers in the galleries, and its layout—a long, narrow rectangle—meant that it was difficult not only for the observing citizens to see or hear the deputies but even for the deputies to see and hear each other. Because the public's scrutiny and even that of their fellow deputies could only be partial and was therefore subject to manipulation, corrupt deputies were free to intrigue and plot in their own particular interest.

Robespierre's solution to the problematic relation of publicity and theatricality is remarkable: rather than excluding spectators from the Assembly, Robespierre wanted to increase their numbers exponentially. The only cure for theatricality, oddly enough, was more spectators:

> Il faudrait, s'il était possible, que l'assemblée des mandataires délibérât en présence de tous les Français. Un édifice fastueux et majestueux, ouvert à douze mille spectateurs devrait être le lieu des séances du corps législatifs. Sous les yeux d'un si grand nombre de témoins, ni la corruption, ni l'intrigue, ni la perfidie n'oserait se montrer; la voix de la raison et de l'intérêt public serait entendue. Mais l'admission de quelques centaines de spectateurs, encaissés dans un local étroit et incommode, offre-t-elle un publicité proportionnée à l'immensité de la nation?[38]

> [It would be necessary, if it were possible, for the assembly to deliberate in the presence of all the French people. A splendid and majestic edifice, open to twelve thousand spectators, should be the site of the meetings of the legislature. Under the eyes of such a great number of witnesses, neither corruption, nor intrigue, nor treachery would dare show themselves; the voice of reason and of the public interest alone would be heard. But admitting a few hundred spectators and hemming them in to a narrow and inconvenient location, is this a kind of publicity that is proportionate to the nation's immensity?]

Robespierre's initial vision of a perfected representative republic is as telling as it is utopically odd. Were it possible, the deliberations of the Assembly should be watched over by the entire French nation. It is clear that this dreamed-of observation is not a mediated one: the Assembly should deliberate "in the presence of all the French people." This is a perplexing scenario since one of the principal justifications for political representation was the practical impossibility of assembling such a large nation. In other words, if "all the French people" could be assembled to witness the National Assembly, then why would they need an assembly of representatives? Why would they not deliberate themselves? The answer seems to be that the act of observing, of watching over those who do deliberate, is as necessary to republican governance as legislating itself. Thus were all the French people to assemble in order to legislate directly, they too would require an observer. Once again, as in his earlier complaint about the paltry number of citizen-observers, the "proportionality"

Robespierre seems so concerned to institute is that between the nation and the body of citizen-observers.

Given the impossibility of an entire nation of witnesses, Robespierre settles here on twelve thousand. The number seems, perhaps, arbitrary; it corresponds to nothing except a sense of sufficient multitudinousness: just as the six thousand pairs of eyes focused on Fouché would pierce his mask and reveal his soul, the twelve thousand pairs in the new assembly would penetrate all dissimulation and, in so doing, protect the Republic. In the "édifice majestueux" Robespierre imagines here, the space of political representation is purged of theatricality precisely because it has been totalized by spectatorship. Here public observation is so overwhelming that it functions as surveillance; indeed, Robespierre warned his colleagues not to imagine that they occupied the same position in relation to the French people that the king had; for with the Revolution came not only new institutions but a new, regenerated people. The free citizens of the Republic would not be bedazzled by the spectacle of its governors but would see through them: "un peuple digne de la liberté n'idolâtre point ses représentants; il les surveille" [a people worthy of liberty does not idolize its representatives; it watches over them].[39] The people's capacity to surveil those who spoke in their name was the best guarantee of the representative's faithfulness. By the same token, only total surveillance could make the Convention a locus of transparency and certainty and thus worthy of a free people. So in the "édifice majestueux" of Robespierre's imagining, no darkened corner, no secret cabal could escape the scrutiny of this nearly universal gaze. Once the penetration of observers rendered the Convention and its participants utterly visible, there would be no space, physical or spiritual, for illusion, deception, or theater to occupy.

As long as popular surveillance of government was not complete, neither was the revolutionary project of freedom. For Robespierre popular supervision over government was as important to the Revolution as the actual institutional forms the new government was to take. For this reason he devoted a substantial portion of his major speech on the new republican constitution to the right of citizens to oversee their government. This right, he demanded, must be written into the constitution and must be construed as broadly as possible:

> Pour moi, je pense que la Constitution ne doit pas se borner à ordonner que les séances du corps législatif et des autorités constituées seront publiques, mais encore qu'elle ne doit pas dédaigner de s'occuper des moyens de leur assurer la plus grande publicité; qu'elle doit interdire aux mandataires le

pouvoir d'influer, en aucune manière, sur la composition de l'auditoire; et de retracer arbitrairement l'étendue du lieu qui doit recevoir le peuple. Elle doit pourvoir à ce que la législature réside au sein d'une immense population, et délibère sous les yeux d'une multitude de citoyens infinie.[40]

[As for my view, I believe that the Constitution ought not limit itself to ordering that the legislature's sessions, as well as those of other constituted authorities, be held in public; in addition, it ought not disdain to seek the means to assure that those sessions will be as public as possible. It ought to prohibit deputies from trying to influence, in any manner, the composition of the observing public, or from trying to restrict arbitrarily the dimensions of the site which is to accommodate the people. It must see to it that the legislature resides in the heart of an immense population and that it deliberates under the eyes of an infinite multitude of citizens.]

Robespierre's insistence that the Assembly must meet in the midst of an immense population is surely a reference to Paris and must be considered a challenge to anyone who would suggest moving the government—a suggestion that was indeed in the air. Not only must the legislature not flee the people's observation, but it must take affirmative steps to ensure it. Such observation must be understood as an integral element of republican governance. Robespierre, moreover, foresees and seeks to forestall manipulation of that scrutiny. What is striking here, as in the previous quotations, is Robespierre's sense that observation alone is insufficient; the number of observers must be immense. We see Robespierre's insistence on the literalness with which he understands the idea of scrutiny. Newspaper reports, no matter how accurate, would not fulfill the mission Robespierre assigns to popular observation, not because newspapers were not "popular" enough but because so much depended, in his view, on the physical presence of observers, on the act of *watching*. So it is important to note that he was referring to the real urban population that surrounded the Assembly (and that he saw and lived with every day) and that could be considered a check on it. The vast number of observers matters because, somehow, the power of the gaze is radically amplified as the number of observers is increased quasi-geometrically. Hence he insists not simply that the legislature's deliberations be open to the public but, more precisely, that they be witnessed by an immense population, an infinite and multitudinous citizenry. For if six thousand focused gazes can render thought itself visible, as Robespierre warned Fouché, then an infinite gaze, like that of the Supreme Being on whose existence Robespierre was soon to insist, must be infinitely powerful. Yet, despite the seemingly magical power he attributed to them, the people Robespierre invokes here were a concrete presence and no mere rhetorical figure.

Popular surveillance of governing authorities must be institutionalized in the constitution, Robespierre argued, because only the continual exercise of popular surveillance could protect popular sovereignty in a representative republic. The scrutiny of the people was the most efficacious tool for the Revolution's preservation. Citizens of the ancient Greek and Roman republics, Robespierre contended, had maintained their liberty by incessantly monitoring the actions of their agents; the French Republic must do the same. Indeed, Robespierre continually, obsessively, sounded the call for a nearly unlimited scrutiny of all the new political institutions, and especially of the National Assembly:

> Etait-ce là la publicité des tribunaux et des assemblées de Rome et des anciennes républiques? Il y avait un moyen simple et infaillible, et le seul peut-être de forcer des mandataires du peuple à être dignes de lui, et d'épargner à la patrie tous les maux qu'elle a soufferts, tous ceux qui la menacent encore; c'était de les faire délibérer au moins sous les yeux de dix mille citoyens: nous n'y avons pas même pensé. Une magnifique salle d'opéra eût été bâtie en six semaines: après quatre ans l'assemblée législative n'a pas encore un lieu décent pour délibérer.[41]

> [Was this the publicity of the tribunals and the assemblies of Rome and the ancient republics? There was a simple and infallible means, and perhaps the only means, to force the people's deputies to be worthy of them and to spare the nation all the ills it has suffered and all those that still threaten it; it was to have them deliberate under the eyes of at least ten thousand citizens: we haven't even thought of that. A magnificent opera house would have been built in six weeks; after four years the legislative assembly still does not have a decent place to deliberate.]

The ten thousand pairs of eyes invoked here—like those of the twelve thousand citizens inhabiting the "majestic edifice," like those of the infinite multitude, and like the six thousand pairs of eyes judging Fouché—do not so much indicate an attempt on Robespierre's part to arrive at and fix the most felicitous number of citizen observers. Rather, the obsessive, continual invocation of such massive figures demonstrates his belief that such observation must be overwhelming, ubiquitous, and thus, in a sense, universal.

Only the gaze of the represented can guarantee that the representatives work for the common good; that safeguard is easily established if those in power are willing to subject themselves to it. The comparison to the theater is odd: on the one hand, Robespierre expresses his belief that corrupt deputies would eagerly and quickly build a magnificent opera rather than a "decent" hall for the National Assembly, yet, on the other, the magnificent opera house had not in fact been built. It is only in Robespierre's imagination that the competition and the rivalry between these two opposed forms of publicity existed.

Surveillance, on Robespierre's account, must be understood as essentially democratic. On the one hand, it allowed revolutionary citizens to exercise their sovereign right to know and to judge the actions of those who governed in their name. On the other hand, in radical contrast to the absolute monarchy's calculus of power—bestowed by Louis XIV on his offspring, and according to which power's magnitude is heightened precisely as it is concentrated in the unique person of the king—surveillance was a species of power that multiplied concomitantly with its extension. Popular surveillance of government on this account was perhaps the best means to reconcile popular sovereignty—a principle hard won and dearly held—with representative government. Direct observation of legislators was crucial, in Robespierre's view, because in its new form—the representative Republic—government was ambiguous.[42] Although the people of France officially held sovereign authority, and ministers, magistrates, and legislators were, in theory, merely the people's agents, the risk that these agents could and would usurp popular power loomed large. Robespierre believed that representative government was far from fully democratic. When the people delegated their power to representatives, rather than exercising it directly, Robespierre argued, it was only "a fiction that the law is the expression of the general will."[43]

The problem those establishing the Republic faced was to bring the fiction that the people made the laws as close to reality as possible. The best solution to that problem, given the impossibility of direct democracy in such a large nation, was the institutionalization, in the French constitution, of vigorous popular surveillance of representatives: "Sous le gouvernement représentatif, surtout, c'est-à-dire, quand ce n'est point le peuple qui fait les lois mais un corps de représentants, l'exercice de ce droit sacré [surveillance] est la seule sauve-garde du peuple contre le fléau de l'oligarchie" (ibid., 146). [In a representative government, above all, that is in a government in which it is not the people who make the laws but a body of representatives, the exercise of that sacred right (surveillance) is the people's only safeguard against the plague of oligarchy.] Representation without surveillance quickly grows into tyranny as the representatives act in their own interests rather than those of the people who elected them. Surveillance, Robespierre argues, distinguishes the republican state from the oligarchic one.

Robespierre was far from alone in his sense that representation and democracy were, or at least tended to be, incompatible. Marcel Gauchet argues in *La Révolution des pouvoirs* that this problem troubled a wide range of revolutionaries—the founders of the *cercle social,* the Girondins Brissot and Vergniaud, and the Cordeliers—and that, in response, they devised a wide variety of solutions. But Gauchet shows that despite their differences all of these republicans believed that it was necessary to create a power *outside* the government that could, in some sense, watch over it or act as a check on it; this power was variously called "censure," "surveillance," and "tribunat." The members of the cercle social, for example, hoped that public opinion organized and diffused by way of the *Bouche de fer,* the newspaper that accepted and printed anonymously deposited commentaries, could serve as a national tribunal. These revolutionaries, Gauchet argues, inherited their conception of the tribunal from Rousseau; for them it would be the institution that stood between the governed and the governors. The tribunal was understood not as a representative but rather as a guardian and a counterweight to the power of government. As the first number of the *Bouche de fer* announced in October 1790:

> La distribution des trois pouvoirs commence enfin à s'établir dans toutes les têtes: mais de quoi vous servira-t-elle, si vous ne parvenez pas à créer un autre pouvoir supérieur, qui ne tenant à aucun d'eux, ait assez de force pour les garder en équilibre?[44]

> [The distribution of the three branches of power is finally starting to become established in our minds: but what good will this do you if you do not succeed in creating another superior power which, being independent of each of them, has enough force to maintain their equilibrium?]

For Bonneville, the editor, this power, exterior but superior to government, was the power of public opinion to act as censor of government. The influential politician and journalist Jacques-Pierre Brissot, on the other hand, suggested instead an American-style convention that would meet periodically to evaluate the actions of the government. Such an institution was necessary, he believed, because without it government authorities could quickly usurp the power that was, after all, only *delegated* to them: "un pouvoir délégué sans un autre qui le surveille et le contrôle, tend naturellement à violer le principe de sa délégation, et à transformer cette délégation en souveraineté" [a delegated power, lacking another power to watch over and inspect it, naturally tends to violate the principle of its delegation, and to try to transform delegation into sovereignty].[45] It was the Cordeliers who most eagerly employed the term *sur-*

veillance and who first conceived of it as a protective tool, as an element of the right of the governed to act as censors of those to whom they delegated their power. The club took the eye of surveillance as its symbol and defined itself as "une société de défiance et de surveillance" [a society of vigilance and surveillance].[46] And although the Cordeliers shared the desire of Brissot and the members of the cercle social to guard against absolute representation, their approach was more radical. With the Cordeliers, Gauchet argues,

> Nous sommes au point virtuel de basculement où la contestation de l'usurpation représentative va retourner en exigence symétrique et inverse d'une réduction-résorption du rôle de représentant au profit de la citoyenneté surveillante. Telle sera en tout cas la trajectoire de Cordeliers. Il ne s'agira pas pour eux, à l'exemple que préconise *La Bouche de fer*, d'aménager un pôle de participation extérieur à la sphère des pouvoirs délégués. La dynamique de leur position les conduira à mettre en question le principe même de la délégation er à réclamer la participation directe du peuple à la législation.[47]

> [We are at the virtual tipping point where contestation of representative usurpation redounds as a symmetrical and inverse requirement for a reduction-absorption of the role of the representative to the benefit of the surveilling citizenry. For them for example, it is not a question of that which the *Bouche de fer* proposed—the creation of a pole of participation exterior to the sphere of delegated authority. The dynamic of their position led them to put the very principle of delegation into question and to demand direct participation of the people in legislation.]

Gauchet's analysis helps us understand and situate Robespierre's recourse to surveillance as a means of preserving, or perhaps even establishing, democracy in a representative system. Robespierre, that is, saw surveillance as that power exterior to government that could guarantee its legitimacy and efficacy. He thus stands somewhere between the Cordeliers' desire for the citizen-surveillant *as* legislator and the more moderate hopes for a harnessed, directed public opinion as censor. For Robespierre the power to surveil governing authority must remain distinct from and outside the power to legislate, yet it remains absolutely integral to the system of government. The danger, according to Robespierre, was that if all the citizens were directly to govern themselves, there would be no one left to watch over them; thus the ideal offered here is not direct democracy but universal and empowered surveillance. Robespierre dreams, strangely, of a legislature deliberating under the eyes of the entire French nation rather than of a deliberating nation. And neither a newspaper nor a specially selected magistrate nor even an elected Convention could serve as the tribunal before which the people's representatives could be called to account. Only the citizenry itself, Robespierre claimed, because it was endowed with the responsibility and capacity for total surveillance, could act as that tribunal:

> Il n'y a qu'un seul Tribun du peuple que je puisse avouer; c'est le peuple lui-même. C'est à chaque section de la République française que je renvoie la puissance tribunienne; et il est facile d'organiser d'une manière également éloignée des tempêtes de la démocratie absolue, de la perfide tranquillité du despotisme représentatif.[48]

> [There is only one tribune of the people that I can avow; it is the people themselves. I commit tribunal power back to each section of the French Republic. And it is easy to organize in a manner equally distant from the tempests of absolute democracy and the perfidious tranquillity of representative despotism.]

Paradoxically, as Michelet pointed out, and as Fabre d'Eglantine learned all too well, Robespierre himself did not like being looked at. Whereas he imagined his fellow deputies as objects of vigilant, popular scrutiny, he imagined himself sharing with his fellow citizens the power and duty of surveillance. Robespierre, for example, named his first, short-lived newspaper *Le Surveillant.* Identifying himself above all as a surveillant allowed him to identify himself with the people: both he and members of the ordinary citizenry carried out the same function. By considering himself a surveillant rather than an agent, Robespierre was able not only to close the gap between himself and the people but also imaginatively to remove himself from the stage of history. He was not there to be looked at; like the citizen-observers who crowded the public galleries he was there to look. Robespierre's sense of his own political identity was inextricably bound to surveillance. Surveillance marked both the beginning and the end of his political career: in his famous last speech to the Convention on 8 Thermidor, Year II, the day before his fall, Robespierre attributed his own impending doom not to having alienated much of his support but to what he believed was his colleagues' fear of what his ongoing observation of them might uncover. He would fall, he believed, because his fellow deputies longed to rid themselves of "un surveillant incommode" [an inconvenient surveillant] (ibid., 10:574).

Robespierre accused his political enemies and counterrevolutionaries of deliberately sabotaging the publicity of the National Assembly's sessions.[49] But while Robespierre may have been alone in his attribution of the salle du Manège's defects to the malevolence of a political opposition seeking to deceive onlookers, his complaints about the hall and the deleterious effects it produced were far from unusual or hyperbolic. Indeed, deputies, commentators, and observers of all political stripes deplored the size, shape, and layout of the Manège; like Robespierre many believed that because it foiled observation, the hall's disposition had unfortunate political consequences.

The hall was the former equestrian ring inside the Tuileries palace, adjacent to the Louvre, where the king and his family were installed as a result of the "October days."[50] The hall was very long and very narrow. Until August 20, 1792, only the galleries at the two extremities were open to the public. These public galleries—together with those set aside for the alternate deputies, the députés de commerce, and the representatives of the commune of Paris— could accommodate only five hundred to six hundred observers.[51] The paucity of space allotted to the public explains Robespierre's aggrieved comparison between the Manège and the Opéra.

The Assembly left the king's palace at Versailles, where the Estates General had met and where it had transformed itself in June 1789 into the National Assembly. After a short stint in the Paris Archevêché, on the Île de la Cité, the Assembly moved into the Manège on November 9, 1789. From the very first, commentators recognized that its size, shape, and design would adversely affect the "publicité" of its sessions. "Ce local . . . ne peut cependant, sous aucun rapport, être comparé à celui de Versailles" [This location cannot in any way compare to that at Versailles], reported the *Journal de Paris* on November 10, 1789:

> C'est un carré très long et très étroit. . . . On a eu beau placer la tribune et les orateurs au milieu, les voix les plus fortes et les plus distinctes ont peine, au milieu même du grand silence, à parvenir aux extrémités de ce carré long.

> [It is a very long and very narrow rectangle. . . . The tribune and the orators were placed in the middle in vain; even when there is great silence, the strongest and most distinct voices can barely be heard at the ends of this long rectangle.]

And a "savant allemand," visiting Paris in 1790 and eager to witness the National Assembly's debates, complained that "les tribunes publiques étant plus élevées que les deux autre galeries, et, par leur situation aux bouts de la salle les plus éloignées du président et de l'orateur, on n'entend pas aussi bien qu'on ne le voudrait" [because the public benches are higher than those of the other two galleries and because of their situation at the ends of the hall farthest from the president and the orator, one does not hear as well as one would wish].[52]

Not only were the proceedings of the National Assembly far from fully visible and audible to the observing citizenry, but the Manège's size and shape meant that the deputies, often invisible and inaudible to those in the galleries, were equally concealed from each other. In October 1791 Antoine Chrysosthome Quatremère de Quincy, art critic and theorist, as well as politician, demanded that the hall be reconstructed, and on the twenty-sixth of that month the *Journal de Paris* applauded his efforts:

> Nous sommes persuadés, comme M. Quatremère, qu'un changement dans la forme de la salle est absolument nécessaire, et que si on négligeait ce soin comme futile, la nation perdrait infailliblement plusieurs des avantages qu'elle doit attendre des vertus et des talents de ses représentants. Dans un carré long et dont les angles fuient dans les extrémités . . . les députés sont très peu en présence les uns des autres.[53]

> [We are persuaded, like M. Quatremère, that a change in the layout of the hall is absolutely necessary and that if this concern is neglected as futile the nation will certainly lose many of the advantages that it has a right to expect from the virtues and the talents of its representatives. In a long rectangle in which the angles recede in the extremities . . . the deputies are very little in each other's presence.]

Even the deputies present, then, were not fully present to the activities of their colleagues. And because visibility and audibility were obscured, artful politicians could potentially manipulate the Assembly for their own private purposes. Despite alterations in early 1792 that shortened the hall and relocated the orator's tribune, as late as August 13, 1792, the eloquent Girondin deputy Pierre-Victurnien Vergniaud lamented the Manège's structure and the ill effects to which it gave rise:

> Je n'ai pas besoin, Messieurs, de vous rappeler le résultat de votre expérience. . . . Notre salle forme un carré long; il y en a grande quantité de places d'où l'on ne peut ni voir le président ni en être aperçu. Il arrive de là qu'on abandonne les grandes objets d'intérêt public.[54]

> [I do not need, Messieurs, to remind you of the result of your own experience. . . . Our hall forms a long rectangle; there are a great many places from which one can neither see the president nor be seen by him. As a result of this we abandon the great objects of public interest.]

Even Vergniaud, a politician less concerned with popular political participation than Robespierre, feared that the hall's structure undermined the publicness of its works. Because the deputies could neither see each other nor be seen, they soon ceased to work for the public interest. If the deputies were not laboring to promote "objets d'intérêt public," then, presumably, they were making use of their public position to further private interests. The salle de Manège's structural flaws thus made it insufficiently public, and its formal deficiencies spawned substantive ones: because the hall effectively baffled public scrutiny, deputies felt free to transact their own personal affairs and leave aside issues of public import. Incomplete publicity bred corruption.

In Robespierre's view the legislature's failure to make its sessions truly available to public observation was purposely contrived. Corrupt deputies resisted reforms to the hall that would lend the sessions greater publicity and would thus bring them under scrutiny because they wanted to protect the illicit power and privilege they had usurped:

> Les hommes superficiels ne devineront jamais quelle a été sur la Révolution l'influence du local qui a recelé le corps législatif et les fripons n'en conviendront pas; mais les amis éclairés du bien public n'ont pas vu, sans indignation, qu'après avoir appelé les regards publics autour d'elle, pour résister à la cour, la première législature, les ait fuis autant qu'il était en son pouvoir, lorsqu'elle a voulu se liguer avec la cour contre le peuple, qu'après s'être en quelque sorte cachée à l'Archevêché ou elle porta la loi martiale, elle se soit renfermée dans la Manège, ou elle s'environna de baïonnettes. . . . Ses successeurs sont bien garder d'en sortir.[55]

> [Superficial men will never see, and knaves will never admit, how important an influence the premises that harbor the legislature have had; but enlightened friends of the public good have seen, not without indignation, that after having called the public's gaze to itself in order to resist the court, the first legislature fled that gaze as much as it was within its power. When it wanted to conspire with the court against the people, after having more or less hidden at the Archevêché where it declared martial law, the legislature enclosed itself in the Manège and surrounded itself with bayonets. . . . Its successors have taken care not to come out.]

According to this highly partisan narrative of revolutionary political events, when political representatives—the deputies to the Estates General—were locked in their initial, risky struggle with the Crown, they turned to the public for authority, power, and protection. They hoped that the watchful gaze of the people would protect them from royal violence. Once it had achieved substantial institutional authority as the National Assembly and had its own power base to protect, however, the legislature made its peace with the Crown in the interest of warding off the real threat to them both, the common citizens.

Robespierre's charges cannot be wholly dismissed as the product of a paranoid mind. After all, many deputies did declare that the Assembly's meetings should be closed to the public altogether. Some, clearly invoking a notion of representation radically alien to that held by Robespierre and many ordinary citizens, argued that removing the spectators from the deliberations would allow deputies the freedom they required if they were truly to act for the public good. According to this theory representatives are more capable of knowing and acting in the public's interest than are the citizens themselves. It is not surprising, therefore, that such arguments were less than warmly received, for they seemed to echo the justifications for the aristocratic government the French had rejected. This argument, the weekly newspaper *Révolutions de Paris* warned in its August 4 issue, was a cynical scheme on the part of conservatives to escape the gaze of watchful citizens in order to legislate in their own interest and against that of the general public: "L'Assemblée national a des tribunes publiques qui ne laissent pas de gêner certains membres. . . . Le côté du roi de la salle de Manège a mis tout en œuvre pour se délivrer de cette incommode surveillance journalière." [The National Assembly has some public benches, a fact that never ceases to bother certain members. . . . The king's side has done everything it could to deliver itself from this uncomfortable daily surveillance.][56]

While Robespierre was announcing that "la publicité est l'appui de la vertu, la sauvegarde de la verité . . . le fléau de l'intrigue" [publicity is the support of virtue, the safeguard of truth . . . the plague of intrigue], by April 1793 some understandably fearful conservative deputies were demanding that the Assembly move back to Versailles to escape the active vigilance and intervention of their constituents, especially that of the citizens of Paris.[57]

Surveillance and Popular Sovereignty

Although Robespierre was opposed by some of his colleagues in the Assembly, he was certainly not bereft of support for his commitment to popular surveillance. Large numbers of revolutionary citizens shared a deeply held belief that they retained the right and responsibility to supervise and censor not only the National Assembly but all official bodies. The exercise of this right was at the heart of their conception of popular sovereignty. And if the year II of the Revolution (1793–1794) can be described, as Richard Cobb has argued, as "an accident of a chance encounter" between the Jacobin revolutionary government and the popular movement of the sans-culottes, that encounter was, for a short while, functional because of a, perhaps coincidental, shared faith in the salutary power of surveillance.[58] Albert Soboul argues that popular politics in the year II of the Republic was guided by two "fundamental principles": "publicity, the people's protector which in the year II constituted the corollary of revolutionary surveillance"; and "unity, which, based on a unanimous sense of purpose, allowed them to achieve concerted action."[59]

In preparation for the meeting of the Estates General in May 1789, Paris was divided into sixty electoral districts. Each district was to write collectively a *cahier de doléance* (notebook of grievances) and to elect electors who would then, in turn, choose the district's deputies. What followed was unforeseeable: the discussions and debates within the district assemblies, rather than ending with the elections, grew apace.[60] The district assemblies resisted all efforts to dissolve them; soon they claimed the right not simply to elect representatives but to regulate local affairs and to comment on issues of national concern. They formed the basis for the new city government of Paris; even more important, the districts, and then the sections that followed them, were a striking innovation and one of the most important revolutionary institutionalizations of direct democracy. These local, neighborhood assemblies were attended by women as well as by men, by those deemed "passive citizens"—that is those who did not pay enough in taxes to have the right to vote—as well as "active ones." Even children were often present. The districts and then the sections elected their own committees so that large numbers of the general citizenry were called on to take part in the administration of the neighborhood. The sections met several evenings each week, and discussions could often stretch late into the night.

The National Assembly tried repeatedly and fruitlessly to disband the districts. Reshaping the sixty districts into forty-eight sections in May 1790 was one such attempt; the new sections, however, quickly came to resemble the old districts. Robespierre opposed the redistricting, but on this occasion he fought a losing battle against conservatives led by Abbé Maury. The districts claimed that they had the right to meet at any time to discuss affairs of importance; they named this right "permanence." The terms in which Robespierre defended the permanence of the districts were certainly not calculated to bring the abbé around. He asked rhetorically: "who can doubt that without the active surveillance of the districts the writing of the constitution would have been slowed down by more effective means?"[61] The argument displays just how large the chasm had grown between those who strove to establish a constitutional monarchy with limited participation and those who sought to accord citizens the greatest possible authority. In the view of Robespierre and his constituents it was the districts' watchfulness—watchfulness over the likes of Maury—that had protected popular interests and prevented the sabotage of the Revolution; by contrast, in the opinion of monarchists the public's surveillance itself constituted sabotage of the state and had brought France to the brink of anarchy.

The districts and then the sections took extremely seriously what they deemed their right to oversee the actions of all those in official capacities. Sections and the political clubs that began to spring up in 1789 made claims to the right of surveillance well before the establishment of the Republic. In February 1792, for example, more than two hundred Parisians went to the Legislative Assembly to demand not only that legislative sessions be subject to public scrutiny but that all kinds of government business—whether carried out by elected or appointed officials—be open to public observation. In their petition they sought to make clear to the legislators "how essential it was that administrative sessions be public, so that the people should know who is not working or watching out [veillent] for their interests, and beware of those who had received their confidence only to further their own ambitions or indulge in their own whimsy."[62] Many of the deputies thought that the scrutiny afforded the public was already excessive, but on July 1, 1792, the Legislative Assembly acquiesced and opened up sessions of administrative bodies so that the people could exercise their right "to watch over [surveiller] the conduct of their administrators."[63]

According to the political creed dominant in the sections—the fervent belief in popular sovereignty—each citizen constituted a part of the sovereign; consequently, the affairs of each citizen, no matter how humble, were elevated to affairs of state. For this reason, after the fall of the monarchy on August 10, 1792, the sections quickly established *comités de surveillance*—committees of local citizens meant to keep an eye out for any counterrevolutionary activities.[64] For the Republic seemed threatened by enemies within who might seek to corrupt the most ordinary citizens as much as by the foreign powers and aristocrats in league against it: for example, the Fraternal Society of Both Sexes demanded the "power of surveillance which every free society of men has the right to exercise directly"; the Théâtre-Français, Croix-Rouge, and Fontaine de Grenelle sections endowed their committees with "all the powers of surveillance so necessary in the present circumstances"; and the Marat section declared itself in a state of "continual patriotic surveillance and solicitude in which all good republicans should remain until liberty is consolidated on unshakable foundations."[65] Many in the sections and the political clubs that sprang up in 1789 believed that it was within their rights as the sovereign to exercise their power directly by policing their neighborhoods themselves: sections worried about what was going on within their own *quartiers* and even within their own local assemblies. The Louvre section, for example, declared that it "reserved the right to police its own territory."[66]

Sectional activists insisted that since everything is public in a republic, everything must be available to the public's surveillance. Indeed, the need for publicity was so total that it had to be extended to areas previously deemed private, such as the ballot. Perhaps unsurprisingly, the secret ballot came under attack; for, as Robespierre explained, "free men want the people to witness their thoughts."[67] Only counterrevolutionaries, lackeys of the monarchy, and bad citizens would want to keep their thoughts to themselves. In the wake of the events of August 10, 1792, the Commune of Paris adopted roll-call voting and made the secret ballot illegal. Ardent republicans took the injunction to render all politics open to scrutiny so seriously that the Lepeletier section arrested those who persisted in calling for the secret ballot, and the Bonne-Nouvelle section went so far as to arrest one of its citizens for voting in a low voice.[68]

Surveillance was thus deeply bound up with the exercise of local power over local activity, and it constituted an important means of direct political participation. But, as we have already seen, the sections also sought to extend their surveillance and thus their capacity for direct participation to national politics as well. With the establishment of the Republic these demands became more comprehensive: for example, in December 1792 the Bon-Conseil section invited the other sections to join it in creating a "committee to watch over [surveiller] ministerial operations" on the grounds that "the actions of the executive powers of all the ministries must be supervised [surveiller] relentlessly."[69] And in March 1793 the Lombards section sought to create a permanent commission to supervise "all the Generals' operations, army maneuvers and troop morale," because "traitorous activity cannot be prevented unless we watch for it more carefully [par une surveillance]" (ibid., 115).

Just as surveillance for Robespierre was essentially democratic in nature—both because it allowed popular supervision of those entrusted with official authority and because it was a power that was enhanced as the number of its practitioners expanded—surveillance, for the sectional militants, was a crucial tool of direct participatory democracy. On the one hand, surveillance protected the neighborhood from malign, antipopular forces, and, on the other hand, surveillance allowed ordinary citizens to exert their supreme authority over all those who wielded state power. Thus in September 1793 the Halles-au-âlé section declared that "only the sovereign people have the authority to scrutinize [scruter] the conduct of officers of bodies they themselves established" (ibid., 117). For these sectional militants surveillance was the best available means to reconcile representation with direct democracy and to make popular sovereignty real and concrete.

The National Convention, jealous of any competition for authority, tried hard to reign in and control the local comités de surveillance. The Convention's Committee of General Security, for example, tried to convince the local committees that they ought to limit their role to aiding and supporting the work of the national government, and the Convention ordered the sectional committees to limit their activities to keeping an eye on resident aliens. The sectional committees, however, were not to be swayed, and the Paris Commune backed them. Despite the directives from higher authorities, and perhaps in reaction to them, the Panthéon-Français section insisted on giving its comité de surveillance "all unlimited and necessary powers so that it can provide efficaciously for the safety of the country and the security of citizens."[70] And because, finally, the central government absolutely lacked the infrastructure that would allow it to carry out the policing functions of the Terror, it left those responsibilities in the hands of club members and sectional activists. Thus, Richard Cobb explains that the Terror was, ultimately, a local and popular affair: "In the absence of a centrally operated, political secret police (not even its embryo existed in the year II), the committee of General Security had to entrust the actual running of the Terror and repression, surveillance, vigilance, denunciation, the control of lodging houses, and the checking of passports to local men: printers, shoemakers, tailors, gunsmiths, innkeepers, and clerks. . . . The Terror was administered on a national putting-out basis, and the local men generally had the last word."[71]

The Eye of Surveillance

On January 2, 1793, the Commune de Paris, the revolutionary city government, ordered that a proclamation urging "bons citoyens de surveiller les traîtres" [good citizens to watch out for traitors] be "imprimée, affichée, et lue dans les places publiques et les carrefours de Paris" [printed, posted, and read in the squares and crossroads of Paris].[72] As we have just seen, Parisian citizens hardly needed such encouragement. It is very likely that on the proclamation ordered by the city there would have appeared one of the Revolution's most frequently seen symbols: *l'oeil de la surveillance* (the eye of surveillance). Up until this point I have been discussing surveillance as an element of political discourse and political practice; I want to turn now to the revolutionary representation of surveillance. In the next chapter I will examine the representation of the practice of surveillance on the Parisian stage, but here I will focus on the symbol that came to stand for that practice, the *oeil de la surveillance*. The eye appeared with great frequency in demonstrations, on badges and *cartes civiques,* on the banner of the Jacobin society, in festivals such as the festival of the Supreme Being, and in engravings and allegorical paintings. The eye began its revolutionary career as a Masonic symbol based on the Egyptian emblem unearthed by Caylus and Winckelmann, but it quickly took on new meaning.[73] This eye represented surveillance as it was conceived and understood by those who practiced it.

Let me begin with an extraordinary allegorical oil painting displaying a plethora of revolutionary symbols (figure 1). Here—above a landscape crowded with a tree of liberty, the fasces, a liberty bonnet, the Gallic cock, an altar to the regeneration of morals supporting a copy of the Declaration of the Rights of Man, a cornucopia, and numerous other such signs—hangs, without any visible means of suspension, a disembodied eye. The eye, complete with brow and lashes, appears immediately below a framed portrait of Jean-Jacques Rousseau. Although Rousseau is obviously a key figure in the revolutionary project of transparency, this is not *his* eye. Still, the eye's proximity to Rousseau seems to guarantee that the eye is a beneficent force rather than a menacing one. Just to the left of Rousseau and the eye is an enormous sun. The eye, at least by reason of its placement, must be a partner in a triumvirate that aids and sustains the Revolution signified beneath it. The meanings attached to the sun and to the portrait of Rousseau are fairly clear: the sun presumably casts out the darkness of ignorance and superstition, enlightens the figures below, and nourishes the growth of the seeds sown by the peasant figure in the lower right corner.[74] Rousseau hovers over revolutionary France as the inspiration and father of its Revolution and, as peculiar as it may seem now, as its moral guide. What, then, does the eye bring to this trio, and whose eye is it, after all? To answer this last question, we will have to examine the eye as it appears in remarkably diverse representations. I should offer one caveat: the images I discuss here all date from 1792 to 1794, but they are not presented in chronological order—indeed it would be impossible to determine exact dates for many of them.

The eye of figure 1 and the eye of figure 2, an engraving celebrating the Declaration of the Rights of Man, are unmistakably related, but they are hardly twins. In figure 2 the eye presides alone above the tablets displaying the Declaration and above a group of personified virtues. The eye itself has changed as well; whereas the eye in figure 1 is uncannily naturalistic, the eye in the engraving does not appear to be quite human. Indeed, in distinctly nonnaturalistic fashion, the eye radiates rays of light in all directions. The winged figure even uses a glass to direct the rays into his body. This eye thus seems to have absorbed and displaced the sun that appeared in figure 1. The eye alone hovers over the Revolution beneath it. Representations of the Declaration of the Rights of Man, a favorite subject for revolutionary artists, regularly included images of an eye in the sky supervising, so to speak, the Declaration's promulgation. Some of these artists placed the eye within a triangle symbolizing equality; some surrounded the eye with highly resonant terms: *equality, unity, indivisibility.* Many represented the powerful rays from the eye pushing back dark clouds or punishing destructive forces of the old regime.

The revolutionary calendar in figure 3 places the eye within the triangle of equality. Here the eye floats above a representation of the deeds of the Mountain, the party of the left in the Convention that was associated with Robespierre. In addition, portraits of Marat and Lepelletier, the two martyred members of the Mountain who appeared on the Declaration of the Rights of Man, look on the scene from either side. Just as in figure 2, the light emanating from the eye pushes back dark clouds. But here, instead of only giving off rays of light, the eye is even more active; it appears to produce lightning that annihilates the symbols of tyranny—the hydra, the crown, the Bastille—depicted below it.

This image, unlike the others we have seen so far, bears a title: *Surveillance.* Although the feats it depicts are attributed to the "sainte Montagne," the active force shown accomplishing them is the ever-watchful and now extraordinarily powerful eye, which is identified neither as Reason nor as Enlightenment but as Surveillance. The eye on the official letterhead stationery of the Committee of Surveillance of Brussels (figure 4), like that on the Republican calendar, sends out mighty bolts of lightning that destroy symbols of oppression, here a crown and a bishop's miter, while it protectively watches over both the figure in the liberty bonnet and the strutting cock. The eyes we see in figures 3 and 4 stand for a universal gaze and the gaze of the universe. Disembodied, this gaze represents a common, rather than an individual, point of view. Hovering in the sky high above the swarm of activity below, it allows nothing to escape its energetic vigilance; like the sun it is omnipresent and nourishing. Capable of scattering clouds and confusion, it reaches everywhere.

In scene after scene the eye of surveillance shines its protective light on the Revolution while it seeks out and destroys the Revolution's enemies. This eye adorned not only the Brussels Committee of Surveillance's stationery but also the seals of the section de l'Arsenal and the revolutionary committee of the droits-de-l'homme section. The eye was stamped on chits and *cartes d'assistance* distributed by local governments like the one in figure 5 that entitled the bearer to various kinds of free aid. In this image the eye is surrounded by a motto that recalls, faintly threateningly, the primacy of popular sovereignty: "obedience to laws accepted by the sovereign people," a motto that clearly implies that obedience is not owed to any laws the sovereign people have not accepted. It was depicted as well in countless allegories of the Republic, and it even decorated common household objects such as china and even books. Was the book whose binding prominently featured the eye meant to be a journal in which, like Rousseau in his *Confessions,* the writer would make visible his or her very soul? Certainly, in this circumstance the eye seems to announce the book's ability to scrutinize its reader rather than vice versa.

The eye, in other words, was a pervasive presence not only in the realm of high politics but also in everyday life. Representations proliferated, finding a place in engravings and paintings with artistic ambition as well as in the ordinary objects made by local artisans that constituted practical existence. It was worn on badges every day; it was carried around every day by ordinary people in the form of official papers and pieces of identification; it decorated the calendars that were meant to help people learn to live according to new, revolutionary time. Thus the eye and the gaze it represented were enfolded into the idea and practice of citizenship.

Remarking the pervasiveness and domestication of the eye of surveillance in revolutionary culture is one way to address the question, To whom does this all-seeing and all-revealing, protective and punishing eye belong? To everyone and to no one in particular. Consider the scene depicting a festival celebrated in honor of the Supreme Being (figure 6). Here the eye, encased in its triangle, radiates its powerful energy onto a republican family and the altar at which they worship. The altar, however, does not exhibit an image of the Supreme Being in the way that, for example, a Catholic altar would.[75] Instead, it bears two figures: the one on the left symbolizes nature with her wheat, her cornucopia, and her bare breasts ready to feed the nation (and the image's caption tells us that the "true priest" of the Supreme Being is Nature); the figure on the right, with her liberty bonnet, tricolor flag, and tablets recording the Declaration of the Rights of Man, stands for revolutionary France. Since the two allegorical figures do not represent the Supreme Being, the eye that presides over the whole scene must. The eye that represents the universal, protective, and penetrating gaze of surveillance would seem to be the divine eye.

Things become a bit more complicated when we turn to the engraving entitled *Hommage à l'Eternel* (figure 7). Just as in the engraving of the Declaration of the Rights of Man, the eye hangs above a long text; here it is the republican profession of faith in the Supreme Being.[76] The eye once again sits within a triangle, signifying equality, from which emanate sunlike rays, but in this case it is not alone; also radiating light are the words "Dieu, Peuple, Loi." This would seem to confirm the supposition that the eye of surveillance is God's eye and thus to render less strange the power associated with it. But why do the people and the law share top billing with God in a document meant to demonstrate the regime's adherence to faith in a supreme being?

Figures 8 and 9 seem to pose the identical problem, but they offer a solution to it. In both engravings the eye alone occupies the triangle and emanates light. Below the eye, in figure 8, the words "Dieu, Peuple, and Loi" are so large that they take up the preponderance of space, and the usual complement of symbols and allegorical figures is pushed to the bottom and sides. Clearly the words and their relation to the eye are the focus of the engraving; moreover, no one word seems more associated with the eye than another. While figure 9 is in a sense more obscure—since it depicts Voltaire on the left and Jean-Jacques Rousseau, having detached himself from his pedestal and come to life, on the right—it is very similar to figure 13. It, too, features the eye, here inside a sunlike circle rather than a triangle, projecting its rays on three phrases: "Etre Suprême," "Peuple Souverain," "République Française." Here again the eye clearly stands in some kind of relation to the phrases, but the words "Etre Suprême" seem no more attached to it than do the other two phrases.

Although the eye in the sky does seem to possess attributes that could be thought of as divine—omnipotence, omnipresence, omniscience, the power to preserve, and the power to punish—figures 8 and 9 imply that the eye of surveillance belongs to the Supreme Being *and* to the sovereign people *and* to the Republic. It is the universal eye that looks down on human beings, searches their hearts, and judges their intentions. But it is also the eye of the citizens who carefully watch over their politicians and their neighborhoods, holding them up to what the Jacobins called "le scrutin épuratoire" (purifying scrutiny) in order to protect the Republic. Finally, the eye represents the eye of the Republic, which judges, rewards, and condemns. So in another version of the republican calendar (figure 10) the phrase "peuple souverain" takes the place of all three, for, after all, the Republic is simply the sovereign people who form it, and the Supreme Being is nothing other than the spirit that emanates from them.[77] The *oeil de la surveillance* is the people's eye, or rather, it represents a new trinity, a new three-in-one.[78] Each element in the republican trinity, like that of the Christian one, is simply an aspect, or an incarnation, of a single whole. This new symbolism helped confer a sacred status on the Republic and the French people; it made revolutionary values themselves sacred.

The eye also appears in a rather different genre of revolutionary images. It is often associated with the allegorical figure of Reason, a favorite for revolutionary engravers. In *La Raison* (figure 11), for example, Reason, a classically garbed woman, accompanied by a lion that indicates her force, holds up a torch over which, in the place of a flame, glows an eye. Like the eyes that hang in the sky, the eye-torch radiates sunlike rays whose brilliance is underlined by the image's dark background. The meaning of the eye in these allegories of Reason seems more straightforward than that of the eye in the sky. This eye symbolizes reason's clear-sightedness, its capacity to repel darkness and confusion, and to see the way to truth. The rather more arcane engraving *The Triumph of Reason and Truth* (figure 12) bears out this interpretation. The scene, described in the caption, portrays "philosophy, in the figure of Jean-Jacques Rousseau, reveal[ing] to the universe reason and truth, which had been hidden by error and lies." Two elevated classical female figures embody reason and truth; from them emanates a glowing light. To their right a particularly virile Rousseau in toga, whose feet crush symbols of tyranny and superstition, exposes reason and truth by lifting a curtain with one hand while his other hand holds a torch.

What seems curious here is the displacement of the glowing light from the eye on the torch to the female figures. Stranger still, at Reason's breast, just where her heart should be, a disk very like the depiction of the eye radiates beams of light. But instead of representing an eye, this disk reproduces a sketchy version of Reason's face. The truth exposed here is the truth of the utter self-identity and transparency of reason. It is as if the very essence of reason is the light that glows within her and that she gives off. For the radiance of the eye here is doubled by the radiance emanating from Reason and Truth. The mirror with which she reflects her own light back on herself emphasizes this sense; the mirror helps her to show herself completely by turning back her own light. And, as is the case in figure 2, this mirror does not connote vanity—those who hold it and direct it toward themselves do not look in it. The mirror accentuates the power of the light of reason and furthers the operation of exposure. Since this particular representation of light is so closely associated with and so closely resembles the power of the all-seeing eye, the engraving suggests that reason itself is the active power of sight. And, at least according to the other revolutionary images of the eye, sight activated is surveillance.

The complicated allegorical scene *Liberty, Supported by Reason, Protects Innocence and Crowns Virtue* (figure 13) repeats the most curious feature of *Le Triomphe de la Raison et de la Vérité*. Here, once again, an engraving represents a figure bearing a glowing eyelike circle at her breast. This picture, however, displays two eyes; Reason, on the extreme right, retains her distinctive eye-torch even as Virtue seems to have incorporated the eye into herself in the way Reason did in the previous figure. The placement of the eye in Virtue's body is intensely meaningful; the eye is located precisely in the place of the heart, which is not only the seat of emotion but also, in revolutionary rhetoric, the place in which the precepts of natural law reside. The heart, rather than the head, can tell what is truly just: thus, the true principles of the Revolution were "written in the heart" of true citizens rather than written in the official declarations of the positive law.[79] The heart was the site of the revolutionary soul. The doubling of the eye here asserts their identity: the glowing, far-seeing eye of Reason is also the glowing heart of Virtue. Moreover, this representation of Virtue must be understood specifically as revolutionary, republican virtue. For from Montesquieu's typology insisting that virtue was the cardinal characteristic of republics, to Rousseau's identification of virtue with citizenship, through the Jacobin notion of a Republic of Virtue, virtue was understood to be a political attribute.

La Liberté soutenue par la Raison represents virtue as the incorporation of the all-seeing, all-penetrating eye of reason and surveillance. It represents that incorporation specifically as the identification or the fusing of the heart with the surveying eye. Figure 14, an engraving given the title *La Raison*, represents even more unequivocally the fusion of the eye of surveillance with the heart. Since the engraving depicts only a bust of the allegorical figure, the usual signs and symbols are yet more condensed. The figure of Reason in a sense absorbs the lion that walked beside her in the other engravings by wearing its skin; and, more stunning, the eye, formerly Reason's instrument, has become her heart. Here Reason not only embodies the eye of surveillance, but reason itself is characterized as the identification of eye and heart. The engraving entitled *La République* (figure 15), perhaps more startlingly still, simply transfers to the heart the characteristics of the eye of surveillance: here the heart itself sheds the telltale illuminating rays usually given off by the all-penetrating eye. The Republic is depicted above all as resting in and depending on the heart, but on a highly singular heart. This is a heart that sees.

This all-seeing heart probably has its origin in the sacred heart of Jesus.[80] But like Jacques-Louis David's famous painting of Marat, which many art historians have likened to a pietà, it demonstrates how Christian imagery could be transformed and transvalued and so lend its sacredness to a new form of social and political imagination. The all-seeing heart that stands for the Republic shows the fusing of the affective and the political. The glowing heart that represents the Republic was meant to glow inside every republican, and like the glowing light incarnated by Virtue and Reason, the radiating heart of the citizen was meant to signify the openness of all republican hearts to one another. Just as the eye in the sky repelled the forces of tyranny, the seeing heart of the citizen would protect the Republic from all its enemies.

The revolutionary images of the eye represent a continuum; at one end the eye represents a universal, disembodied, objective view—the gaze of justice and posterity. At the other end the eye represents the soul of the revolutionary republican citizen. The movement from the image of the eye as sun to the eye in the breast—the eye that occupies the heart and the soul—represents the existence within every individual of the universal gaze; that gaze was not universal simply because it hung in the sky; it was universal because, like the power of surveillance, it belonged to everyone. The internal eye did not simply look outward to assess others; the eye was represented *within* the body because surveillance also required self-examination, and only self-examination could produce virtue. Like the allegorical figures directing their own light back toward their bodies, the citizen must turn his or her eye back on him- or herself. The revolutionary soul is constituted through surveillance, by the turning inward of the same scrutinizing gaze that was to preserve the virtue of politics.

I do not mean to suggest that the duped citizen simply internalized an externally generated overseer. On the contrary, the citizens who carried out surveillance on their political representatives and who subjected themselves to the same searching gaze were not internalizing any preexisting disciplinary Law; they were in the midst of creating for themselves a new regime in which they would be both subject and object of the gaze because they were both subjects and makers of the laws. These were the selves Rousseau described as divided—at once subject and citizen. These revolutionary citizens were trying to bring into being freedom as Rousseau had defined it: "obedience to a law one prescribes to oneself."[81]

"[T]o oneself": this self-reflexive generation of the law makes the dividedness of revolutionary subjectivity new. In *The Renaissance Bible* Deborah Shuger argues that the Reformation created a splintered and conflicted subjectivity, one in which the Christian identified both with the crucified Christ and with his tormentors. The reformed Christian thus continually occupied the position of sinner and punisher of sin. While the revolutionary subject of surveillance might look like a politicization of the Christian conscience, it is in fact both more and different. For what the secularization of this self-scrutiny means is that there is no higher judge, no minister, no priest, no king, no God to guarantee reward or punishment, to approve or disapprove of the individual's self-policing endeavors. Nor can the state be said to have taken on that role, for the state itself at this point was precisely what was coming into being and cannot be said to have been institutionalized. The state, at least as it was theorized, was identical to the citizenry. The revolutionary images we have been examining may create the impression that the citizen internalizes a type of surveillance that comes originally from without, but the universal gaze was always already nothing other than the citizens' gaze united and turned outward.

But if the republican subjectivity created through the practice of surveillance is not assimilable to Christian conscience, neither, despite first appearances, can it be likened to the Althusserian model of subjectivity Judith Butler assesses in her book *The Psychic Life of Power*. According to Butler's reading of Althusser, the self is formed in relation to the Law: "[t]he turn toward the law is thus at once a turn against oneself, the turning back upon oneself that constitutes the movement of conscience."[82] The moment at which one simultaneously turns back upon oneself and toward the Law, for Althusser, is the moment in which the subject is constituted. Since by this account the subject does not exist prior to the moment it encounters and accepts the Law, Althusser and Butler believe that this model escapes the determinism that characterizes psychoanalytic and other theories of subject formation according to which the subject is produced through the internalization of external injunctions. Althusser, according to Butler, avoids the pitfall of determinism since "the model of internalization takes for granted the 'internal' and the 'external' as already formed," whereas the Althusserian approach insists that the subject comes into being only in the moment when it embraces the Law (ibid., 115).

The logical problem with this model, in relation to revolutionary subjectivity, is that if it does not assume the preexistence (or transcendence) of the subject, it does assume the preexistence and autonomy of an all-powerful Law. And because the Law is oppressively immutable and omnipresent (that is to say, that particular laws may be changed, but the structure of the Law cannot be), there is no room in Althusser's account for what Butler calls "bad subjects." For to be a subject, Butler concurs with Althusser, is inevitably to be complicit with the Law. To be a subject is to be an Orwellian figure who is not only "ensnared by [her] own state" but who loves the state for having ensnared her. The Law is thus so inescapable that to be a rebellious or "bad" subject is an impossibility. The only avenue to rebellion, Butler argues, is to cease to be a subject at all. To rebel, she claims, requires a "willingness not to be . . . a critical desubjectivation" (ibid., 130).

But what can this account of the impossibility of the "bad subject" mean in relation to revolution? Certainly, French revolutionaries ceased to be subjects—they became citizens.[83] But in ceasing to be subjects of the king they did not cease to be subjects in Butler's sense. What does it mean, in other words, for subjects to come into being by overturning and demolishing the Law? One answer might be that even in changing the most fundamental of laws—even, for example, those of time and space—as the French revolutionaries did, they did not really rebel against the Law. Perceived in this way, the revolutionaries suffered a bad case of false consciousness. This account denies that revolutions, no matter how overwhelming and world-historical, can ever be truly revolutionary. But the French Revolution would seem to offer an insuperable obstacle to that view. The Revolution destroyed the fundamental laws that had shaped daily existence for hundreds of years. Revolutionary subject formation was therefore a truly reflexive process; the new citizen-subjects were engaged in making the Law that formed them.

Surveillance and Sympathy

The figure of the eye in the breast recalls one of Robespierre's most curious locutions. Within the heart of every good citizen, he declared, there lodged an "accusateur invisible" (invisible prosecutor) who scrutinized and passed judgment on that individual's thoughts and actions. The "accusateur invisible" would seem to have found its visual expression in the image of the internal, radiating eye of surveillance. The lawyer Robespierre's use of juridical language is noteworthy; the "accusateur" was the official position held by the citizen who prosecuted crimes in the criminal courts and, more notoriously, before the revolutionary tribunal. Robespierre's conception of the internal judge thus seems to come clearly from the secular realm rather than the divine one so often associated with the voice of conscience. Or rather, the "accusateur," like the eye of surveillance, would appear to perform a melding of the secular and the sacred since it, above all else, protects the Republic, which itself had gained sacred status.

If Robespierre's term for this form of internal regulation seems creepy, especially given its association with the grotesque violence of the revolutionary judicial apparatus, it is even stranger to note its powerful resemblance to Adam Smith's famous "man within the breast."[84] According to Smith we can only judge our own behavior by considering it as another would view it. The imagined spectator to our actions must not be a party to them; he or she must be impartial.[85] The identity of Smith's impartial spectator cannot be defined precisely: he is not God, since Smith explains that we have need of the man within because we are not fully capable of perceiving divine justice (128); nor is the man within simply the representative of public opinion, since often the internal judge rightly overturns the decisions of the public (129). The man within expresses something like a purified human faculty of judgment. Smith calls him "this inmate of the breast, this abstract man, the representative of mankind, and the substitute of the Deity" (130).

When the individual considers and seeks to judge his or her own actions, he or she consults the man within the breast:

> When I endeavour to examine my own conduct, when I endeavour to pass sentence upon it, and either approve or condemn it, it is evident that, in all such cases, I divide myself, as it were, into two persons, and that I, the examiner and the judge, represent a different character from that other I, the person whose conduct is being examined into and judged of. The first is the spectator, whose sentiments with regard to my own conduct I endeavour to enter into, by placing myself in his situation, and by considering how it would appear to me, when seen from that particular point of view. (113)

Smith deploys the same juridical language—judging, passing sentence—we saw at work in Robespierre, but I am even more interested in the way in which judgment operates for Smith through spectatorship and sympathy. Self-scrutiny requires an act of the imagination that divides the self into "characters" and that arrives at its conclusions by having one "character" act as spectator to the other. But it is perhaps even more important to note that judgment itself is nothing other than sympathy. Judgment requires not one but two acts of sympathy: one judges by "endeavour[ing] to enter into" the sentiments or situation of another (or of oneself as another). The man within the breast tries to sympathize with the actions of the person, or character, who is being judged. If the judge can indeed sympathize with those actions, the conduct is approved; if the judge cannot "enter into"—cannot sympathize—with the conduct, it is condemned. But sound moral judgment also requires that the individual enter into—sympathize with—the sentiments of the spectator or judge. As David Marshall points out in his reading of *The Theory of Moral Sentiments,* sympathy has a *social* function for Smith: "it forces us to moderate our passions in order to create a 'harmony and concord with the emotions' of those who are watching us."[86] Because we long above all else for others to enter into our feelings, because such a community of sentiment offers relief from even the most miserable of woes, and because we fear so strongly the withholding of that sympathy that comforts us, we seek to moderate our actions according to what we know is worthy of the sympathy (and thus approval) of others.

In Smith's scenario, as Marshall argues, spectatorship paradoxically has the capacity to create a sympathetic community, just as in the case of Fabre d'Eglantine a dethéatricalized theater could create a new purified type of spectatorship that would help forge fraternal bonds. But if consideration of Smith's "man in the breast" leads us back to spectatorship, it also reveals the underlying connection between sympathy and surveillance. The community of sentiment Smith imagines resulting from the moral efficacy of the impartial spectator is not so distant from the transparency of hearts Rousseau dreamed of. And Smith's spectator is not so very distant from the scrutiny of the reader or the public that will ensure and affirm Rousseau's essential goodness or from the eye of surveillance that protects the Republic and ensures the virtue of its citizens. Smith describes the truly good man and citizen:

> He has never dared to forget for one moment the judgement which the impartial spectator would pass upon his sentiments and conduct. He has never dared to suffer the man within the breast to be absent one moment from his attention. With the eyes of the great inmate he has always been accustomed to regard whatever relates to himself. This habit has become perfectly familiar to him. He has been in the constant practice, and indeed under the constant necessity, of modeling or endeavouring to model, not only his outward conduct and behavior, but as much as he can, even his inward sentiments and feelings according to those of this awful and respectable judge. He does not merely affect the sentiments of the impartial spectator. He really adopts them. (*Theory of Moral Sentiments,* 146–147)

Just as Rousseau worried lest he disappear for one moment from the reader's eye, Smith's virtuous man never "dare[s] to suffer" that the man within the breast remove his gaze for an instant. In both cases, establishing morality means establishing sympathy between self and other even within oneself. And in both cases this morality and sympathy are made possible only by ongoing surveillance. But perhaps Smith's man within the breast resembles even more nearly the spirit of the internal eye of surveillance than he does Rousseau's reader. For while the identity of the man within the breast refuses absolute definition, the man within the breast, like the eye of surveillance, amalgamates the personal, the social, and the divine and introjects that amalgamation. The man within the breast is at once part of the individual (he or she divides himself and one part plays the "character" of the judge), the representative of an abstract humankind with all its social requirements, and that which, given the limitations of humanity, stands in for the divine.

While Smith would no doubt be appalled by any parallel drawn between Robespierre and himself, his man within the breast, like the eye of surveillance and the "invisible prosecutor," offers the possibility of a transparent, sentimental community through the practice of surveillance. This surveillance must be carried out by each individual. It is a right and a responsibility that inheres in the individual. Surveillance carried out by an external power alone would only produce external conformity that would, in turn, disguise immorality or crime. Only voluntary surveillance practiced as an integral form of citizenship, directed toward the community and toward oneself, could produce both the virtue and the fraternity necessary to a republic.

Conclusion

It is pleasantly ironic and even satisfying that Fouché, who came to stand for the opacity, illegibility, and omniscience of the nineteenth-century police, should have been subject to the powerful, surveilling gaze of the people, even if only in Robespierre's imagination. But, in fact, the confrontation between the two men led to Fouché's rise, to the demise of popular surveillance, and to the beginning of the repressive surveillance with which we are familiar. Fouché, fearful for his life because of Robespierre's undoubted enmity, began to agitate secretly against Robespierre and eventually helped engineer the Thermidorian coup that brought Robespierre to the guillotine. Despite his earlier violent excesses, he assumed the position of minister of police under the Directory in 1795. His difficult mission was to root out conspiracies on both sides, royalist and Jacobin, and to keep the "petit peuple" quiet. He writes in his memoirs of his very first steps: "I resolved to suppress the clubs first. I began by a kind of proclamation, or circular, in which I declared that I had just taken upon myself the duty of watching for all, and over all, in order to re-establish tranquillity at home."[87]

Fouché's first act was to suppress the political clubs because, as we have seen, they claimed that as citizens and part of the sovereign, they had the right to carry out surveillance. No longer would surveillance be a right and responsibility of all. Now the power of surveillance would be centralized: the citizens would be relieved of their duty; Fouché would perform it for them. He would watch in their place. Fouché's pronouncement that he would watch "for all, and over all" in the interest of tranquility, his expropriation of what was seen as a political right and an individual duty, effectively ended a radical republican vision of popular participation and self-government. It announced the beginning of the nineteenth century.

Figure 1. Revolutionary allegory with Jean-Jacques Rousseau, the eye of surveillance, and numerous revolutionary symbols below. © Photothèque des Musées de la Ville de Paris / Berthier.

Figure 2. *Déclaration des droits de l'homme et du citoyen* [Declaration of the Rights of Man and of the Citizen] (engraving, 1793). Bibliothèque nationale de France.

Figure 3. Engraving of the Republican calendar (spring and summer months) dedicated to the glory of the "mountain," the party of the left in the National Convention (1794). Bibliothèque nationale de France.

Figure 4. Letterhead stationery of the Brussels surveillance committee (1794). Bibliothèque nationale de France.

Figure 5. "Carte d'assistance," or a chit delivered by a neighborhood sectional government in Paris to local resident. The chit declares that the bearer is entitled to various forms of aid (1793). Bibliothèque nationale de France.

FÊTE CÉLÉBRÉE EN L'HONNEUR DE L'ÊTRE SUPRÊME.
Le 20 Prairiale l'an 2me de la Rep

Le véritable Prêtre de l'Être suprême, c'est la Nature, son temple l'Univers, son Culte
la Vertu, ses fêtes la joye d'un grand Peuple rassemblé pour resserer les doux noeuds de
la Fraternité, et Jurer la mort des tirans

Figure 6. Engraving inspired by the Festival in Honor of the Supreme Being. Depicts a republican mother teaching her children the new values of the Republic. The family stands before an "altar of the Nation" bearing republican symbols (1794). Bibliothèque nationale de France.

Figure 7. Engraving inspired by Robespierre's attempt to establish a republican "cult of the Supreme Being." Depicts the new revolutionary profession of faith (1794). Bibliothèque nationale de France.

Figure 8. *Dieu. Peuple. Loi.* [God. The People. The Law.] (engraving, 1794). Bibliothèque nationale de France.

Figure 9. Engraving in which Voltaire points to the words, "Supreme Being, Sovereign People, French Republic." The image has been cropped, but it is clear that Rousseau originally appeared on the opposite side of the page (1794). Bibliothèque nationale de France.

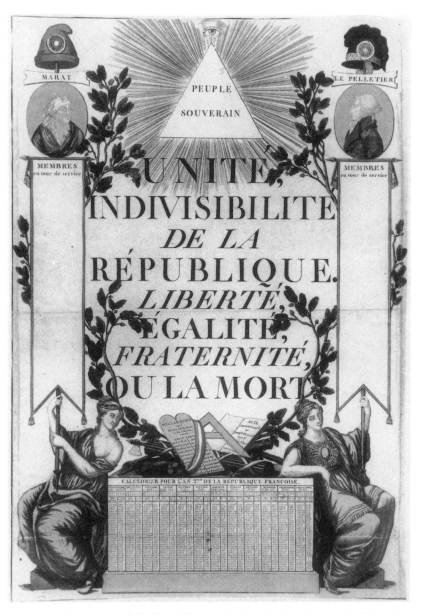

Figure 10. Engraving of the Republican calendar bearing the words "Peuple souverain" [Sovereign People] (1793). Bibliothèque nationale de France.

Figure 11. Allegorical figure of Reason (1794). Bibliothèque nationale de France.

LE TRIOMPHE DE LA RAISON ET DE LA VÉRITÉ

La Philosophie sous la figure de J.J. Rousseau,

Découvre à l'Univers la Raison et la Vérité, voilée par l'erreur et le mensonge.

Figure 12. *Le Triomphe de la raison et de la vérité* [The Triumph of Reason and Truth], with Jean-Jacques Rousseau (engraving, 1793). Bibliothèque nationale de France.

Figure 13. *La Liberté soutenue par la Raison protège l'Innocence et couronne la Vertu* [Liberty, Supported by Reason, Protects Innocence and Crowns Virtue] (engraving, 1793). Bibliothèque nationale de France.

Figure 14. The allegorical figure of Reason (engraving, 1794). Bibliothèque nationale de France.

La République

A Paris chez Ballet, *rue Jacques au coin de celle des Mathurins N.º 670*

Figure 15. *La République* [The Republic] (engraving, 1794). Bibliothèque nationale de France.

4 The Home and the World
Domestic Surveillance and
Revolutionary Drama

Mieux l'état est constitué, plus les affaires publiques l'empor-
tent sur les privées dans l'esprit des citoyens. Il y a même beau-
coup moins d'affaires privées, parce que la somme du bonheur
commun fournissant une portion plus considérable à celui de
chaque individu, il lui en reste moins à chercher dans les soins
particulier.
Jean-Jacques Rousseau, Du Contrat social, *book 3, chapter 15*

Although others have studied the ways that experts or the state have deployed surveillance to subject and govern individuals, briefly, during the French Revolution, the founding moment of political modernity, surveillance was understood by many ordinary citizens to constitute a powerful democratic means by which to exercise their right and their capacity to govern. Surveillance was one key means by which many citizens exerted their authority over those who governed in their name, as well as over their cities, towns, and neighborhoods. But surveillance had an important role that went beyond the realms of politics and policing. Or, put another way, because the degree to which the personal was the political during the Revolution can hardly be overstated, surveillance was deemed necessary to protect every aspect of life. Citizens' conceptions of just what surveillance was could be very broad indeed; thus, for example, when audiences insisted that the Comédie-Française perform *Charles IX* or insisted that the Théâtre du Vaudeville not perform *L'Auteur d'un moment*, they could be said to be exercising surveillance over the theaters. For while *surveillance* is a rather technical and rigid word in English, in French its meaning is richer and less restrained: *surveiller* includes the word *veiller,* meaning to watch over or to hold vigil. *Veiller* in no way evokes the domination of authorities but, in fact, suggests a sense of protectiveness; hence its implied subject is familial or communal.

Revolutionary drama represented private, domestic life as utterly continuous with public, political life, and it represented surveillance—a practice that linked individual and local action to the protection of the Revolution—as a crucial element in forging this continuity. Numerous dramas told stories of individuals or families whose personal happiness is threatened by antagonists who also pose a threat to the Republic. Time and again, surveillance defeats these personal and political foes.

It is not incidental that *drame,* a form invented in the mid-eighteenth century precisely to publicly explore and expose the private, served as the vehicle for the representation of surveillance. Throughout the second half of the century those who made arguments on behalf of this new and ill-defined genre had to start by asserting that the private was a legitimate object for artistic ambition and an important object for public interest. For those who held fast to the traditional hierarchy of theatrical genres, tragedy, theater's highest form, portrayed the great and thereby treated issues and problems of great magnitude. Indeed many aesthetically conservative critics complained that tragedy, under the influence of that most nefarious of literary inventions, the novel, had lost sight of its ancient mission and had degenerated into a frivolous exhibition of languid love stories. In other words, by turning to the representation of private emotion tragedy had diminished its stature; it could only be regenerated by studiously avoiding the personal and taking up subjects of public importance. Nor, despite a shared focus on the middle classes, was it any more suitable for comedy to delve into the private in the way that drame sought to do; comedy's proper object was the social or, in the hands of Molière, the critique of character.

Proponents of drame, like Diderot, argued that the private realm was an object of public interest and importance and therefore a legitimate object of artistic representation. Representations of the interior life of ordinary people not only afforded a singular pleasure—the pleasure of shedding tears—not offered by either of the two traditional genres, but they also helped destroy prejudices (such as that which stigmatized illegitimate children) and provided touching examples capable of instructing fathers, mothers, and children how best to fulfill their familial responsibilities and, in so doing, find happiness. Private happiness, in turn, contributed to making a happier community, one less at risk from the excesses and disorders to which unhappy families can give rise. On this argument Sedaine's play *Le Philosophe sans le savoir* attained the highest level of artistic achievement as conceived by the Enlightenment: it instructed while it gave pleasure.[1]

If artistic representations were to be judged on the basis of the effects they produced on spectators, the innovators argued, drame ought to hold a respected rank. For while tragedy was meant to produce catharsis in its spectators and comedy was, through its salutary laughter, meant to correct certain social or character flaws, drame's effect was to expand and heighten the spectators' sensibility. The critic and defender of both novels and drames, Mistelet, drew a distinction between passions and sensibility: passion always leads to egotism whereas sensibility leads to pity and to identification with others. The man driven by passions is destructive, but

> [c]elui dont l'âme est sensible, n'est point reduit à de sentiments destructeurs des autres: il s'inquiète de tout, approfondit tout, étend ses regards sur la nature entière: rien n'est étranger à son cœur. La sensibilité est le principe qui met toutes les passions en mouvement; mais qui, en les opposant les unes aux autres, en adoucit toujours les effets; et de ce choc à peu près égal, de cet équilibre entre tant de sentiments divers, naît la vertu.[2]

> [he whose soul is *sensible* is not reduced to sentiments that are destructive of others: he is concerned about everything, goes into everything, and extends his regard to all of nature: nothing is foreign to his heart. Sensibility is the principle that puts all passions into movement, but that, in opposing them to each other, always softens their effects; and from this nearly equal shock of forces, from this equilibrium among so many different sentiments, virtue is born.]

The man of sensibility, not the noble warrior, is the man of virtue—a good citizen, a good friend, a good father, and a good husband—and drame is one of the most powerful means by which sensibility can be cultivated. Why then, Mistelet asks, do so many critics disapprove of drames: "Pourquoi, enfin, s'élever contre les Drames, dont le but doit être d'éclairer et d'attendrir, et qui, par l'illusion du spectacle, sont plus propres que tout autre ouvrage, a bien remplir cet objet?" (ibid., 11). [Why, then, rise up against drames, whose purpose is to enlighten and to touch and which, by means of the illusion of theater, are the most fitting of all works to achieve this purpose?] Moreover, Mistelet remarked, audiences loved drames. Indeed, perhaps one reason critics opposed the drame was its essentially democratic character. Not only did it appeal to the bad taste of the lower orders, they complained, but, more important, it also raised the interior experiences of ordinary people to a matter for public concern. In drame the troubled lives of these characters were important in themselves, not simply as reflections of the social order, and the shared state of heightened emotion bonded the audiences of drames into a sentimental community.

With the advent of the Revolution, audience authority over theaters, the abolition of privileges for the Comédie-Française, the Comédie-Italienne, and the Opéra, and the emergence of a host of new theaters, critical opinion no longer stood in the way of drame. And, perhaps more to the point, the stiff competition among Parisian theaters helped dissolve not only the hierarchy of genres but even the strict demarcations among them. By the spring of 1791 Toussaint Mareux, director of the Théâtre Saint-Antoine, worried about surviving in this new world in which the market decided the fate of theaters: "On every side theaters are being built and we are going to be inundated by them after Easter. There will be thirty-eight."[3] These new theaters could be very large; the Théâtre de la Cité, built across from the Palais de Justice, and the Théâtre du Vaudeville, near the Tuileries, each seated eighteen hundred to two thousand patrons.[4] In order to survive, they had to build and retain an audience. Drames, dramelike comedies, and parodies were well-received because, in publicly exposing the interior lives of characters representing ordinary citizens and ordinary families in the theater, these plays both represented and enacted the continuity between interior and exterior, private and public, that many considered the heart of the revolutionary experience. Furthermore these plays represent surveillance as the crucial link between private life and public good.

La Chaste Suzanne *and the Problem of Surveillance*

In January 1793, a scant seven days after the execution of Louis XVI, the fédérés—the volunteer soldiers brought to the capital from all corners of France to protect the National Convention in the event of a counterrevolutionary attack—rebelled. They menaced citizens, destroyed property, presented petitions, and swore solemn oaths. Was this fédéré violence the result of some rekindled monarchism? Far from it. The events that stirred the soldiers were theatrical, not political: their wrath was aroused by what would seem the unlikeliest of objects—a Vaudeville production of the biblical story of Susannah and the elders called *La Chaste Suzanne*. This is not the only case in which the fédérés, who had been active in and around Paris since the Fête de la Fédération in the summer of 1790, took the lead in the tumultuous events that occurred regularly in Parisian theaters from the very beginning of the Revolution. It is, however, to my knowledge, the only case in which a riot was provoked by a sacred drama—or what we should perhaps call a play based on a biblical theme, since we are considering a Vaudeville production.[5]

One of the Vaudeville actors, Delpeche, brought this complaint to the Commune, the revolutionary Paris city government:

> Depuis plusieurs jours on nous menaçait de faire interrompre la représenta-tion de *La Chaste Suzanne*. . . . Ils ont commencé par forcer le passage et en-trer sans payer. . . . Quelques-uns d'entre eux sont descendus des premières loges à l'orchestre, et ont tenu les propos les plus injurieux sur le public, les auteurs, les acteurs, et les pièces. Le commissaire de police de la section des Tuileries leur a représenté qu'ils doivent respecter les propriétés. Un partic-ulier lui a répondu qu'on ne venait point empêcher la représentation, mais s'opposer aux allusions indécentes.[6]

> [For several days some people have been threatening to interrupt the per-formance of *La Chaste Suzanne*. . . . They began by forcing their way in without paying. . . . Some of them came down to the orchestra from the loges and vehemently insulted the public, the authors, the actors, and the play. The police commissar from the Tuileries section explained to them that they must observe the proprieties. . . . One of them responded that they hadn't come to obstruct the performance but to oppose indecent allusions.]

Delpeche came to plead for the Commune's protection, explaining that the fédérés' hostility to *La Chaste Suzanne* and to the theater company that per-formed it seemed implacable:

> Quelques-uns de ces particuliers, après le spectacle, sont montés sur le théâtre, cherchant ceux à qui ils en voulaient, et sont sortis en promettant de faire un hôpital de ce théâtre. Juste ciel! Verrions-nous se renouveler les scènes sanglantes de 2 et 3 Septembre, et les spectacles seraient-ils sur la liste des proscriptions? (ibid.)

> [After the play some of these people climbed up on the stage looking for those with whom they were angry. They left vowing to turn the theater into a hospital. Good heavens! Would we see the bloody scenes of the second and third of September all over again and would the theaters be on the list of the proscribed?]

But Delpeche, apparently no astute politician, had miscalculated. The histrionic references to the gruesome prison massacres of the previous September struck no responsive chord. Rather than finding a sympathetic audience for his tale, Delpeche faced Jacques-René Hébert, the deputy procureur of the Commune and ally of the fédérés, who joined the soldiers in demanding the suppression of the play on the vague but crucial grounds that "elle corrompt les mœurs républicaines" [it corrupt(ed) republican morals].[7] A newspaper reporting the event denounced Delpeche, claiming that having failed to satisfy his need for applause on the stage, the actor sought it at the Commune.[8]

When the Vaudeville Theater directors capitulated and withdrew the play, the troubles came to an end in a manner less spectacular than that Delpeche had foreseen. The triumphant fédérés sent word to the newspaper *Révolutions de Paris* of their renewed oath to be faithful to their post; to defend liberty, equality, and the Republic; and to die rather than allow the rebirth of tyranny. And to that oath they added, "Sur l'invitation qui a été faite aux auteurs et directeurs du Théâtre du Vaudeville, de suspendre la représentation de *La Chaste Suzanne*, motivés sur les troubles qu'elle pourrait causer, ils y ont acquiescé. Nous te prions, citoyen journaliste d'insérer de même cette note." [The actors and directors of the Théâtre du Vaudeville have acquiesced upon being invited to suspend the performance of *La Chaste Suzanne* because of the troubles it might provoke. We beg you, Citizen journalist, likewise, to insert this notice.][9]

Why should *La Chaste Suzanne* have occasioned a crisis? Why should such a trivial play have aroused such deep and violent fury, especially at a time when events of the gravest nature were taking place? Marvin Carlson has argued that the Vaudeville play provoked anger because one of its lines seemed to allude critically to the deputies of the National Convention: the judge at Suzanne's trial, in the line in question, admonishes the accusing elders that they may not act as her judges: "You are her accusers you cannot be her judges" (2.2). Audiences apparently understood this rebuke to the elders as a reference to the deputies who both brought the king up on charges and sat in judgment of him.[10] Similarly, Emmet Kennedy claims that *La Chaste Suzanne* "had nothing to do with Revolutionary politics but had two lines that were taken as a denunciation of the Jacobins."[11] According to this explanation nothing inherent in the *story* told in *La Chaste Suzanne* angered revolutionary audiences; the spectators merely responded to obvious, superficial allusions to contemporary events. But this interpretation cannot account for the play's travails, for the contentious line was removed from the play after the performance of January 5, and the riots did not occur until January 28.[12]

Something more profoundly disturbing about *La Chaste Suzanne* must have caused the riots. The play, despite its seeming frivolity, took up one of the period's most important concerns: surveillance. Revolutionary citizens' practice of surveillance was deeply bound up with their aspirations for truly meaningful popular sovereignty. As we saw in chapter 3, to be sovereign meant to retain supreme authority over all those whom the people entrusted with authority. Surveillance seemed to offer one of the very best means by which to preserve that supreme authority. As a consequence of the doctrine of popular sovereignty, each citizen was considered to bear some portion of the right to govern; surveillance allowed citizens to exercise that right. But popular sovereignty also carried with it another consequence: if each citizen was, in a sense, a ruler, then each citizen's life became a matter of vital state interest, and each citizen's home became a place of state importance. So if we understand the term *private* in the Habermasian sense as designating that which has no official state function or office, it follows that in the Republic there were no longer any *particuliers* (private individuals), nor were there any *maisons particulières* (private homes). Ordinary citizens and ordinary lives must, consequently, be subject to the same surveillance that preserved the integrity of the National Assembly. *La Chaste Suzanne*'s representation of the elders' gaze was understood by the fédérés and many others as a counterrevolutionary attack on surveillance and thus on Robespierre and the Jacobins who promoted surveillance as the key to the defeat of theatrical, counterrevolutionary politics and as the cornerstone of republican culture.

The case of *La Chaste Suzanne* does more than illuminate the deeply problematic nature of spectacle and theatricality in revolutionary culture. It helps us to understand the high stakes that were attached to it. These unlikely riots surrounding a seemingly innocuous play took place at perhaps the most anxious moment in the revolutionary period. Not only were the toppling of the monarchy and the trying and executing of the king momentous political and psychic events, but they also revealed and hardened the deep rift between Jacobins and Girondins that was to prove so harmful to the future of the Republic.[13] This rift is relevant to my discussion here, for the soon-to-be-defeated Girondins did not harbor warmer feelings for Louis XVI than did the Jacobins. What separated the two groups was their relation to what they would call "le peuple"—the mass of urban workers, artisans, and small shopkeepers perhaps best described by the contemporary term "sans-culottes"—and to political representation. Jacobins, unlike their Girondin colleagues, were willing to make an alliance with the sans-culottes. Some historians have argued that this alliance was nothing but a temporary strategic maneuver on the part of the Jacobins, and this may well be true. Cynical ploy or genuine heartfelt belief, however, the result was not only Jacobin support for wage and price controls, as Marxist historians have emphasized, but also Jacobin espousal of popular aspirations for full, participatory democracy.[14] From the Revolution's earliest days the leading Jacobin, Robespierre, had argued against property qualifications for the vote and had railed against the notion that the population could legitimately be divided into two political classes: active and passive citizens. But both the Jacobin and the popular conception of active citizenship went far beyond voting: Jacobins supported the "permanence" of the sections, and they backed demands for popular oversight of political, military, and administrative institutions. In the phrase of Lucien Jaume, the Jacobins and the sans-culotte militants shared "a passion for surveillance" (209; my translation). The Girondins, on the contrary, feared such direct interventions, which they believed to be anarchic and destabilizing.

Moreover, the political motivation for rejecting the play was continuous with an aesthetic motivation for the riots. The overt, unabashed theatricality of *La Chaste Suzanne*—manifest most powerfully in the spectacular display of Suzanne undressing for her bath—constituted a stunning rejection of the antitheatrical dramatic theory and practice that I discussed in chapter 2, developed by leading radical playwrights such as Fabre d'Eglantine. The theatricality of Suzanne's bath was particularly incendiary in the historical context of the profound antitheatricalism of radical revolutionary drama and politics. The play's critique of revolutionary surveillance and its rehabilitation of spectacle together constitute the corruption of republican morals so feared by Hébert.

The riots caused by *La Chaste Suzanne* reveal the tensions and conflicts generated as the Revolution transformed France from a society of spectacle into a society of surveillance. The battle over *La Chaste Suzanne* and the contest over the nature and status of surveillance that it opens up allow us to grasp the pervasiveness and the relevance of surveillance to modern Republican culture, a culture that was displaced by liberal, capitalist culture yet continued to haunt the French political imagination throughout the nineteenth century.

I will focus here on dramatic representations of surveillance, specifically on the way those representations construct the role of surveillance in the domestic sphere. For the Revolution developed a distinct new theatrical genre—what I call the drama of domestic surveillance—which staged and restaged surveillance's place in everyday life. The drama of domestic surveillance represented the cultural anxieties that attended surveillance and the dangers that surveillance was meant to suppress. These plays about citizens and their homes and families explored the relation between ordinary lives and public affairs. They were the descendants of Diderot's *drame bourgeois:* serious plays about common people that made private, family concerns a matter for public sympathy and interest. But these plays differed from their predecessors as well, for the revolutionary dramas of surveillance, unlike those earlier plays, are also dramas of state. In the revolutionary plays the affairs of the family are no longer the subject only of moral interest; they are also of paramount political importance because family members are now citizens not subjects. And because the home is a place of political significance and political activity, it requires surveillance for its protection. When we place *La Chaste Suzanne* in the context of these plays, we can begin to understand why it was so inflammatory. The play presents a vision of surveillance that was fundamentally at odds with the one extolled by the dramas of domestic surveillance.

The Drama of Domestic Surveillance

The extension of surveillance from the political sphere to the neighborhood and domestic spheres was staged again and again in numerous popular dramas, and the drama of domestic surveillance makes manifest the logic I have been describing.[15] Once subjects become citizens, the private sphere contains as many threats to the Revolution as does the sphere of high politics; likewise, the private sphere is as vulnerable to counterrevolutionary corruption as is the National Assembly.[16]

Consider, in this respect, *L'Époux républicain* (The Republican Husband), a highly successful play by Maurin de Pompigny. The hero is Franklin, retired locksmith, president of his sectional assembly, virtuous and ardent revolutionary. Indeed, Franklin embodies exemplary revolutionary citizenship, for he makes no distinction at all between the personal and the public. He has, for example, jettisoned his own name and taken that of the revered, recently deceased American patriot in order to mark his new freedom. Franklin's professional life has also changed with the revolution; the play emphasizes that Franklin has retired from his trade at the relatively young age of forty-five. The new regime presumably does not require the secret coffers, the iron chains, and the dismal dungeons that would have kept a locksmith busy in the Old Regime. More telling still, after years of widowhood Franklin has remarried precisely because he believes that celibacy is a threat to the Republic. Thus he urges his prospective daughter-in-law, Rosalie, to the altar on the grounds that marriage is good for the new nation, and he even thinks that the Republic should require marriage legislatively: "Aussi, j'espère bien qu'avant peu nous aurons un bon décret qui proscrira le célibat" [so I hope that before long we will have a good decree outlawing celibacy].[17] That Franklin has married a former nun, Mélisse, powerfully signals his disavowal of the Old Regime and his commitment to the new one. And, naturally, Franklin has married Mélisse only because he believes that her repudiation of the Old Regime is as categorical as his own:

> Tu sais que quoique je t'aimasse déjà de tout mon cœur, je ne t'aurais jamais épousée si tu ne m'avais bien assuré que c'était au fond de ton âme que tu abjurais toutes les mômeries monacales, et que tu regardais comme le plus beau de ta vie, ce jour qui t'avait rendu à la liberté.[18]

> [You know that although I already loved you with all my heart, I would never have married you if you hadn't assured me that you repudiated all that monastic mummery and that you regarded the day that your liberty was restored (i.e., the Revolution's abolition of monastic vows with the law of February 13, 1790) as the most wonderful day of your life.]

But Franklin begins to discover that his wife does not share his identification of personal and public interest:

> FR. Qu'as-tu, ma femme? tu me parais rêveuse; toutes les fois que je parle de *nos* affaires, il me semble . . .
> MÉL. De quelles affaires?
> FR. Parbleu! des seules qui doivent nous intéresser; du salut, du bonheur de la République. (1.9; my emphasis)

> [FR. What's wrong wife? You seem distracted; whenever I talk about *our* affairs it seems that . . .
> MÉL. About what affairs?
> FR. My goodness! The only affairs that ought to interest us: the safety and happiness of the Republic.]

Mélisse's failure to recognize instantly that "our affairs" are the Republic's affairs clearly indicates that she does not share Franklin's identification with the Republic. In fact, Franklin has been deceived. For we discover that Mélisse and her adulterous lover, Brumaire, a former church canon, are conspiring with counterrevolutionaries and are planning to flee France. Worse still, Mélisse has lured Franklin's young son Floréal into her plot.

Mélisse's machinations against Franklin and his family and against the Republic are thwarted by surveillance. Hyacinthe, a household servant, advises Romarin, Franklin's *homme de confiance,* that she has doubts about Mélisse's politics and her morality—Hyacinthe suspects the illicit liaison between Mélisse and Brumaire and believes that they have concocted a counterrevolutionary plan. For this reason, Hyacinthe reports, she has tried to win Mélisse's confidence in order to learn more: "Il fallait bien les écouter et dire comme eux; sans cela que sais-je?" (1.3). [It was necessary to listen to them and to agree with them; otherwise what could I know?] Romarin, deeply concerned, urges Hyacinthe to continue spying. Moreover, rather than immediately informing Franklin of Mélisse's suspicious behavior, Romarin goes to the neighborhood section and persuades it to authorize further surveillance: "J'ai dit que je connaissais un projet de conspiration, et je demandais d'être autorisé à en suivre la trame" (2.4). [I said that I knew about a conspiracy, and I asked for authorization to unravel the plot.]

Despite Hyacinthe's qualms about spying on others and publicizing their personal lives, Romarin convinces her to cooperate in this course of action by insisting on the total character of the public interest. Everything, even family matters, must be public in a republic: "Se taire est quelquefois une crime; rien n'est indifférent dans une République, un seul mot peut donner le clé d'une grande conspiration et sauver la patrie. Achève donc de m'éclaircir, et compte sur mon prudence" (1.3). [Keeping quiet can be a crime; nothing is unimportant in a Republic. One word can be the key to unlocking a grand conspiracy and saving the country. Continue to keep me informed and count on my prudence.] In the new regime even seemingly private matters are of concern, Romarin reminds Hyacinthe, for even the intensely private may turn out to have public ramifications. Hence whereas Hyacinthe considers keeping her suspicions quiet so as not to wash dirty linen in public, Romarin finds such discretion potentially dangerous and criminal.

Romarin knows that Franklin fully shares his view of surveillance and would endorse his conduct. For when he is still unaware of his own household's counterrevolutionary and adulterous infestation, Franklin discusses the very issue of surveillance with his enemy and rival, Brumaire. Brumaire, feigning allegiance to the Revolution, worries aloud about the possible injustices that might result from malignly motivated surveillance. Franklin, however, dismisses Brumaire's concerns citing, on the one hand, the Republic's inherent justice and, on the other, its vulnerability to enemies: "Ne vaut-il mieux dans les circonstances ou nous sommes qu'un prévoyance salutaire nous fasse commettre une erreur facile à réparer, que si par une délicatesse mal entendue, nous laissions échapper un coupable . . . ? Nous avons grand besoin de surveillants" (1.10). [Isn't it better, in our present circumstances, that out of salutary foresight we make a mistake that can be easily rectified than that, because of some misplaced delicacy, we let a guilty person escape . . . ? We are in great need of surveillants.] Franklin thus confidently asserts the Republic's capacity to sort out the guilty from the innocent effectively (a confidence that is vindicated in the play's subplot involving Franklin's eldest son, Fervidor). At the same time, Franklin balks at recognizing the value Brumaire has proposed protecting: privacy. In Franklin's view personal privacy is not a countervalue in need of legal protection; it is a mistaken idea, a "misplaced delicacy" that lingers from the Old Regime.

The play's climax fully justifies Franklin's view. Armed with the intelligence Hyacinthe and Romarin produce, Franklin confronts Mélisse, who revealingly insists that her criminal correspondence is really a feminine secret and therefore beyond the purview of the state and its citizens. But Mélisse's coquettishness falls flat because femininity no longer exists outside the public realm. Franklin thus follows the same logic he employed earlier with Brumaire: "[R]ien ne gêne les gens honnêtes: il n'y a que les malintentionnés qui craignent les surveillants" (2.10). [Nothing bothers honest people: only malefactors fear surveillants.] For secrets per se—feminine or political—are a crime in revolutionary culture. Anything legitimate welcomes exposure, and only crime tries to avoid public knowledge. "Point de secrets pour la République" [No secrets in the Republic], intones Franklin as he orders Mélisse taken away, surely to the guillotine: "son salut dépend de la publicité" (2.10) [its safety depends on publicity].

L'Époux républicain insists on an identity between threats to the family (here, Mélisse's adultery) and threats to the Republic (conspiracy). Indeed, Mélisse's adultery and her treason are not merely analogous; they are wholly indistinguishable, and both are manifested in a single act—leaving France. For that is the only crime with which Mélisse and Brumaire are charged. The criminal but canny Brumaire tries to turn this fact to his advantage; certainly, he concedes, running off with another man's wife is immoral, but, he asks, should this personal decision be considered treasonous: "Il est vrai que ta femme, ton fils et moi avons formé le projet de partir; mais s'éloigner de sa patrie est-ce donc la trahir?" (2.11). [It is true that your wife, your son, and I have decided to leave; but is leaving one's country betraying it?] In a republic, however, Franklin argues, private decisions always have public implications; "Yes," he replies to Brumaire's query; "Oui, quand on peut la défendre ou mourir pour elle" (2.11) [when one can defend it or die for it].

The play's subplot revolving around Franklin's younger son, Floréal, reveals the danger of failing to understand the fundamentally indissoluble bond between private happiness and the safety of the Republic. Floréal almost becomes a counterrevolutionary traitor because he balances personal and public concerns against each other rather than understanding them as continuous. Floréal becomes involved with the conspirators because he believes, mistakenly, that it is the only way to gain access to his beloved Rosalie, also a former nun: "Je leur avais confié mon amour pour Rosalie. . . . ils crûrent pouvoir profiter d'un moment d'impatience et de faiblesse pour me révéler leurs horribles complots" (2.14). [I had confided my love for Rosalie to them. . . . They thought they could take advantage of a moment of weakness and impatience to reveal their horrible plots to me.]

Floréal's first mistake is to have thought that personal happiness could be purchased by and could exist despite the commission of a crime against the public happiness. He learns of his error when he finds that Rosalie, who considers herself "a child of the nation," will have nothing to do with the conspirators. His second mistake is his failure, despite Rosalie's exhortations, to denounce the traitors even after his decision not to join them. He commits this second blunder for reasons similar to the first: his delicacy of feeling will not permit him to cause his father the pain he knows the revelation will bring. These personal considerations paralyzed him: "Ils me mirent dans la cruelle alternative d'être leur dénonciateur ou leur complice; je n'aurais pas hésité; mais percer moi-même le cœur d'un père en lui annonçant qu'une épouse criminelle . . . je n'osais" (2.14). [They gave me the cruel alternative of being their denouncer or their accomplice; I would not have hesitated, but to pierce the heart of my father by announcing to him that his criminal wife . . . I didn't dare.]

Floréal's irresolution, his tendency to put personal and public concerns into competition with one another, almost brings about his downfall. Floréal's confusion contrasts with the clarity of Franklin's priorities: on hearing his son's story, Franklin exhibits no grief at his wife's betrayal. Instead, he exclaims against his son's near willingness to allow a crime to be committed: "Insensé! un moment plus tard et tu recevrais le prix d'un coupable silence" (2.14). [Fool! A moment later and you would have paid the price for your guilty silence.] Floréal's inability to recognize the public character of seemingly private matters and his reluctance to take part in the surveillance and the publicity that safeguard both almost cost him his love and nearly send him to the guillotine. The story of Franklin's family shows that there is no distinction between private and public crimes. Hence the resolution of the domestic plot and the resolution of the political plot are the same; surveillance protects the family and preserves the Republic's safety.

L'Époux républicain was a very successful play.[19] It was certainly not alone in its representation of the practice of surveillance. It is, in fact, an exemplary instance of a revolutionary subgenre—of what I am calling the drama of domestic surveillance—that proved abundantly fruitful and bears witness to a deep and widespread social and theatrical preoccupation. Plays featuring plots that hinged on the undoing of conspiracies by means of surveillance abounded, and these conspiracies were, as in the case of *L'Époux républicain*, double. They operated simultaneously in the private and the public domains. Indeed, far from separating the home from politics and relegating it to insignificance, revolutionary culture was especially anxious about what went on in what we might now consider private life.[20] For if the Revolution were to regenerate the nation, it must regenerate individuals and families. The fact that these plays for the most part link sexual offenses such as adultery, seduction, and fornication to counterrevolutionary crimes, instead, for example, of depicting theft, swindling, or fraud, attests to the significance of what Habermas calls the intimate sphere in the revolutionary imagination.

One of these plays, *La Veuve du républicain, ou, Le Calomniateur* (The Widow of the Republican, or, The Slanderer), which *Les Spectacles de Paris* called an "ouvrage soigné de style" (work of meticulous style) and a "succès brillant" (brilliant success), treats concerns similar to those prominent in *L'Époux républicain*—personal and political betrayal—but in a different setting.[21] No longer in a domestic interior, it tells the story of a poor, virtuous widow and mother, Cécile, who falls victim to a conniving suitor. Cécile and her children are living in a *hotel garni* (boardinghouse) in Paris, whence they have come in the hopes of securing a pension. The boardinghouse is, by its nature, an ambiguous space: in it people carry on their domestic lives alongside complete strangers. The house opens its doors to all those who can pay and refuses all those who cannot, thus underlining the commercial character of its domesticity.[22] The boardinghouse is thus neither fully private nor fully public and by its very existence calls into question any notion of a preserved private interior.[23] The play confirms the interdependence of private and public that the boardinghouse incarnates, for the denizens of the boardinghouse require surveillance for their protection, just as did Franklin's family. The boarding-house is no safer than Franklin's private house, but neither is it any more dangerous; *La Veuve* does not draw a distinction between some putatively safe private home, in which women are protected, and the commingled world of Cécile.

Like Franklin, the widow Cécile exemplifies the republican attributes appropriate to her sex. She is open, affable, and honest; she is sorrowful over the loss of her heroic husband yet uncomplaining and fervently patriotic; most important, despite her poverty she helps others and dedicates herself to her children. A boardinghouse domestic sings her praises:

> Triste de ses malheurs; craignant d'en affliger
> Les cœurs dont la pitié pourrait la soulager
> Du peu qu'elle possède, allégeant la misère
> Donnant à ses enfants tous les soins d'une mère
> Comment ne pas l'aimer?[24]

> [Sorrowful because of her misfortunes,
> fearing to afflict the hearts of those whose pity could comfort her,
> easing the misery of others with the little she has,
> giving to her children every maternal care,
> how can one not love her?]

In this Rousseauian age "every maternal care" is almost certainly a reference to breast-feeding, and breast-feeding is *the* sign of female virtue. Yet breast-feeding is not an act of private virtue alone: the Comédie-Française's fund-raising performances on behalf of *mère-nourrices* (breast-feeding mothers), Madame Roland's self-glorifying account of heroically nursing her daughter, and the startling revolutionary images of female goddesses who sustained the people with the milk from their engorged breasts demonstrate the degree to which breast-feeding was understood to be an act of communal virtue.[25] Like Franklin, then, the most profoundly personal aspects of Cécile's life are fully integrated into the public life of the Republic.

The villainous Vernon plots to obstruct the pension Cécile deserves as the widow of a war hero by blackening her late husband's reputation and having him declared a traitor. Vernon's goal is to force Cécile to turn, out of desperation and destitution, to him. Vernon admires neither Cécile's virtue nor the devotion with which she tends her children; he covets her beauty. His devious plan is thwarted by the vigilance of the late husband's devoted friend and fellow soldier Beauval, who, staying in the same boardinghouse with the widow

and the villain, manages to intercept letters, look through keyholes, and, by re-
counting glorious stories of the war, to enlist the boardinghouse domestic to
take part in the surveillance. They trail the malefactor as he scurries around
the capital eavesdropping, gossiping, and provoking in his effort to slander
Cécile's late husband, until, together, they gather enough evidence of the
malefactor's wrongdoing to turn him over to the authorities.

Like Brumaire in *L'Époux républicain,* the villain of *La Veuve du républicain*
acts the role of the honest patriot while he conspires against the Republic and
good republicans: "Aucun ne me soupçonne. On croit à mon civisme" (1.5)
[No one suspects me. Everyone believes in my patriotism], he reassures himself. And he, too, makes reasonable sounding speeches about the potential
dangers revolutionary surveillance poses to blameless people. Surveillance can
be misused for personal ends, Vernon suggests; wrongful accusations can be
lodged on purpose since "on a des ennemis" [people have enemies]. "L'injuste
calomnie" [An unjust calumny], he warns, can destroy an innocent citizen:
"Un soupçon nous expose" (2.4) [One suspicion jeopardizes us]. Vernon thus
tries to confuse his foe by confounding what to Jacobins and their supporters
and sympathizers were two very different matters: calumny and civic denunciation. Accusations made to advance private interests such as greed, jealousy,
and revenge constituted calumny and were not only dangerous but criminal.
And, of course, Vernon is guilty of just this crime when he spreads false rumors about Cécile's late husband.

Denunciations, on the contrary, were accusations made to protect the public good, never to advance a personal desire. Denunciation was a civic responsibility closely tied to the popular practice of surveillance. "[D]enunciation
was a manifestation of revolutionary vigilance," according to Albert Soboul; it
was an important means by which good citizens protected the Republic.[26]
Hence many citizens who had been particularly active during 1793 and 1794
were confused and disconcerted when, after Thermidor and the fall of the revolutionary government, they were reproached or even arrested for having denounced others. Soboul cites Michel, a painter from the Bonne-Nouvelle section, who petitioned authorities after his arrest in the year III (1795): "[I]s it
therefore a crime to have exposed and denounced facts that were true and useful to the public safety? Will disorder, anarchy and confusion reach such a
point that civic denunciations will be likened to those dictated by vested interests, vengeance or cupidity? . . . Nothing short of love of my country guided
me in my denunciations."[27] Like the militant painter Michel, who is puzzled
by the accusations made against him, *La Veuve du républicain* draws a sharp

moral and political distinction between the actions of the defamer Vernon and
those of the patriotic hero Beauval. In the Old Regime the denouncer was de-
spicable because his or her actions helped a corrupt and tyrannical regime to
maintain its illegitimate power. But in the Republic he or she who denounced
a probable criminal protected the public good since the public, the public
good, and Republican authority were, in theory, identical.

Even the methods by which these two types of accusations were lodged
confirmed their profound difference: Vernon goes to work secretly and indi-
rectly, dropping a word here and a hint there:

> Il me faut aux aguets poster la calumnie,
> Jetter sur sa conduite un peu d'ignominie.
> On devient scrupuleux, même en ce pays-ci:
> Ravissons-lui l'honneur d'un ci-devant mari.
> Je suis bien connu de certaine personne,
> La chose ira très bien. (1.5)

> [I must be on the lookout to leak the calumny,
> to cast some disgrace on his conduct.
> They are becoming scrupulous even in this country:
> I'll steal the honor of her former husband from her.
> I'm well-known by a certain someone.
> The plan will come off nicely.]

On the other hand, like Franklin, the patriot with a denunciation to make acts
directly, calls on authorities, and confronts the suspect face-to-face. *La Veuve*'s
hero, Beauval, sees through Vernon's obfuscations and rejects the argument
against surveillance with the same refutation Franklin made to Brumaire:
"Doit-il offenser quand il sert notre cause? Le traître, le méchant craint l'œil
de la vertu; L'honnête homme le cherche, il veut être connu" (2.4). [Should it
(surveillance) give offense when it serves our cause? The traitor, the scoundrel
fears the eye of virtue; the honest man seeks it, he wants to be known.] Beauval, like Franklin, has faith in the Republic's capacity to distinguish between
guilt and innocence. And just as Franklin believed that secrets were necessarily nefarious, since nothing honest would be kept from the public view, Beauval believes that honest people welcome surveillance, and only the dishonest
shun the people's scrutiny, "the eye of virtue."

These plays express the belief that republicanism makes protection of the
individual, the family, and the nation the responsibility of both citizens and
their communities. Communities therefore are called on to practice surveil-

lance just as are individuals. In *Plus de bâtards en France* (No More Bastards in France), a drama by Citoyenne Villeneuve inspired by the law of 12 Brumaire, Year II (November 2, 1793), giving illegitimate children inheritance rights, the misery of an abandoned, illegitimate boy is the concern of a an entire village.[28] The villagers, by spying and pooling their intelligence, discover that the local *ci-devant seigneur* (former lord), having seduced and abandoned a young peasant girl (now dead) years before, is the father of the beloved, penniless, virtuous waif. The former lord, Deternis, is described as a "vieux célibataire" (old bachelor); instead of forming a legitimate union and founding a family, Deternis destroys the lives of poor, vulnerable girls and fails to acknowledge the children he has by them since he considers them of a lower order. The villagers uncover his ongoing project to seduce yet another innocent girl with the aid of a procuring priest. They foil his plans, call official punishment down on him, and remind each other that "un père dénaturé ne pouvait être un bon citoyen" (3.6) [an unnatural father is inherently a bad citizen]. Furthermore, the story ends happily not only because the villain is punished but also because the youth Colas comes to realize that he is no longer a bastard. When Colas tells a village boy that he is all alone in the world, asking, "Je n'ai ni parents, ni famille: à qui tiendrai-je?" [I have neither parents nor family: to whom do I belong?] The good lad responds: "À la République, c'est la mère à tous les bons français, ils sont tes frères" (1.10). [To the Republic, it is the mother of all good Frenchmen and they are your brothers.] This play thus significantly reconceives the family by extending it beyond traditional, biological connection. All the good villagers and, indeed, all good citizens now form a national family. Affective ties that bind spring not from blood—as the example of Deternis demonstrates—but from the shared values of citizenship. The family is therefore, by its very nature, a matter for public concern. For if all the French people (or at least all good French people) now constitute one family, it becomes impossible to distinguish between what is public and what is private.

In *L'Époux républicain* adultery and treason were indistinguishable; similarly, in *La Veuve* and *Plus de bâtards* moral crimes and political crimes go hand in hand. The heartless seducer and unnatural father of *Plus de bâtards* is also a former aristocrat who curses the Revolution and longs for the old days when he could oppress peasants openly and without interference. The exploitative, dishonest suitor of *La Veuve* claims that human beings are so weak they can be happy only as slaves and that therefore Revolution was a mistake (2.6). And just as the villagers of *Plus de bâtards* understand that a bad father is per se a bad citizen, Beauval chastises himself for not having grasped Vernon's plot more quickly: "J'aurais dû le prévoir; un mauvais citoyen ne peut, a nul égard être un homme de bien" (*La Veuve du républicain,* 3.8). [I should have foreseen it; a bad citizen cannot be, in any respect, a good man.]

In another successful play, P.-A.-A. de Piis's *La Nourrice républicaine, ou les plaisirs de l'adoption* (The Republican Wet Nurse, or, The Pleasures of Adoption), the connection between good citizenship and "private" morality is made even more plainly.[29] The eponymous wet nurse and her husband take in the infant son of a rich, aristocratic neighbor, whom, they believe, has left his motherless child and gone away to join the republican army. The good couple discovers that the absent father has, in fact, fled across the border to join enemy forces. They adopt the abandoned baby despite the fact that they are simple peasants and already parents of a large brood. The play ends with the newly constituted, happy family singing together onstage:

> Qu'il faut avoir le cœur méchant
> Qu'il faut avoir de barbarie
> Pour laisser là son pauvre enfant
> Et pour laisser là sa patrie. (1.8)[30]

> [You have to have a wicked heart
> You have to be a barbarian
> To desert your poor child
> And to desert your country.]

These plays share Robespierre's assertion of the fundamental inseparability of "homme" from "citoyen": "Un homme qui manque des vertus publiques, ne peut avoir les vertus privées" [a man who lacks public virtues cannot have private ones].[31] The drama of domestic surveillance thus insists on the identity of personal and political interests and offers one means to protect them both: surveillance.

The dramas of domestic surveillance make clear a persistent revolutionary anxiety about the most private aspects of life, about love, betrayal, and sexuality. These seemed to pose a nearly insuperable obstacle to revolutionary transparency. The closeness of the domestic circle, the intimacies of friendship, and the depths of the human heart potentially blocked the revolutionary will to know and to unveil far more effectively than any deceptions practiced by corrupt politicians could.[32] So these familiar, intimate obstacles exacerbated the need to reveal and the need for surveillance.

When domestic dramas represented characters efficaciously employing surveillance to defend their families, their homes, their communities, and the Republic, they solicited audience members to join them in their efforts to "unravel the plot," for, as we have seen, in these plays the conspiratorial plots and the narrative plots were deeply imbricated. But spectators' surveillance was not only invited in dramas of treason and immorality. Fictional households were opened up to the scrutiny of audiences in comic tales of everyday life. In such cases surveillance was not represented in the intrigue; rather, these plays transformed the fact that plays are meant to be performed before spectators into the play's subject. That is, these plays were all about presenting domestic scenes to audiences' scrutiny. One remarkable and very successful play that exposed an ordinary home to the spectators' observation was *L'Intérieur d'un ménage républicain* (The Interior of a Republican Household) by Armand-Marie-Jacques de Chastenet, marquis de Puységur.[33] Clearly, Parisians enjoyed their position as observers—the play had a healthy run of forty-six performances. *L'Intérieur,* as the title implies, is built less around plot than situation; the play represents the home life of an affluent, patriot family and, through the device of a long-absent governess, demonstrates the happy changes that the Revolution has wrought in the family. The play is sentimental; it enthusiastically appealed to the revolutionary ideals of parental, filial, and conjugal affection. The appreciative review in *Le Moniteur* noted:

> On y trouve en effet des tableaux charmants, d'un intérêt doux et pleins de sensibilité, ceux d'un père et d'une mère parfaitement unis, et qui n'ont pas de meilleur moyen de se temoigner leur tendresse, que de concourir ensemble, chacun suivant ses moyens, à l'éducation de leurs enfants.[34]

> [In fact, one finds charming tableaux full of sensibility and sweetness in the play; those of a father and a mother perfectly united who have no better way to show their tenderness to each other than to work together, each according to his own means, to educate their children.]

L'Intérieur not only stages the continuity of public and private by opening up the domestic interior to public scrutiny; it explicitly takes the coextension of revolutionary politics and private life as its subject. Under the Old Regime the Mirville family—mother, father, Paul, and Amélie—were archetypically unhappy, if not desperately dysfunctional: the children paid no attention to their lessons and felt neglected by their father; the father showed little interest in his wife and children and sought amusement and occupation outside the family circle. While family life under the Old Regime seemed to penalize wife and children especially, *L'Intérieur* emphasizes that fathers and husbands also suffered real losses, even if unwittingly.

Before the Revolution, education in the Mirville household was largely religious. As a result the children felt mystified and stymied. Amélie explains that she could never understand the religious books she was to read and that when she asked the governess, Rose, to explain them, she was denied any enlightenment: "Elle me disait: c'est que ce sujet ne peut se comprendre à votre age" (sc. 1). [She always said to me: it is a subject that you cannot understand at your age.] On the contrary, in the new regime the children's books are "[b]ien plus clairs et bien plus amusants" (sc. 1) [much clearer and much more amusing], and the children's mother always provides honest, comprehensible explanations.

The new world of domestic transparency in the play thus stems at least in part from the revolutionary reaction against what revolutionaries called obfuscation, superstition, and fanaticism, that is Catholicism. But the family's happiness owes even more to the Revolution's destruction of another Old Regime prejudice: aristocratic disdain for the pleasures of family life. In the old days Madame Mirville used to look at her children and sigh, "Hélas! Où donc est leur père?" (sc. 12). [Alas! Where is their father?] Monsieur Mirville was a bad husband and careless father, but the Revolution changed all that, as his wife recounts:

Je te le disais souvent, mon ami; lorsque mille affaires, mille soins étrangers t'occupent sans cesse hors de chez toi, tu ne savais pas ce que tu perdais de jouissances. Ah! Tu dois beaucoup à notre Révolution qui t'a forcé de devenir heureux malgré toi, en remplissant le plus doux de tes devoirs. (sc. 12)

[When a thousand affairs, a thousand outside cares kept you occupied constantly away from your home, I told you often, my friend that you did not know the joys you were missing. Ah! You owe much to our Revolution that forced you, despite yourself, to become happy by fulfilling your most pleasing duties.]

Citizen Mirville owes his personal and familial happiness to the Revolution because it was the Revolution that, in abolishing a social and political order based on aristocratic privilege, also undermined the highly formal, "artificial" aristocratic model of the family, which placed no value on conjugal or filial companionability.

Citizen Mirville acknowledges the profound effect of political life on personal life and even on personal character:

Quand sous un pouvoir arbitraire
Le Français vivait avili
Aux préjugés son caractère
Se trouvait sans cesse asservi.
C'est sous les lois des Républiques
Que l'homme, ayant sa dignité,
Sait jouir de sa liberté,
En reprenant les mœurs antiques. (sc. 12)

[When Frenchmen lived abased,
under an arbitrary power,
their character found itself
ceaselessly subjected to prejudices.
It is under the laws of Republics that man,
regaining his dignity,
knows how to exercise his liberty
by returning to ancient ways.]

Mirville voices an explanation of his conduct that is not so distant from Rousseau's famous insight that "everything depended fundamentally on politics."[35] When he was weak and subservient under the monarchy, Mirville disregarded his family responsibilities in his efforts to succeed and to impress others according to the corrupt standards of the day. Now that he has regained the dignity of republican citizenship, Mirville "exercises his liberty" by joining with his wife to create the kind of family on which the moral and political success of the Republic depends. Home and politics, far from belonging to different spheres, are inextricably and chiastically bound together: no happy home without republican morals; no happy nation without republican homes. Revolutionary politics has a place in every aspect of the Mirville home life—it entered not as an alien force but as a felicitous and integral element.

Within the conceit of *L'Intérieur d'un ménage républicain* the Mirvilles set about to disabuse the newly returned governess, Rose, of her old ideas and to convince her of the rightness of the new order. Rose, a deeply devout woman, has been away on a long pilgrimage and is at first shocked to find the family neglecting religion; the vision of the newly happy, united, and virtuous family, however, brings about a revolution in her ideas. The transformation is so profound that Rose decides to marry, despite the vow of celibacy she made on the death of her husband fourteen years previously. Furthermore, she allows herself to be persuaded by the Mirvilles to marry the new constitutional curé Germance.[36] Germance wants to marry so that he may be a better republican: "Je suis un vieux célibataire, des vains prestiges dégagés, dans mon état il fallait faire, ce qu'exigeait le préjugé, pour tenir rang dans sa patrie, d'hymen il faut subir la loi." [I am an old bachelor, freed from vain distinctions. In my position I had to do what prejudice required; to take one's place in the nation one must wed.][37] Priestly celibacy, Germance now sees, was not only an unhappy state, but it also served no function, except to create social distinctions that separated priests from their fellows. Playwrights must have returned time and again to the theme of the marrying priest or nun in order to offer audiences a sensational thrill, but the abolition of monastic vows was also an extraordinarily serious and contentious political issue. *L'Intérieur* clearly takes marriage to be a political act: the decision to marry on the part of Rose and Germance is a decision to fully participate in the new French nation. For it is only through marriage that these two characters quit the reclusion in which they both had lived and enter into the community. The spouses will be happier for their newfound society, and the lives of their fellow citizens will be enriched by the expansion of the fraternal order. Just as Franklin encouraged Rosalie to marry for her own good and that of the nation, Mirville promotes this marriage, knowing that expanding the number of republican families not only adds to the stability of the nation but also enhances republican citizens' "interior" lives: "Allons ma femme, occupons-nous tout de suite à faire dresser un contrat de mariage, et que l'union de ce nouveau ménage avec le notre augmente encore le bonheur de notre intérieur" (sc. 18). [Come along, my wife, let us get busy right away having a marriage contract drawn up, and may the union of this new household with our own increase the happiness of our interior.][38] That interior, as we have just seen, is one that is perpetually externalized and manifested for its scrutinizing audience.

La Chaste Suzanne *and the Politics of Surveillance*

We can now begin to see why the Vaudeville's *La Chaste Suzanne* provoked such surprising fury. The subject of the play is looking, and it treats this subject in a radically different way from the prosurveillance dramas I have discussed. Indeed, the Vaudeville play thematizes surveillance in ways that conflict with the republican ethos of surveillance—the ethos the fédérés had sworn to uphold. The charges the fédérés and their allies in the city government leveled against *La Chaste Suzanne* were the following: that the play drew parallels between the elders and the deputies at the Convention; that its Suzanne was an allusion to Marie-Antoinette; and, finally, that it "corrupted republican morals," the very morals, I believe, we see upheld in popular domestic dramas.[39]

The Vaudeville play modifies the biblical story of Susannah and the elders only slightly. In the play, Suzanne, an extraordinarily beautiful and virtuous wife and mother, is left alone at home when her husband, Joachim, goes off to lead the armies of Israel. One day Suzanne's maids prepare her bath in the garden and then withdraw to the house, for modesty forbids her to undress and bathe in their presence. Two of the elders, or judges, of Zion, Accaron and Barzabas, have, however, hidden in the garden. They try to make use of Suzanne's surprise and exposure to extort her sexual favors. When Suzanne does not succumb, the elders threaten blackmail. This is, in other words, a biblical story of sexual harassment.

In retaliation for Suzanne's steadfast refusal to meet their demands the elders publicly denounce her: having heard disturbing rumors about Suzanne's behavior, they claim, they personally put her garden under surveillance to discover whether the stories had any merit. There, they allege, they observed her with a young man who escaped and whom they were unable to identify. Suzanne is accused of adultery and brought to trial in the public square. The charges are false, of course, but based on their reputations for wisdom, austerity, and rectitude, the lascivious elders carry the day. Suzanne patiently awaits death by stoning when the intervention of Daniel, with his lawyerly skills, trips up the elders and reveals their slanderous fabrication. Daniel separates the two accusers, and when, in response to his precise questioning, they offer differing accounts of the crime they claim to have witnessed, their plot is revealed, Suzanne is vindicated, and the elders are condemned.

La Chaste Suzanne stages surveillance, but it does so in a manner that contrasts markedly with the surveillance dramatized in *L'Époux républicain.* Unlike Franklin's home, for example, which is represented as porous and completely continuous with the *quartier,* Suzanne's garden is marked out as a private, sacred domain, forbidden to men, which the elders knowingly violate. Thus even while he excitedly awaits the spectacle of Suzanne bathing, Accaron worries: "Je ne puis me défendre d'un certain frémissement à l'aspect de cette enceinte sacrée, ou nul Israélite, nul homme ne peut pénétrer sans crime." [I can't keep myself from shuddering at the sight of this sacred place which no Israelite, no man, can penetrate without committing a crime.][40] Privacy, an inherently suspicious idea in *L'Époux républicain,* is a sacred value in the world staged by *La Chaste Suzanne.* Thus the mere presence of any man, or any outsider, in Suzanne's private realm is criminalized.

The Vaudeville play departs significantly from its biblical source in its representation of Suzanne's house and garden; indeed, the Vaudeville playwrights invented the garden's private, sacred character. In the Bible story Susannah's garden is described explicitly as a public place: "Or Joachim étoit fort riche, et il avoit un jardin fruitier près de sa maison; et les Juifs alloient souvent chez lui, parce qu'il étoit le plus considérable de tous." [Joachim was very rich and he had a fruit garden adjoining his house, and the Jews frequently met at his house because he was the man of greatest distinction among them.]⁴¹ Furthermore, Joachim and Susannah's house had a public function: "Ces vieillards alloient d'ordinaire à la maison de Joachim, et tous ceux qui avoient des affaires à juger venoient les y trouver." [These men (the judges) were constantly at Joachim's house, and everyone who had a case to be tried came to them there.]⁴² The Bible, unlike the play, depicts the house and garden as heavily trafficked places continuous with the larger world of the community. The playwrights altered the story to separate the private from the public and to emphasize the violation of the private.

Not only does the Vaudeville play insist on the absolute privacy of the home, however; it also self-consciously invokes surveillance. For the elders employ the political language of surveillance in jest, poking fun at their own illicit enterprise. Barzabas, who spent the entire night in the garden hoping for a peek at the object of his weary desire, reports that "pendant toute cette nuit éternelle; à mes yeux rien ne s'est offert; J'ai vainement fait sentinelle" [throughout this eternal night there was nothing to see; I played the sentinel in vain].⁴³ Rather than seeking to expose crime, as does Franklin's faithful servants' surveillance, the elders' spying is itself criminal in intent. Indeed, the elders' spying is not simply the prelude to an erotic act—it *is* their erotic act. For the play mercilessly mocks the elders' physical infirmities; as they themselves constantly remind each other, their rheumatism, their gout, and their fatigue will inevitably preclude the possibility of acting on their desires. And when Suzanne does appear and begin to undress, the two are reduced to inarticulate cries of "Voyez-vous? voyez-vous?" (1.7) [Do you see? Do you see?].

The crisis of the play, and the crisis I think for the soldiers whom it enraged, springs from the fact that these lecherous elders are respected politicians entrusted by the people with the preservation of community morality: the judge at Suzanne's trial reminds them: "Vous avez été élevés à la dignité de juges par le suffrage du peuple; il vous a nommés entre tous les sages de Babylone" (2.2). [You have been elevated to the dignified position of judges by the people's suffrage; the people chose you from among all the sages of Babylon.]

The people, gathered in the public square to witness Suzanne's trial, are thus shocked by the betrayal of their faith and by the true character of their wise men: "Quoi! Barzabas, le modèle des sages! L'incorruptible et sévère Accaron! Quoi, ce sont eux!" (2.2). [What! Barzabas, the model of sages! The incorruptible and severe Accaron! What, it is they!], exclaims the crowd.[44] And if the elders' moral character is put into question, is not also the surveillance that they practice? For it is they who have invoked surveillance as a valuable tool of the state in controlling crime—here Suzanne's supposed adultery—only to have it revealed that surveillance was just a clever political camouflage for their own compulsion to look.

La Chaste Suzanne seems to offer a full-fledged critique of surveillance and of the Jacobin politicians who advocated it.[45] Surveillance, as the play represents it, is nothing other than officially sanctioned voyeurism. This was a critique bound to unnerve the fédérés especially. For the fédérés were closely tied to the Jacobins and shared their political ideals; the January 13, 1793, issue of the *Moniteur* reports that:

> Des fédérés de divers départements de la République arrivés à Paris . . . sont venus [à la Commune] déclarer qu'ils se réuniraient tous les jours, depuis onze heures du matin, jusqu'à quatre heures du soir, dans la salle de la Société des Amis de la Liberté et de l'Egalité, aux Jacobins, pour se concerter entre eux sur les moyens de conserver les droits imprescriptibles des hommes et l'unité indivisible de la République.[46]

> [Some Fédérés who have come to Paris from the diverse departments of the Republic . . . went to the Commune to announce that they will convene every day from eleven o'clock in the morning until four in the afternoon in the hall of the Society of the Friends of Liberty and Equality (the Jacobin club) in order to work together toward the conservation of the inalienable rights of man and the indivisible unity of the Republic.]

Not only did the play suggest that the Jacobin politics to which the fédérés were committed was a cynical hoax, but it suggested something far worse; for while the soldiers were away from home defending the Republic, they counted on the Republic to care for and defend their families. But *La Chaste Suzanne* implied that the politics of surveillance was all a maneuver to disguise republican politicians' lascivious looking and that, just as in Joachim's case, the political leaders who sent them off to war might, in fact, seek to take advantage of their absence from home. Joachim's absence and his military vocation— both innovations of the playwrights lacking in the biblical story—suggest a resemblance between Suzanne's husband and the volunteer soldiers. In *Révolutions de Paris* Louis-Marie Prudhomme hints that the play makes this suggestion when he reminds his readers that the fédérés had been away from home for more than eight months and were naturally anxious to see their wives.[47] The play's implication that Jacobin surveillance was not the exercise of true democratic patriotism but that, on the contrary, it masked the oldest, Tarquinian form of tyranny was too much for the soldiers to bear.

But the play did not attack "republican morals" only in its critique of surveillance; it also undermined them by exalting the spectacularly beautiful Suzanne. For if the play condemns surveillance in its condemnation of the elders, it also celebrates spectacle, the same theatrical power revolutionaries associated with the monarchy, when it acquits Suzanne. For although Suzanne does not knowingly present herself to the elders' gaze, she does deliberately make herself an object of the audience's gaze. *La Chaste Suzanne* frequently acknowledges the audience's presence, and, especially in the musical numbers, it appeals to the spectators directly. Thus if within the action of the play Suzanne is seen by the elders without her knowledge, outside of the plot but within the structure of the play *qua* play Suzanne self-consciously exhibits herself and solicits the spectator's gaze.[48] Suzanne seduces the spectators even as she struggles against the elders' aggression.

This, I think, accounts for the otherwise startling assumption that the figure of the chaste Suzanne alluded to the anything-but-chaste Marie-Antoinette. I say startling because, after all, as a newspaper article dismissing the association pointed out, "[L]e surnom d'Antoinette donné depuis dix ans à toutes les filles de la rue Saint-Honoré, montre assez combien il y a peu de rapport entre la veuve Capet et la chaste Suzanne." [That the surname 'Antoinette' has been given to all the girls of the rue Saint-Honoré (i.e., prostitutes) for the last ten years demonstrates how little there is in common between the widow Capet (Marie-Antoinette) and the chaste Suzanne.][49] But the association of the two is less surprising if we remember that Marie-Antoinette was *the* focal point for revolutionary male anxiety about the power of the spectacular woman. Marie-Antoinette's beauty and charm were considered so seductive that many republicans feared she could entice nearly anyone into her web of counterrevolutionary intrigue. She was also thought to be a skilled actress, and along with her beauty, her prodigious powers of dissimulation made her one of the Republic's greatest threats.[50] Her physical presence, her appearance, exercised enormous power: "Marie-Antoinette's force of attraction," argues Chantal Thomas, "analogous to that which movie stars of the twentieth century radiate, had its source in the queen's intimate passion for the magic of appearance."[51]

What the chaste Suzanne and Marie-Antoinette share is the power of spectacle—the tyrannical power over others that their appearance lends them.[52] For even while Suzanne seems to be a defenseless victim of the elders' illicit desire and misappropriated authority, the Vaudeville play refers constantly to the disarming, indeed, unmanning effects Suzanne's beauty produces on her tormenters. In the first scene in the garden, for example, Accaron warns Barzabas not to look on Suzanne's unveiled beauty for fear that it will overpower him and render him incapable of carrying out their nefarious plot. Later, in the public square, when the judges demand that Suzanne remove her veil, the better to ascertain her guilt or innocence, the two accusers, according to stage directions, "[R]estent comme pétrifiés à l'aspect de Suzanne" [remain as if petrified by the sight of Suzanne], and Barzabas confesses his weakness before Suzanne's beauty to his accomplice: "Ah mon ami, qu'elle est belle! je ne saurais soutenir sa vue" (2.2). [Oh my friend, she is so beautiful! I cannot withstand the sight of her.] This, too, is a departure from the Bible. In the biblical story the elders themselves demand that Susannah remove her veil "afin qu'ils se satisfassent au moins en cette manière par la vue de sa beauté" [so that they could satisfy themselves in this manner at least with the sight of her beauty].[53] In other words, the force Suzanne's beauty exerts over those who look at her is the playwrights' invention. And finally, Accaron and Barzabas claim that, innocent at heart, they have in fact been victimized by Suzanne's great beauty: "C'est vous, oui, vous, qui me rendez coupable, beauté trop aimable" (1.7). [It's you, yes you, who have made me guilty, too adorable beauty.]

But while in the case of Marie-Antoinette the power of spectacular female beauty is—medusa-like—inherently malevolent, the story of Susannah and the elders shows that God himself condones, indeed celebrates, the power of beauty.[54] There is no incompatibility between Suzanne's status as spectacle and her purity. Certainly, the elders' attempts to portray themselves as victims of beauty's tyrannical force fail miserably. And neither Suzanne's beauty nor the power it has to compel all to look at her is indicted. The play does not deny that Suzanne's beauty produces these spectacular effects; indeed, it underscores the theatrical force of her beauty—its powerful, perhaps overpowering, effect on viewers—and finds it nonetheless innocent. In a sense, Suzanne stands for the seductive power of theater itself; the figure of the beautiful woman often served as an allegory for the work of art. Certainly, theater seemed to possess such a dangerous feminine power for Rousseau, Jean Starobinski argues: "Le spectacle-objet nous volait notre liberté et nous nous immobilisions comme des choses dans la salle obscure: nous étions pétrifiés par un regard de Méduse." [The spectacle-object stole our freedom and immobilized us, like things in the darkened theater: we were petrified by Medusa's gaze.][55] For antitheatricalists of the Rousseauian strain theater itself acts like a Medusa's head: it stupefies, objectifies, and disempowers. When *La Chaste Suzanne* acquitted Suzanne, it acquitted theater. For the fédérés, who saw Suzanne as a figure for Marie-Antoinette, *La Chaste Suzanne*'s celebration of spectacle and demonization of surveillance amounted to a rehabilitation of the twin pillars of the ancien régime: spectacle and monarchy.

The rise of the drama of domestic surveillance and the violence provoked by the performance of *La Chaste Suzanne* expose the tensions generated as revolutionary French society sought to establish publicity as a primary cultural value. The notion that publicity was the Republic's most vital safeguard against its enemies and that it therefore must be extended to every household, the idea that "nothing is unimportant in a Republic," as Romarin asserts in *L'Époux républicain,* inevitably required a rethinking of the home and its relation to the world beyond it. Dramas like *L'Époux républicain* sought to allay fears about opening up the private to public scrutiny; *La Chaste Suzanne* exacerbated those fears with its depiction of surveillance as voyeurism. Moreover, publicity per se, not only when publicity meant publicizing private lives, produced anxiety. For theatricality, as a particular mode of public representation, threatened to subvert publicity from within by transforming a mode of exposing truth into a method of deceiving and manipulating. Such anxiety made surveillance—the practice meant to detect and defeat theatricality—a central element of the revolutionary imagination as well as of revolutionary practice.[56]

The violence produced by *La Chaste Suzanne* makes manifest a clash between two visions of surveillance and privacy. The successful domestic dramas presented a republican conception according to which surveillance was a popular practice exercised by ordinary citizens in defense of their homes, their families, their neighborhoods, and their Republic. The Vaudeville play, on the other hand, represents surveillance not only as criminal and invasive but also as a clever deception practiced on credulous dupes by corrupt politicians. And while domestic dramas imagine a continuity between the home and the world, the domestic and the political, *La Chaste Suzanne* suggests that the home must be protected, even walled off, from politics. When the fédérés attacked *La Chaste Suzanne,* they were defending a republican conception of surveillance and a republican idea of the home against a view they could only characterize as counterrevolutionary. That such a conflict found its representation in the theater (and that such a confrontation occurred in a theater) attests both to revolutionary drama's seriousness and meaningfulness and to theater's centrality in revolutionary culture.

Totality and Fragmentation

If under the Old Regime what we would now call private life was conceived of as a lower domain, necessary for the reproduction of life, while the public sphere was the higher realm in which civilization was created and advanced and in which, therefore, the self could realize his or her highest capacities, as Richard Sennett has famously argued, then we must conclude that the radical Republic did not so much reverse the priority of the two spheres as seek to integrate them.[57] The nineteenth century eventually elaborated an ideology of individual freedom that depended on a strict demarcation of the home and the world, that is on the idea of a sacrosanct domestic space that seemed to operate according to principles antithetical to those of the market and, perhaps most crucially, that no state intrusion could violate.[58] During the first French Republic, on the contrary, popular drama, especially the drama of domestic surveillance, expressed a desire for an essential union of private and public and a belief that the same principles were at the heart of both.

This drama imagines a culture in which the individual's division into "man" and "citizen"—a division the nineteenth-century bourgeois orders would enshrine—is not so much transcended as erased. These plays represent the degree to which the revolutionary culture expressed the desire to make "public affairs as such . . . the general affair of each individual" and "the political function . . . the individual and the general function," as Marx put it, since this very theme—that is, the way in which public affairs become the affair of each individual and the political function becomes the individual and the general function—was explicitly staged in them. The fact that they drew large, enthusiastic, participatory audiences further reveals this desire.[59] If a play like *L'Époux républicain* seems frightening for the ease with which the protagonist is able to dispense with his wife and the politicization of human relations that this ease implies, the favor with which it was received does not necessarily attest to the cold-bloodedness of revolutionary spectators, as nineteenth-century critics contended. It could demonstrate spectators' embrace of something akin to Marx's definition of true emancipation. For the young Marx, very much interested in the French Revolution, true emancipation occurs only when "the real, individual man re-absorbs in himself the abstract citizen, and as an individual human being has become a species-being in his everyday life, in his particular work, and in his particular situation."[60] Liberation, according to Marx, means the union of the abstract, juridical being—the citizen—and the sensual, concrete being—the man—in the individual's particular, concrete existence. But for Marx this unified individual must also overcome the artificially produced isolation that prevents the realization and expression of an essential human connectedness in order to be truly free. The realization of this human community by characters whose particular and political existences are inextricable is precisely the subject of the revolutionary dramas I have discussed here. And that inextricability is often manifested through surveillance. It was perhaps this optimistic vision of liberation and fraternity that revolutionary audiences espoused when they applauded and cheered these plays.

At its most radical, revolutionary culture did not conceive of the individual citizen as an atom emptied of all concrete particularity, as Hegel argued famously in the *Phenomenology of Spirit;* rather, this culture sought to break down barriers between the individual and the community. As one Paris section put it: "Nothing about the patriot is simply personal; he shares everything with the larger community: happiness, sadness, everything is openly communicated in the arms of his brothers, and here you see the source of the publicness that distinguishes fraternal, that is republican, governance."[61] The republican citizen was not imagined to be void of emotional and biographical particularity; on the contrary, the emotions and states we tend to ascribe to the private domain—love, familial betrayal, and so forth—were, at least in theory, to be lived and shared in public, by the community. Fraternity, for staunch republicans, meant that all French people now belonged to one national, revolutionary family; consequently, not only all their interests but also all their sentiments were shared.

With the fall of the Jacobin Republic and the onset of the Thermidorian reaction in the summer of 1794, a new view of the relation between the home and the world began to emerge. What had seemed a natural interconnection between the political and the personal in revolutionary republican plays now appeared to be dangerous invasion of the private by political power just as *La Chaste Suzanne* had asserted. Jean-Antoine Lebrun-Tossa's *Arabelle et Vascos, ou les Jacobins de Goa,* an event-packed gothic drama that failed when it premiered in July 1794 but succeeded a year later, registers this shift.[62] *Les Jacobins de Goa* portrays Jacobin politicians in the guise of their namesakes, Jacobin monks, and characterizes their surveillance as a power-hungry, vaguely sexually charged, inquisition. The play opens with the heroine's nurse, Cymbeline, trying to elude the Jacobin:

> CYMBELINE. Quelqu'un paraît. . . . C'est le père jacobin. . . . O le vilain homme! Il ne vient que pour épier les secrets de la maison, évitons sa rencontre.
> LE JACOBIN. Où allez-vous donc, Cymbeline? Vous me fuyez, je crois.
> CYMBELINE. Mes occupations m'appellent ailleurs, mille pardons.
> LE JACOBIN. Vos occupations! Vous en avez donc beaucoup?
> CYMBELINE. J'en aurais bien de plus si je me mêlais, comme tant de gens, de celles des autres. (1.1)

> [CYMBELINE. Someone is coming. . . . It's the Jacobin father. . . . Oh the vile man! He only comes here to spy on the secrets of the house, I'll avoid him.
> LE JACOBIN. Where are you going Cymbeline? You are running away from me I believe.
> CYMBELINE. My responsibilities summon me elsewhere, a thousand pardons.
> LE JACOBIN. Your responsibilities! You have many of them then?
> CYMBELINE. I would have many more if I interfered, as so many other people do, in those of others.]

In the domestic dramas I discussed earlier secrets were inherently criminal, and those who harbored them were double-dealing villains. In *Les Jacobins de Goa*, however, it seems natural that houses would have secrets that they would want to protect and that those who would seek to uncover those secrets were "vile" interlopers. Cymbeline's smart remark tells the Jacobin priest that good people take care of their own responsibilities, mind their own business, and keep their noses out of the affairs of others. This opening dialogue marks a brusque shift in sensibility; no longer are the affairs of the household legitimate matters of interest for the wider community; no longer are troubles to be shared with one's fellows. Now it is ethical to limit one's sphere of interest to one's household and unethical to "interfere" in the lives of one's neighbors. Perhaps most telling of all, the figure of the spy is wholly altered. The loyal companion, the friendly villager, the heroic soldier have been replaced by the hypocritical, power-driven priest. If the malicious but comic elders of *La Chaste Suzanne* are the crude precursors to the Jacobin priest of Goa, he, in turn, is the not-so-distant ancestor of Balzac's diabolical master spy Vautrin.

The drama of domestic surveillance expresses a longing for and a vision of revolutionary totality.[63] In these plays virtuous characters belong to a larger whole, and interests that could be seen as competing—for example, those of the individual against those of society, those of the private against those of the public—are in fact concordant. Indeed, the plays put forward the view that the Revolution makes it possible for the individual to overcome the fragmentation of his or her existence: to be a good citizen, a good mother, a good neighbor, a good republican are all one. With *Les Jacobins de Goa,* on the other hand, we see emerging a new liberal conception of society and identity. Here emotional life and family life are not only utterly severed from the larger community and from the political; they are necessarily so. This is a glimpse of the world to come, a world in which freedom requires precisely the fragmentation of life the revolutionaries tried to overcome.

▊ Notes

Introduction

1. On participatory democracy see Pateman, *Participation and Democratic Theory.* The literature on the French Revolution is too vast to list here. For a helpful overview see Doyle, *Origins of the French Revolution.*

2. *Du Contrat social,* bk. 3, chap. 15. "Le peuple Anglais pense être libre; il se trompe fort, il ne l'est que durant l'élection des membres du parlement; sitôt qu'ils sont élus, il est esclave, il n'est rien" (Rousseau, *Œuvres complètes,* 3:430). Maurice Cranston translates this passage: "The English people believes itself to be free; it is gravely mistaken; it is free only during the election of Members of Parliament; as soon as the Members are elected, the people is enslaved; it is nothing" (Rousseau, *The Social Contract,* 141).

3. Unfortunately, Paul Friedland's *Political Actors* was published after the completion of this book, so I cannot address it in the body of this study. (1) Friedland asserts that representative democracy was established on firm and stable grounds in 1789; he argues that the revolutionary government easily pacified and excluded the citizenry. Occasional "disturbances" did not undermine or threaten the hegemony of representation. I argue that representative politics remained deeply unstable during the revolutionary period, that politicians remained anxious and ambivalent about political representation, and that many citizens persisted in rejecting the representative model. (2) Friedland argues that the French Revolution was highly theatrical and that politics and theater were indistinguishable, and theater, for Friedland, means actors, not plays. I oppose this view—which is held by many others, most importantly by Marie-Hélène Huet (see note 4 of this chapter below) and develop an alternative account of the relation between politics and theatricality in chapters 2 and 3. While I will not rehearse that argument here, I will note that Friedland's use of the term *theatricality* is vague: for example, for Friedland events that take place in public seem necessarily to be theatrical, or the participation of an actor in the military or in politics (not qua actor but rather as a citizen) by necessity implies a theatricalizing of those spheres. In fact, as I discuss in chapter 2, the term *theatricality,* as it was conceptualized in the eighteenth century, is extraordinarily complex. (3) Friedland argues that spectators in theaters were passive, with the insignificant exception of a few audience disturbances. I have not found this to be the case; indeed, the actions of audiences in theaters

were central to the development of alternative democratic theories and practices. (Ravel, in *The Contested Parterre,* also argues for an undisciplined and active audience.) Moreover, when Friedland himself cites contemporaries complaining that politics too closely resembled theater, in every case their point is that the spectators to political debates were too raucous, active, and interventionist. In other words the very contemporaries Friedland cites viewed theater audiences not only as far from passive but indeed as overly empowered and threatening. Finally, while Friedland presents deeply interesting work on actors, he does not discuss revolutionary plays at any length.

4. See Huet, *Rehearsing the Revolution.*

5. For my thinking on theatricality I am most indebted to Michael Fried, *Absorption and Theatricality;* and David Marshall, *The Figure of Theater.*

6. Denis Diderot is probably the most important source for the aesthetics of a touching, moving theater, as well as for the conceptualization of its potential social effects. Diderot elaborates his vision of a new drama in the *Entretiens sur le fils naturel* and *De la poésie dramatique.* The opposition between manipulating and touching can be seen as roughly analogous to the opposition Diderot makes between *coup de théâtre* and *tableau.* See chapter 2 for more on this distinction. Diderot later problematizes the opposition between touching and manipulating in *La Religieuse.*

7. For the term *transparency,* and the problematic of transparency and obstacle, I am indebted to Starobinski's absolutely crucial book *Jean-Jacques Rousseau.* On transparency and revolutionary theater see the excellent essay by James H. Johnson, "Revolutionary Audiences and the Impossible Imperatives of Fraternity."

8. Cited in Habermas, *Between Facts and Norms,* 466–467.

9. Clark, "Painting in the Year Two," 20.

10. See Vovelle, *Idéologies et mentalités;* and Vovelle, *La Mentalité révolutionnaire: Société et mentalités sous la Révolution française.*

11. See below note 24; and Carlson, *Theatre of the French Revolution.*

12. For an excellent account of the development of the political culture approach to French Revolution studies see Desan, "What's after Political Culture?"

13. Hunt, *Politics, Culture, and Class,* 1.

14. Ragan and Williams, *Re-Creating Authority in Revolutionary France,* 3.

15. Cited in ibid.

16. See Kennedy, *Cultural History of the French Revolution.* Some of the results of this ongoing research have been published in Emmet Kennedy et al., *Theatre, Opera, and Audiences.*

17. Greenblatt, *Learning to Curse,* 158.

18. Gallagher and Greenblatt, *Practicing New Historicism,* 9.

19. Habermas, *Between Facts and Norms,* 486.

20. Before the advent of Marxist and other socioeconomic interpretations, historians often attributed the creation of a revolutionary impulse and the content of

revolutionary ideas to the major thinkers of the Enlightenment such as Montesquieu, Voltaire, and Rousseau. See, e.g., Alexis de Tocqueville, *The Old Regime and the French Revolution;* Hippolyte Taine, *Les Origines de la France contemporaine;* and Mornet, *Les Origines intellectuelles de la Révolution française.* On the press and the Revolution see Censer, *French Press in the Age of Enlightenment;* Censer and Popkin, *Press and Politics in Pre-Revolutionary France;* and Darnton and Roche, *Revolution in Print.*

21. In *The Contested Parterre* Jeffrey Ravel shows that from the seventeenth century through the eighteenth the theater was a central public institution and that it was in no way simply a repair for the aristocracy. Ravel demonstrates that even during the height of absolutism, the theater was often active and unruly; the pit often successfully exerted its authority.

22. The theater clearly was beyond the means of the poor, but John Lough argues in *Paris Theatre Audiences in the Seventeenth and Eighteenth Centuries* that the middle class made up the "backbone of the parterre" (188) and that schoolboys and students regularly attended. In addition, he argues that there is "evidence to show that a slightly more plebeian element found its way into the two main theatres" in the last two decades of the Old Regime (206). On the social composition of the theater public see also Ravel, *The Contested Parterre;* and Rougemont, *La Vie théâtrale,* 213–233.

23. On the popular boulevard theaters see Root-Bernstein's excellent study, *Boulevard Theater and Revolution.*

24. Of these only Olympe de Gouges has generated any recent critical interest. Although Chénier was considered the most important literary figure of his time during the early years of the Revolution, his reputation was diminished even before his death, and his literary historical position has been eclipsed by that of his less fortunate brother, the poet André Chénier. On Olympe de Gouges see Court, "Un Mélodrame d'Olympe de Gouges"; Nesci, "La Passion de l'impropre"; Ratsaby, "Olympe de Gouges et le théâtre de la Révolution française"; Scott, "The Imagination of Olympe de Gouges"; Vanpée, "The Trials of Olympe de Gouges"; Verdier, "From Reform to Revolution"; and Trouille, "Amazons of the Pen."

25. Etienne and Martainville, *Histoire du théâtre français.* Perhaps because of their personal acquaintance with many of the people and events they describe, this history is more evenhanded than most. See also Ernest-Charles, "L'Action du théâtre"; D'Estrée, *Le Théâtre sous la Terreur;* Fournel, "Le Parterre sous la Révolution"; Hérissay, *Le Monde des théâtres pendant la Révolution;* Jauffret, *Le Théâtre révolutionnaire;* Lumière, *Le Théâtre français pendant la Révolution;* Pougin, *La Comédie-Française et la Révolution;* Welschinger, *Le Théâtre de la Révolution.*

26. Camus, *The Rebel,* 253.

27. Ernest-Charles, "L'Action du théâtre sur l'opinion publique," 583.

28. Goncourt and Goncourt, *L'Histoire de la société française pendant la Révolution,* 140.

29. There are some notable exceptions. See, e.g., Hyslop, "The Theater during a Crisis"; and Carlson, *Theatre of the French Revolution.* Carlson's book poses a problem for a history of the scholarly literature on the revolutionary theater. Although it was published in 1966, the book seems to belong more to the nineteenth century than to the twentieth. On the one hand, it is based overwhelmingly on nineteenth-century histories rather than on original research. On the other hand, Carlson sometimes outdoes conservative nineteenth-century critics in his contempt for his subjects. Olympe de Gouges, a playwright who had four plays performed in major theaters during the Revolution and who died on the scaffold in 1793 at the age of thirty-eight, is described as "an ugly and irascible old lady whose works proved that *pièces de circonstance* were not necessarily successful even in the receptive surroundings of revolutionary Paris" (148); theater audiences are described as "the fickle and violent mob" (v). Carlson is also uninterested in the plays themselves (vi).

30. The expression "there is nothing outside of the text" [il n'y a pas de hors-texte] comes from Jacques Derrida. See Derrida, *Of Grammatology,* 158.

31. *Rapport des MM. les commissaires nommés par la commune relativement aux spectacles,* 10.

32. This tract was originally published in 1772. I have consulted the reprint that was presented to the imperial Institut de France (Paris, 1807), 1–2.

33. Although Paris had three official theaters, only one, the Théâtre français, performed French tragedies and high comedies. The Opéra was, obviously enough, a musical theater, and the Comédie-Italienne, which had originally staged plays in the Italian language, had largely become by the late eighteenth century a home for comic opera.

34. On the status of actors see Duvignaud, *La Sociologie de l'acteur.* Duvignaud argues that the Revolution marked an important transition, indeed a rupture, in the condition and in the consciousness of the actor. See also Rougemont, *La Vie théâtrale,* 193–212.

35. Millin de Grandmaison, *Sur la liberté du théâtre,* 6.

36. Ibid., 7. The *Mercure français,* Dec. 1, 1792, similarly argues that tyrannical governments forbid the theatrical representation of important problems or events and that the theater suffers aesthetically as a result:

Toutes ces entraves éteignirent presque entièrement le génie dramatique; aussi de nos jours, la scène comique n'a presque plus à nous présenter que des intrigues romanesques, ou, ce qui est encore pis, des intrigues de boudoirs, de petites jalousies, et toujours des mariages entre des comtesses et des marquis, des baronnes et des chevaliers. . . . Sous un gouvernement Monarchique, où la cour est tout . . . on n'a sans doute rien de mieux à faire que de toucher des ressorts amoureux pour arriver au cœur. Mais dans une République, et surtout dans une République naissante, le Génie doit parcourir une plus vaste carrière, et c'est surtout au théâtre qu'il a des moyens de se déployer.

[All these obstacles nearly extinguished dramatic genius altogether; hence today the comic stage hardly presents anything other than romanesque intrigues or, even worse, tales of boudoirs, petty jealousies, and always marriages between countesses and marquis, baronesses and knights. . . . Under a monarchic government, where the court is everything, . . . no doubt one has nothing better to do than to play the strings of love in order to touch hearts. But in a republic, and especially in a nascent republic, genius must have a vast career, and it is above all in the theater that genius can show itself.]

See chapter 1 for more on the idea that the theater had been corrupted by the novel.

37. See Kennedy et al., *Theatre, Opera, and Audiences.*

38. Attributed to Citoyenne Villeneuve (Paris, An III [1795]). The play was first performed at the Théâtre de la Cité on the fourth jour complémentaire, an II (Sept. 20, 1794).

39. On the origin of melodrama in the French Revolution see Brooks, *The Melodramatic Imagination.*

40. It does seem fair to say, however, that the largely bad theater of the Revolution is no worse than the largely bad theater of the decades preceding the Revolution, none of which, with the important exception of Beaumarchais, is read or performed today. The fact that the theater of the Revolution is singled out for scorn seems to indicate the persistence of the belief that worthwhile art is incompatible with politics.

One   Resisting Representation

The epigraph to this chapter has been translated by Maurice Cranston: "One can judge, however, the embarrassment the crowd sometimes caused from what happened at the time of the Gracchi, when a great part of the citizens voted from the rooftops" (Rousseau, *The Social Contract,* 142).

1. *Séance* of Dec. 27, 1792, *Archives parlementaires,* 1st ser., 55:710, 724. Although Treilhard was the elected president of the Convention for the period from December 27 to January 19, Barère, as *ancien président,* took the chair on December 26 and 27, when former president Defermon had vacated the position and Treilhard had not yet taken his place. All translations are my own unless otherwise indicated. For an extensive account of the development and evolution of the rules governing the legislative sessions see Brasart, *Paroles de la Révolution.*

2. *Séance* of Dec. 26, 1792, *Archives parlementaires,* 1st ser., 55:634.

3. *Séance* of Dec. 14, 1792, *Archives parlementaires,* 1st ser., 55:45–48. Manuel was an early minor hero of the Revolution. Under the Old Regime he had been imprisoned in the Bastille for his unacceptable writings. In 1789 he turned this ex-

perience to his advantage with the publication of a successful book about the Bastille. His views, however, were moderate, and he was executed in 1793.

4. See esp. Baker, *Inventing the French Revolution;* and Gauchet, *La Révolution des pouvoirs.*

5. Furet, *Interpreting the French Revolution,* 48. Keith Michael Baker shows that eighteenth-century concepts of representation were complex and often in conflict. Baker identifies, in addition to Rousseau's political theory, a judicial theory of representation (put forward by the *parlements*) and a social theory of representation (largely associated with the physiocrats). Baker argues that revolutionary politicians for the most part accepted representation: he attributes to Emmanuel-Joseph Sièyes the elaboration of the revolutionary theory of representation that combined elements from the physiocrats, Adam Smith, and Rousseau (see Baker, "Representation"). For more on the variety of theories of political representation from Hobbes through the present see Pitkin, *The Concept of Representation.*

6. This is surprising given the important and authoritative work that has shown just how difficult and profound a problem representation posed for eighteenth-century French culture. Lynn Hunt demonstrates that the French Revolution provoked a "crisis of representation" in which revolutionaries "came to question the very act of representation itself" (Hunt, *Politics, Culture, and Class,* 88). Representation seemed to occlude—to establish difference between the object and the subject of representation—which was unacceptable in a society obsessed with transparency, unmasking, and unveiling. Thus, Hunt cites an anonymous newspaper writer who urged that "the people should be accustomed to see in a statue only stone and in an image only canvas and colors" (91). In *Absorption and Theatricality* Michael Fried shows that from the mid-eighteenth century French painters increasingly believed that painting must surmount the potential theatricality inherent in artistic representation—i.e., that paintings are meant to be exposed to the view of beholders—in order to be successful. Artists therefore devised a variety of strategies, notably the portrayal of absorption, that would negate the presence of the viewer. This painterly imperative corresponded to a widespread critical sense (articulated most importantly by Denis Diderot) that theatricality vitiated artistic and dramatic representation. Finally, Jacques Derrida has demonstrated that what troubled Jean-Jacques Rousseau, the single most important intellectual figure for the French Revolution, so greatly about the theater "is not the content of the spectacle, the sense *represented* by it, although that *too* he criticizes: it is re-presentation itself. Exactly as within the political order, the menace has the shape of the representative" (Derrida, *Of Grammatology,* 304).

7. See Soboul, *The Sans-Culottes,* 95–134. Although Soboul's work goes a long way toward demonstrating the coherence and breadth of this popular political philosophy, Soboul himself, because of the rigidity of his Marxist framework, hesitates to recognize it fully. The classic work on crowd actions during the Revolution is George Rudé, *The Crowd in the French Revolution;* unfortunately Rudé's ac-

count is a material-social determinist one. For Rudé, riots are meaningful only in that they reflect (i.e., represent) the class interests of the rioters; the meaning of riots can be determined by ascertaining the (preformed) class interests of the rioters. For an extremely influential cultural materialist interpretation of riots, especially food riots, see Thompson, *Customs in Common,* chap. 4. Thompson argues that food riots cannot be understood as merely instinctual responses to hunger; rather, crowd actions must be understood within the complex framework of the actors' beliefs about food and about their culture's economic and social organization.

8. Huet, *Rehearsing the Revolution,* 3.

9. Bryson, *The Chastised Stage,* 114.

10. Huet, *Rehearsing the Revolution,* 35.

11. This view is not without justification. At different times various revolutionary political authorities did seek to harness the theater and transform it into a means of what they termed "public education." For example, in his memoirs Bailly explained that he opposed freedom of the theater because he believed that "[l]e spectacle est une partie de l'enseignement public qui ne doit pas être livrée à tout le monde, et que l'administration doit surveiller" (Bailly, *Mémoires,* 2:286) [the theater is a part of public education that should not be handed over to just anyone and that the administration should watch over]. In 1793–1794 the government ordered the regular performance of certain plays such as Voltaire's *La Mort de César* and Antoine-Marin Lemierre's *Guillaume Tell* "par et pour le peuple." But what is notable, in every instance, is that such efforts to control the theater proved largely ineffective.

12. See Habermas, *Structural Transformation.* Habermas's concept of the public sphere—especially his emphasis on the centrality of writing to its construction— has been important to the work of many scholars of eighteenth-century France. In addition to Chartier, *Cultural Origins of the French Revolution,* see, e.g., Baker, *Inventing the French Revolution;* Darnton and Roche, *Revolution in Print,* esp. Darnton's introduction to the volume and his essay "Philosophy under the Cloak"; and Landes, *Women and the Public Sphere.* For the relationship between a public sphere of letters and the American Revolution see Warner, *Letters of the Republic.*

13. For more on the distinction between public opinion and the opinion of the people see Ozouf, "L'Opinion publique."

14. Habermas, *Structural Transformation,* xviii. Arlette Farge takes this statement as the point of departure for her book *Dire et mal dire.* In an important alternative to the print-centered interpretation of political culture, Farge attempts to recover a popular public opinion of the spoken word.

15. Marie-Joseph enjoyed significantly greater literary success during his life than did his brother, the poet André Chénier. Marie-Joseph was also more politically radical; he was a member of the Jacobin club and a deputy to the Convention Nationale. André, who was guillotined in July 1794, belonged to the constitutional monarchist Feuillant club and was an active journalist.

16. Both Carla Hesse and Daniel Roche, for example, cite Chénier as a forceful advocate of freedom of the press without mentioning his overriding concern for freedom of the theater. See Hesse, "Economic Upheavals in Publishing"; and Roche, "Censorship and the Publishing Industry."

17. Chénier, "Discours prononcé devant MM. les représentants de la commune" (Aug. 23, 1789), 130.

18. Chénier, "De la liberté du théâtre en France," 137–138.

19. This Lockean philosophy was widely disseminated among French intellectuals. For French contributions to sensationalist philosophy see Etienne Bonnet de Condillac, *Traité des sensations* (1754) and *Essai sur l'origine des connaissances humaines* (1746).

20. For more on the relation between sensibility and artistic production in the Enlightenment see Vila, *Enlightenment and Pathology.*

21. See Boltanski, *Distant Suffering.*

22. La Harpe, *Discours sur la liberté du théâtre.*

23. Millin de Grandmaison, *Sur la liberté du théâtre,* 22–23.

24. The classic study of the Revolution's intellectual origins is Mornet, *Les Origines intellectuelles de la Révolution française.*

25. Darnton, *Forbidden Bestsellers,* 172. Darnton rightly points out that other European countries developed public spheres, but none experienced a revolution. Darnton argues that "if cultural history is really to explain the Revolution's origins, it must establish connections between attitudes and behavior patterns on the one hand and revolutionary action on the other" (173). James Swenson provides a thorough account of this debate, as well as of the historiography of the Revolution's intellectual origins, in *On Jean-Jacques Rousseau,* 1–52.

26. Chartier, *Cultural Origins of the French Revolution,* 68.

27. "The people" is a notoriously tricky term. In the different contexts of this study it can refer to the lower classes—as when the aristocratic characters of *La Critique de Charles IX* complain that Chénier's play appeals only to "le peuple"; it can mean the French people or the French nation; it can mean the people of Paris, specifically the activist militant Parisians who were likely to take to the streets; or it can be an abstract figure, conjured up by a politician in an effort to legitimize his position. On the ways in which "the people" can be invoked for use by politicians or experts see Bourdieu, "Uses of the 'People'"; the limitation of Bourdieu's essay is that it only considers "the people" as put to use by others.

28. See Mason, *Singing the French Revolution,* for her argument that song was a powerful medium for the production and expression of revolutionary political beliefs.

29. Chartier, *Cultural Origins of the French Revolution,* 32.

30. Ibid., 33–34. Chartier is essentially performing a reading of eighteenth-century views of the formation of the public sphere that assert theater's exclusion, but his later endorsement of the argument that books made the Revolution creates

the impression that there is an imbrication here of Chartier's views with those he cites.

31. This is perhaps one of the dangers of considering cultural objects solely in terms of form or function and leaving aside content.

32. It is evidence for the extraordinary power of print-based interpretations of eighteenth-century culture that so fine a reader as Roger Chartier could overlook the presence of the theater in this discourse, which, of course, was meant to be performed on a stage. For an interesting account of the place of Beaumarchais in the public sphere see MacArthur, "Embodying the Public Sphere."

33. Bailly, *Mémoires*, 2:283–286.

34. Framéry, *De l'Organisation des spectacles*, 238.

35. Chénier, *De la Liberté du théâtre*, 146 (my emphasis).

36. *Charles IX* is discussed extensively in the nineteenth-century histories of the revolutionary theater. Recent accounts are fewer; in addition to Carlson's *Theatre of the French Revolution* see Boncompain, "Théâtre et formation des consciences"; and Walton, "*Charles IX* and the French Revolution."

37. Chénier, *De la Liberté du théâtre*, 146.

38. Cited in Chénier's letter to the *Chronique de Paris*, no. 169, June 18, 1790.

39. For more on the rules that governed French classical theater and the idea of the *bienséances* see Scherer, *La Dramaturgie classique en France*. For the history of French tragedy in the late eighteenth century see Lancaster, *French Tragedy in the Reign of Louis XVI*.

40. Chénier, *De la liberté du théâtre*, 148.

41. *L'Année littéraire et politique*, no. 8, Feb. 1790, 2:5.

42. Ibid., 2:8–9. This seems a contentious claim at best.

43. Chénier, *De la liberté du théâtre*, 152.

44. See May, *Le Dilemme du roman au XVIIIe siècle*.

45. Millin de Grandmaison, *Sur la liberté du théâtre*, 7.

46. *Année littéraire et politique*, no. 8, 1790, 9, 30.

47. I have found no evidence that this play was ever performed. It was reviewed in the periodical literature only as a printed text. Subsequent references to the play will be made parenthetically in the text.

48. Carlson asserts that the voice from the pit was that of Danton (*Theatre of the French Revolution*, 22). Although this is possible, and it is certain that Danton attended the theater that night, no sources I have examined have definitively identified the voice as that of Danton. Moreover, it seems clear that there were many shouts, not one. Carlson sees the relationship between Chénier and Danton as evidence that "Chénier had abandoned literary goals to seek the support of a political group" (23). I am arguing, and I think it is clear from the preceding discussion of the relation between theater and tyranny, that Chénier and many others never understood the pursuit of "literary goals" to be contradicted or undermined by an engagement with politics. Had Chénier allied himself with the Cordeliers solely as

a means to gain political backing, he would have to have been either an extraordinarily gifted prophet or unbelievably stupid since the Cordeliers (Danton, Camille Desmoulins, Marat, et al.) were fairly marginal figures in the summer and fall of 1789.

49. Cited in Bingham, *Marie-Joseph Chénier*, 2.

50. Lafitte, *French Stage*, 2:198.

51. For an extensive treatment of the *Charles IX* affair and its effects on the Comédie-Française see Carlson, *Theatre of the French Revolution.*

52. Palissot, "Considérations importantes sur ce qui se passe," 7.

53. "Relation de ce qui s'est passé," 5.

54. This public confrontation led to a duel the next day between the two actors. No one was hurt.

55. "Relation de ce qui s'est passé," 7.

56. "[D]es citoyens armés, abusés toujours par les ruses de ceux qui s'en emparent (& il est si facile de s'emparer de l'esprit de cette brave, loyale garde nationale), & qui, dans les spectacles devraient se tenir à l'écart . . . avait dit, ou plutôt on leur avait fait dire qu'il y avait un cabale, que M. d'Anton en était; ce M. d'Anton, ce citoyen courageux, dont le nom seul fait pâlir les ennemis de la liberté; que le cabale se serait renouvelée hier: & voilà tout de suite l'aristocratie en l'air, & tous ses satellites" ("Relation de ce qui s'est passé," 6). [Some armed citizens, abused by the ruses of those who gained a hold over them (and it is so easy to gain a hold over the spirit of this brave, loyal national guard), and which should remain withdrawn in theaters . . . had said, or rather someone had them say, that there was a cabal and that Monsieur Danton was a participant in it; M. Danton, that courageous citizen whose very name makes the enemies of freedom go pale; that the cabal would meet again yesterday: and suddenly there we have aristocracy and all its henchmen in the air.]

57. Ibid., 8.

58. Palissot, "Considérations importantes sur ce qui se passe," 13.

59. The mayor, Bailly, also ordered the company to readmit Talma temporarily until the matter could be adjudicated; this order was met with blank refusal. See the *Chronique de Paris*, no. 264, Sept. 21, 1790.

60. Ibid.

61. Etienne and Martainville, *Histoire du théâtre français*, 1:156.

62. *Chronique de Paris*, no. 264, Sept. 21, 1790.

63. Ibid. The actor Fleury's account of the reaction is also interesting:

Scarcely had Dugazon ceased to speak, than the most Babel-like confusion of tongues proceeded from every corner of the theater. Some stretched themselves over from the upper boxes to address persons in the tier below; others maintained dialogues by bawling from one side of the theater to the other, keeping up a kind of cross-fire of voices, amidst which some menacing expressions fell upon my ear. . . . The tumult increased, and some of the audience were prepared to climb from the pit to the stage.

The whole house was now in a perfect uproar, the female portion of the audience had fled the scene of riot, and the men in the pit were evidently providing themselves with missiles by tearing up the benches. . . . Fortunately at this juncture the military made their appearance, in time to save the theater from destruction.

Next day our company was summoned to appear before M. Bailly. We felt it no small humiliation that we comedians in ordinary to the King, should be thus summoned before the municipal bar. (Lafitte, *French Stage,* 2:206–208)

64. See, e.g., *Chronique de Paris,* Sept. 21, 1790; *Les Révolutions de France et de Brabant,* no. 44, 1790; and Etienne and Martainville, *Histoire du théâtre français,* 1:156–157.

65. See, e.g., *Chronique de Paris,* no. 264, Sept. 21, 1790: "Les comédiens, d'un autre coté, ont pu distribuer un grand nombre de billets et cartes; ce moyen leur est facile, puisqu'ils en ont le magasin." [The actors, on the other hand, were able to distribute a large number of tickets; this is an easy method for them, since they own the store.] See also *Les Révolutions de France et de Brabant,* no. 44, 1790: "En effet, on assure qu'il y avait bien eu 300 billet de données et la partie n'était pas égale." [In fact, they say that 300 free tickets were handed out and that the sides were not equal.]

66. Etienne and Martainville, *Histoire du théâtre français,* 156–157. The *Chronique de Paris* (no. 264, Sept. 21, 1790) describes the scene this way: "Suleau, le Lucas des aristocrates, s'est permis des bouffonneries qui ont fait rire, et pourtant très indécentes, en ce qu'il ridiculisait l'Assemblée nationale." [Suleau, the Lucas of the aristocrats, allowed himself some antics that made some people laugh but that were, nevertheless, very indecent in that they ridiculed the National Assembly.]

67. *Les Révolutions de France et de Brabant,* no. 44, 1790.

68. Ibid.

69. *Révolutions de Paris,* no. 63, Sept. 18–25, 1790.

70. *Chronique de Paris,* no. 271, Sept. 28, 1790.

71. Things were not so tranquil within the theater company, however; by early 1791, in the wake of the January 1791 law on the freedom of theatrical performance, the troupe had split in two. The royalists remained in their theater, which they renamed the Théâtre de la Nation, whereas those with revolutionary sympathies (including Talma, Mme. Vestris, and Dugazon) left to form the new Théâtre de la rue de Richelieu, later named the Théâtre de la République. This theater is the current home of the Comédie-Française. See Carlson, *Theatre of the French Revolution,* for a thorough account of the schism in the theater.

72. *Journal des théâtres,* no. 18, Feb. 24, 1792.

73. Jeffrey Ravel shows in *The Contested Parterre* that, most certainly, many voices were raised in the theater under the Old Regime. Nevertheless, it remains

interesting and important that Millin insists that the Old Regime sought to silence audiences.

74. Millin de Grandmaison, *Sur la liberté du théâtre*, 3–4.

75. *Chronique de Paris*, no. 85, March 26, 1790. The *Chronique* went on to advise its readers: "Ne nous laissons donc pas ramener à cette impassibilité que nous portions autrefois au spectacle, où nous étions sans cesse entourés de bayonnettes menaçantes." [Let us not allow ourselves to be brought back to the impassiveness with which we used, formerly, to attend the theater, where we were constantly surrounded by menacing bayonets.] And the *Chronique* resisted assimilating the theater to anything like a market structure: "Les entrepreneurs auront beau dire qu'ils peuvent donner telle ou telle pièce, comme un marchand peut exposer telle ou telle marchandise; ils doivent plus de respect à l'opinion de la majorité" (cited in Hallays-Dabot, *Histoire de la censure théâtrale*, 167). [The entrepreneurs claim, vainly, that they present this or that play like a merchant offering this or that merchandise; they owe more respect to the majority opinion.]

76. *Le Courrier des 83 départements*, Feb. 24, 1792.

77. This account appeared in *Révolutions de Paris*, no. 138, Feb. 25 to March 3, 1792.

78. *Le Courrier des 83 départements*, Feb. 27, 1792.

79. *Caius Gracchus* was first performed on Feb. 9, 1792, at the Théâtre de la rue de Richelieu.

80. Léger, *L'Auteur d'un moment*, 1.2.

81. Chénier, *Fénélon, ou les religieuses de Cambrai*, iii.

82. Chénier, *Caius Gracchus*, 2.2. Subsequent references to the play will be made parenthetically in the text. There is of course the irony that Caius has to tell the people that they no longer need fathers.

83. *Chronique de Paris*, no. 58, Feb. 27, 1792. The *Chronique de Paris* clearly assumed that *L'Auteur*'s attack on Chénier's popularity was meant as an attack on the popular politics celebrated in *Caius Gracchus*. The paper explained:

M. Chénier venait de donner *Caius Gracchus* au théâtre de la rue Richelieu; il est un de ceux qui ont le mieux servi la Révolution, et sous prétexte qu'il a quelques ridicules, que ses succès liu donnent trop d'orgueil, il est aussitôt traduit sur le théâtre du Vaudeville. . . . Certainement, cette conduite n'est rien moins qu'impartiale, et on semblait vouloir ridiculiser l'écrivain patriote, pour atténuer l'effet de ses ouvrages, qu'il aurait été plus dangereux d'attaquer.

[M. Chénier has just given *Caius Gracchus* at the Théâtre de la rue de Richelieu; he is one of those who has best served the Revolution, and on the pretext that he has some foibles, and that his success has given him too much pride, he is suddenly hauled onto the stage at the Théâtre du Vaudeville. . . . Certainly this conduct is less than impartial, and they seem to wish to ridicule the patriotic writer in order to attenuate the effect of his works, which it would be more dangerous to attack.]

84. *Chronique de Paris,* no. 58, Feb. 27, 1792.

85. *Archives parlementaires,* 1st ser., 57:28.

86. Laya, *L'Ami des lois,* 2.3. Subsequent references will be made parenthetically in the text.

87. *Décret de la commune,* Jan. 11, 1793. Cited in Hamiche, *Le Théâtre et la Révolution,* 160.

88. Cited in Lumière, *Le Théâtre-Français pendant la Révolution, 1789–1799,* 138–139.

89. This version of events gained wide credence. Someone pasted this note into the inside cover of the Bibliothèque de l'Arsenal's copy of *L'Auteur d'un moment:* "édition originale, rare, de cette pièce où Chénier était désigné de manière à ce qu'on ne pût se méprendre et dont la représentation occasionna un tumulte effroyable de la part des fanatiques révolutionnaires. A peine parvint-on à sauver le théâtre de l'incendie et d'une déstruction totale" [rare, original edition of this play in which Chénier was designated in an unmistakable manner, and the performance of which occasioned a dreadful tumult on the part of fanatical revolutionaries. The theater was barely saved from fire and complete destruction].

90. Santerre, the commandant of the national guard whose uniform so failed to move the spectators, later complained to the municipal council that the audience was made up not of the people of Paris but of "le peuple de Coblentz." See the *Journal de Paris,* no. 14, Jan. 14, 1793. Coblentz was the base of counterrevolutionary operations for Louis XVI's brothers, the comte d'Artois and the comte de Provence.

91. The insightful Ferdinand Brunetière remarked that one of the most striking characteristics of this period was "l'envahissement du populaire sur les droits de l'ancien censure" (Brunetière, "Critique de Welschinger, 478). I take "popular censorship" to be roughly equivalent to *taxation populaire.* Audiences, like crowds at markets, broke official laws in order to enforce what they believed were more fundamental laws, the responsibility for the execution of which rested with them.

92. *Révolutions de Paris,* no. 138, Feb. 25 to March 3, 1792.

93. *Archives parlementaires,* 1st ser., 56:206.

94. See Robespierre's speech "Sur la Constitution," 146. Robespierre, like many deputies influenced by Rousseau, remained deeply ambivalent toward political representation. See chapters 2 and 3.

95. On this very old question see Pitkin, *Concept of Representation,* 144–167.

96. Roger Barny makes this argument in "Démocratie directe en 1793."

97. See, e.g., Vergniaud's famous speech of December 31, 1792:

[I]ci le vœu de la volonté générale s'est manifesté; elle s'est déclarée pour l'inviolabilité. Exprimez un vœu contraire si le salut public vous semble le commander; n'entreprenez de substituer ce vœu particulier à la volonté générale déjà connue, que lorsque celle-ci aura donné son consentement. Autrement, vous usurpez la souveraineté, vous vous rendez coupables de l'un des crimes dont vous voulez punir Louis. (*Archives parlementaires* 56:91)

[Here the wish of the general will has expressed itself; it declared itself for inviolability. Express a contrary wish if the public safety seems to demand it, but do not undertake to substitute your particular will for the already declared general will unless the general will has consented. Otherwise you usurp its sovereignty, and you will be guilty of one of the crimes for which you want to punish Louis.]

Robespierre's argument against trying the king (and for skipping straight to his punishment) illustrates the difference between his position and Vergniaud's. Whereas Vergniaud argued that the people must decide the king's fate and that that decision could be made by *voting*, Robespierre argued that the people had, in fact, already announced its will regarding the king by *acting*. The popular insurrection of August 10, 1792, that brought down the monarchy was, in Robespierre's view, the clearest possible expression of the people's will. So Robespierre managed to take a position against the referendum and, simultaneously, take a position for the direct intervention of the people. I develop this point further in chapter 3.

98. Fabre d'Eglantine, *Opinion de P.-F.-N. Fabre d'Eglantine*.

99. Cited in Genty, "Pratique et théorie de la démocratie directe," 17. In another article Genty points out that it was during the Revolution that the notion of representative democracy began to emerge (and that at the Revolution's outset the words *representation* and *democracy* were mutually exclusive). Thus by the year IX (1802), Genty shows, Pierre-Louis Roederer, Girondin and then Bonapartist, could claim "l'aristocratie élective dont Rousseau a parlé il y a cinquante ans, est ce que nous appelons aujourd'hui démocratie élective" (see "1789–1790," 37–38). Paris was divided into sixty electoral districts for the Estates General. These districts quickly assumed important governing powers; in 1790 the districts were abolished, and Paris was redivided into forty-eight sections.

100. This text is cited in Claudine Wolikow's excellent article, "1789–An III," 59. Wolikow shows how the terms *representation* and *democracy*, slowly and with much dispute, came to shed their aura of mutual exclusion.

101. Gueniffey, *Le Nombre et la raison*, 250. When Gueniffey says these practices were abolished in 1789, he also means that they had only originated in 1788–1789 as well. The practices that were resurrected were those that came into being in preparation for the Estates General and in the immediate circumstances of the Revolution's outbreak.

102. Soboul, *Mouvement populaire et gouvernement*, 505.

103. Genty, "1789–1790," 40.

104. Genty, "Pratique et théorie de la démocratie directe," 20. Michel Foucault

comments very interestingly on the role of Charlemagne in early revolutionary discourse and remarks that the assemblies of the people at the champ de Mars were understood as a "court instant de retour à la démocratie germanique." See Foucault, *"Il faut défendre la société,"* 181–187. Foucault argues that scholarly focus on classical references and revivals during the Revolution has led us to overlook the vital presence of what he calls a "rêve carolingienne"; for Foucault, the fête de la fédération, held at the champ de Mars on July 14, 1790, should be understood as a "fête carolingienne" because it was meant, principally, to reunite the now free people with a king who accepted and celebrated the people's freedom and their right to participate. The fête, Foucault writes, "[c']est bien un certain rapport du peuple ainsi assemblée à son souverain, ce rapport de modalité carolingienne, qu'elle permettait, jusqu'à un certain point, de reconstituer ou de réactiver" (187). [It is a certain relation of the people thus assembled to its sovereign, the Carolingian mode of relation that the fête permitted up to a certain point, to reconstitute or to reactivate.]

105. Furet, *Penser la Révolution Française,* 48.

106. Edmund Burke, *Reflections on the Revolution in France,* 92.

Two   The Comic Revolution

The epigraph to this chapter has been translated by J. M. Cohen: "That first meeting with violence and injustice has remained so deeply engrained on my heart that any thought which recalls it summons back this first emotion. The feeling was only a personal one in its original, but it has since assumed such a consistency and has become so divorced from personal interests that my blood boils at the sight or at the tale of injustice, whoever may be the sufferer and wherever it may have taken place, in just the same way as if I were myself its victim" (Rousseau, *Confessions of Jean Jacques Rousseau,* 30).

1. Aulard, "Figures oubliées de la Révolution française," 60.

2. Ibid. Little has changed since Aulard lodged his complaint. Fabre d'Eglantine (1750–1794) has received little new critical attention. When he is mentioned by literary critics, he is usually dismissed as an abject failure. Thus, for example, Angelica Goodden, citing as evidence only an anonymous pamphlet published in Switzerland in 1793, writes: "Fabre d'Eglantine, too, was both playwright and actor, although the *Anecdotes curieuses* (Geneva, 1793) observes that he achieved little success in either" (*Actio and Persuasion,* 56). In fact, Fabre was an extremely successful playwright. For the statistics on the number of performances of Fabre's plays see Tissier, *Les Spectacles de Paris pendant la Revolution.*

3. A comprehensive list of works that fall into this category would be inordinately long as the assertion that revolutionary politics were theatrical has by now become an assumption. See, e.g., Huet, "Performing Arts"; Goodden, "The Dramatising of Politics"; and Blanchard, *Saint-Just & Cie,* esp. 51–52 and 69–105.

Blanchard, despite his adherence to the theatrical view of politics, does have a nuanced and historical understanding of the revolutionary theater. Alan Liu, in "The Power of Formalism," explains that the English Renaissance and the French Revolution have been the most fertile areas for the theatrical model of culture. I have found Liu's analysis extremely suggestive.

4. Michelet, *Histoire de la Révolution française*, 1. The translation is from Furet, *Interpreting the French Revolution*, 194.

5. For her description of the Convention as a theater Huet depends on Michelet's quotation of Louis-Sébastien Mercier, but she does not mention that Mercier was himself a playwright or that he was jailed by the revolutionary government. She therefore misses the possibility that Mercier's depiction was a form of critique—that, in other words, he was calling the deputies hypocrites and the observers in the galleries callous pleasure seekers—rather than an impartial description. Incidentally, Hazlitt, relying on similar descriptions of the atmosphere in the Convention, likened it to a coffeehouse rather than a theater. Hazlitt is quoted in Carlson, *Theatre of the French Revolution*, 143.

6. Of course it is only in Arasse's conception that the Place de la Révolution is a backdrop, and certainly those going to their deaths were not acting—they were real victims. Like Huet, Arasse overlooks the critical uses of the concept of theatricality. Among his many illustrations, for example, the two that clearly portray the scaffold as a theatrical stage and show the victims, Louis XVI and Marie-Antoinette, in classical theatrical postures are both English engravings. They were made by someone imagining the events with horror from the safety of London rather than by someone who had actually witnessed them. The engravings, in other words, were attacks on the French revolutionary government. Engravings of the same events made in France are far from theatrical: they establish a very distant point of view from which it is difficult to identify individuals on the scaffold. Furthermore, most French engravings are so teeming with people and incidents that the guillotine barely holds sway. Finally, Arasse makes nothing of the fact that the images prepared for the proposal to build the guillotine not only show the executioner looking away from the execution but specify in writing that the executioner would look away and that the people would be kept far away by barriers. See the plates in Arasse between pages 116 and 117.

7. Bryson, *The Chastised Stage*, 114.

8. Landes, *Women and the Public Sphere*, 125. Landes sees the efforts of women to participate in the public sphere as attempts at self-dramatization, and she interprets revolutionary antitheatricality as misogyny. Hence she argues that the Revolution was bad for women since in the Old Regime some women, like Marie-Antoinette, had access to privileged positions of theatrical visibility. Madelyn Gutwirth, in *Twilight of the Goddesses,* follows the same logic.

9. For recent scholarship on Olympe de Gouges see my introduction note 24.

10. See Montrose, "New Historicisms," 410.

11. For more on the relation between Rousseau and Robespierre see Blum, *Rousseau and the Republic of Virtue.*

12. The ways in which opening up both public and private life to public scrutiny was diversely conceived is discussed in chapters 3 and 4.

13. If actorly representation, with its institutionalized disjoining of appearance and reality, was the antithesis of revolutionary representation, the broader structure of theatrical representation suggested a relationship between representatives and represented—between actor/politician and audience/people—even more deeply disturbing to revolutionary ideology. As we have seen, politicians understandably regarded the audiences in revolutionary theaters as alarmingly powerful.

14. The terms *transparency* and *opacity* come from Starobinski, *Jean-Jacques Rousseau.*

15. *Le Présumptueux* was revived in 1790 with moderate success. For more on the dispute between Collin d'Harleville and Fabre over this play see Fabre d'Eglantine, *Protestation inédite de Fabre contre les Comédiens* (July 8, 1790), and Fabre d'Eglantine, *Lettre de M. Fabre d'Eglantine à Monsieur . . .* (Paris, 1789).

16. In addition Fabre wrote a very popular song entitled "Il pleut, il pleut bergère."

17. "Célébré dans les journaux avec une sorte d'adoration, puisque l'auteur n'y est plus nommé que le Molière du siècle" (La Harpe, *Répertoire de la littérature,* 199). La Harpe's text is an excerpt of his *Cours de littérature,* which was written under the Directory.

18. Etienne and Martainville, *Histoire du théâtre français,* 1:84. Etienne went on to become an extremely conservative *ultra* with the Restoration; Martainville wrote plays mocking republicans and republicanism.

19. See Aulard, "Figures oubliées de la Révolution française," 75.

20. Darnton, *What Was Revolutionary about the French Revolution?* 39. For more on Molière during the French Revolution see Barny, "Molière et son théâtre dans la Révolution."

21. Darnton, *What Was Revolutionary about the French Revolution?* 37–47.

22. John Lough notes that "as in the previous period [pre-1715], tragedy remained the dramatic genre in the eyes of serious theater-goers and of critics in general; and yet not a single tragedy out of a total of very nearly 200 which were performed at the Comédie-française between 1715 and 1789 can be said to be still living today" (*Paris Theatre Audiences,* 163–164).

23. Molière, *Le Misanthrope, ou l'Atrabilaire amoureux,* 1.1. Subsequent references to the play will be made parenthetically in the text. Translations are from Richard Wilbur's translation, *The Misanthrope and Tartuffe.*

24. Jean Goldzinck makes the point that Rousseau trumps Bossuet even while agreeing with him by resituating the antitheatrical argument in a purely secular register. Goldzinck also argues that this crucial shift in argument underlines how radically secularizing the philosophes' project was. See Goldzinck, *Les Lumières et l'idée du comique,* 55–56.

25. On the *Lettre à d'Alembert* see Barish, *The Antitheatrical Prejudice,* 256–294; Coleman, *Rousseau's Political Imagination;* Derrida, *Of Grammatology;* Marshall, *The Surprising Effects of Sympathy,* 135–177; and Starobinski, *Jean-Jacques Rousseau.* For more on the circumstances surrounding the composition of the *Lettre* see Max Fuchs's introduction in his edition of *La Lettre à M. d'Alembert sur les spectacles.* Pierre Force argues in *Molière ou le prix des choses* that Rousseau's critique has structured the critical reception of Molière from its appearance to our own day. Suzanne Gearhart provides an excellent reading of the *Lettre* in relation to recent literary criticism and theory, especially that of Paul de Man, in *The Open Boundary of History and Fiction,* 261–284. The authoritative English translation of the *Lettre* is Allan Bloom, *Politics and the Arts.* See also Goldzinck, *Les Lumières et l'idée du comique,* for a fine reading of the *Lettre* in relation to Enlightenment conceptions and practices of comedy.

26. Rousseau, *Œuvres complètes,* 5:17. Translation is from Bloom, *Politics and the Arts,* 18–19.

27. Rousseau's argument against the theater was widely disseminated. For example, it is paraphrased in a letter published in the newspaper *L'Année littéraire et politique* in October 1789. In response to the proposal that the city governments regulate theaters put forward in a pamphlet entitled "Discours et motions sur les spectacles par M. M . . . , membres de la Commune de Paris," the writer asserts:

> Les spectacles, dit M. M . . . , par l'influence qu'ils ont sur l'esprit et les mœurs des citoyens, méritent de fixer, au moins quelques instants, l'attention des législateurs. Les spectacles ainsi que les lettres, ont très peu d'influence sur l'esprit et les mœurs des citoyens: c'est l'esprit, ce sont les mœurs des citoyens qui ont, au contraire, la plus grande influence sur les spectacles et sur les lettres. Les livres et les pièces de théâtre ne s'attachent qu'à flatter le goût dominant, mais ils ne peuvent créer ce goût ni le reformer. (*L'Année littéraire et politique,* 37:73)

> [Because of the influence that it exerts over the spirit and the morals of citizens, the theater deserves the attention of the legislators, at least for a few instants. The theater, like letters, has very little influence on the spirit and morals of citizens; on the contrary, the spirit and morals of citizens have the greatest influence on theater and letters. Books and plays seek only to flatter prevailing tastes; they cannot create or change this taste.]

28. Rousseau, *Œuvres complètes,* 5:23.

29. Marshall, *Surprising Effects of Sympathy,* 144.

30. Rousseau, *Œuvres complètes,* 5:14.

31. This profoundly alienated being is as distant as can be from the citizen as fully integrated species-being imagined by the dramas of domestic surveillance I discuss in chapter 4.

32. Primal, but not originary—that is to say that the desire to be recognized

emerges as soon as a human being becomes conscious of the gaze of others, and that consciousness emerges only when an individual lives in society. Original, natural humans lack all awareness of others as their fellows.

33. Marshall, *Surprising Effects of Sympathy,* 139. Coleman argues similarly: "If theater is pernicious, it is because it exacerbates the kind of fragmentation characteristic of social life" (*Rousseau's Political Imagination,* 51).

34. See, e.g., Marshall, *Surprising Effects of Sympathy,* 154; Coleman argues that Rousseau identifies with Molière, as well as with Alceste (*Rousseau's Political Imagination,* 170–173). See also Wellek, *A History of Modern Criticism,* 1:62. The importance of Molière for Rousseau is also treated in Hamilton, "Molière and Rousseau," 100–107.

35. Rousseau is very clear in his insistence that he is not evaluating the theater in and of itself—the notion of art for art's sake is almost an incoherent one for Rousseau: "Demander si les spectacles sont bons ou mauvaises en eux-mêmes c'est faire une question trop vague. . . . Les Spectacles sont faits pour le peuple, et ce n'est que par leurs effets sur lui qu'on peut déterminer leurs qualités absolues" (Rousseau, *Œuvres complètes,* 5:14).

36. For more on the debate set off by the *Lettre à M. d'Alembert* see Moffat, *Rousseau et la querelle du théâtre au XVIIIe siècle,* 112–179.

37. Marmontel, "Apologie du théâtre," 739.

38. For more on politeness in seventeenth- and eighteenth-century France see Peter France, *Politeness and Its Discontents.* France discusses the importance of theater in the generation and inculcation of models of politeness (57) and mentions the case of *Le Misanthrope* specifically (61).

39. "Cette même probité s'irrite, passe les bornes et tombe dans l'excès. Le Misanthrope déraisonne et devient ridicule, non pas dans sa vertu, mais dans l'excès ou elle donne" (Marmontel, "Apologie du théâtre," 765).

40. *Œuvres complètes de Marmontel,* 2:239.

41. "Le premier besoin d'une société est d'être en paix avec elle-même" (Marmontel, "Apologie du théâtre," 741). The 1790 play by C.-A. Demoustier, *Alceste à la campagne, ou le Misanthrope corrigé,* based on the Marmontel rewriting, is even more distant from Rousseau's (and Fabre's) sensibility. Demoustier's play ends happily, with Alceste begging Ursule to teach him how to get along in society:

> Donnez-moi votre humeur et votre égalité,
> Et ce vernis charmant de la société.
> Daignez m'en rappeller le ton, les convenances,
> Et de mon caractère adoucir les nuances.

> [Give me your humor and your even temper,
> And that charming social veneer.
> Deign to recall for me the tone, the conventions,
> And soften the nuances of my character.]

The first lesson Ursule imparts is never to let people know what he really thinks: "D'abord il faudra d'un sourire / Accompagner toujours ce que vous voudrez dire" (Demoustier, *Alceste à la campagne*, 3.6) [First you must always accompany with a smile / Everything you wish to say].

42. Gossman, *Men and Masks*. Gossman convincingly links Alceste's need for sincerity with his tyrannical impulses. Ambiguity allows others a freedom that Alceste cannot accept. Alceste is punished because he is an impostor: "His sincerity, his disgust, and his indifference are thus the poses of an independence he does not in fact possess, while the sincerity he demands from others is the indispensable condition of the recognition he desires from them. All the contradictions in Alceste's behavior can be traced back to this fundamental and initial imposture" (72).

43. "Ce qu'Alceste attaque se trouve en lui. Il prétend être sorti des 'bienséances' mensongères, et il tombe dans l'illusion de ce que Hegel nommera la 'morale abstraite.'" (Starobinski, *Le Remède dans le mal*, 89). Lionel Trilling argues, "Alceste's point of pride is his sincerity, his remorseless outspokenness on behalf of truth. The obsessiveness and obduracy of his sincerity amount to hubris, that state of being in which truth is obscured through the ascendancy of self-regarding will over intelligence. It is to his will and not, as he persuades himself, to truth that Alceste gives his stern allegiance" (Trilling, *Sincerity and Authenticity*, 17).

44. Rousseau, *Œuvres complètes*, 5:38. Translation is from Bloom, *Politics and the Arts*, 41.

45. Bloom, *Politics and the Arts*, 39.

46. Ibid. ("Gens si doux, si modérés, qui trouvent toujours que tout va bien, parce-qu'ils ont intérêt que rien n'aille mieux" [Rousseau, *Œuvres complètes*, 5:36]).

47. Rousseau, *Œuvres complètes*, 5:39.

48. Fabre d'Eglantine, *Le Philinte de Molière*. Subsequent references to the play will be made parenthetically in the text.

49. *Moniteur*, Feb. 24, 1790.

50. *Chronique de Paris*, Feb. 24, 1790.

51. *Journal de Paris*, Feb. 24, 1790.

52. *Chronique de Paris*, Feb. 24, 1790.

53. The capital letters are Fabre's.

54. Rousseau, *Œuvres complètes*, 5:36. Translation is from Bloom, *Politics and the Arts*, 39.

55. Bolingbroke cited in Vereker, *Eighteenth-Century Optimism*, 113.

56. The *Lettre*, along with R. A. Leigh's presentation and textual history of it, can be found in Besterman, *Studies on Voltaire*, 30:247–311.

57. Rousseau, *Les Confessions*, 507–508.

58. Here Rousseau's belief that human suffering, in large measure, was the product of human actions rather than of divine wrath or punishment was particularly useful.

59. Cited in Starobinski, *Le Remède dans le mal*, 67. Translation is from Goldhammer, *Blessings in Disguise*, 41.

60. Starobinski, *Le Remède dans le mal,* 69. Translation is from Goldhammer, *Blessings in Disguise,* 42.

61. Collin d'Harleville, *L'Optimiste.* The play was first performed at the Comédie-Française on February 22, 1788. Lough reports that 1,548 tickets were sold for the first performance of *L'Optimiste* (*Paris Theatre Audiences,* 173).

62. Fabre d'Eglantine, *Le Philinte de Molière,* ii.

63. Ibid., i.

64. Ibid, ii–iii. Here Fabre quotes from *L'Optimiste,* 5.13.

65. Ibid., iv–v.

66. In his short preface Collin writes that *L'Optimiste* "serait bien plus défectueuse encore, sans les conseils sages et sévères d'un digne Académicien, recommandable par son goût exquis, par le don heureux de sentir finement, et de s'exprimer avec grâce; d'un Académicien, d'abord mon censeur seulement, puis mon guide, puis enfin mon ami" (6) [would be even more defective without the wise and severe counsel of a worthy member of the Academy known for his exquisite taste, his gift of refined sentiments, and his ability to express himself gracefully; a member of the Academy who was at first only my censor, then my guide, and then finally my friend]. The censor Collin praises is Jean-Baptiste-Antoine Suard, who banned Chénier's *Charles IX* and his *Henri VIII* among many other works.

67. Ibid., i.

68. Collin d'Harleville, *L'Optimiste,* 1.8.

69. Redman, *Portable Voltaire,* 230.

70. Fabre d'Eglantine, *Le Philinte de Molière,* xlvii.

71. Diderot, *Entretiens sur le fils naturel,* 88. I am influenced greatly by Michael Fried's analysis of the tableau in *Absorption and Theatricality.* For more on the tableau see Caplan, *Framed Narratives;* Frantz, *L'Esthétique du tableau dans le théâtre du XVIIIe siècle;* and Szondi, *"Tableau* and *coup de théâtre."*

72. Diderot, *Entretiens sur le fils naturel,* 88.

73. Fried, *Absorption and Theatricality,* 78.

74. Fabre d'Eglantine, *Le Philinte de Molière,* xvii.

75. Ibid., xxvi.

76. Ibid., xxxi ("Cette tartufferies puérile a surtout gagné le théâtre").

77. Rousseau, "Origin and Foundations of Inequality," 127.

78. See Arendt, *On Revolution;* and Boltanski, *Distant Suffering.* Although Arendt and Boltanski agree on the rise of the politics of pity in the eighteenth century, they have entirely different estimations of it. Arendt blames the failure of the French Revolution on what she sees as the misguided turn of French revolutionaries from the task of establishing liberty to the (impossible) mission of eradicating misery. With this turn, Arendt argues, the French Revolution (in contradistinction to the American Revolution) disastrously slid from the political into the social. The makers of the American Revolution, Arendt argues, were wisely blind to the suffering around them (notably embodied in the black slave population).

Because of this blindness the American founders were able to concentrate on building an institutional structure for liberty. For building liberty, according to Arendt, is within the capacities of humankind, whereas the elimination of suffering is beyond our powers. The politics of pity is interesting to Boltanski, however, precisely as a possible practical aid to formulating an ethical obligation on the part of witnesses, especially, for example, television viewers, toward the suffering they see. Because the politics of pity is based on vision and narrative and presumes distance between beholder and the suffering object, Boltanski believes that it can be of help to us today as we, on the one hand, are capable of viewing suffering half a world away yet, on the other hand, remain perplexed about the proper response to make to it.

79. Boltanski, *Distant Suffering*, 48.

80. Fabre, *Le Philinte de Molière*, xliii.

81. Boltanski, *Distant Suffering*, 99.

82. Fried, *Absorption and Theatricality*, 97.

83. Watelet, "Grimace."

84. Bloom, *Politics and the Arts*, 81.

85. Aulard, "Figures oubliées de la Révolution française," 74. ["L'habit pauvre et le maintien gauche, n'est-ce pas une figure déjà vue? N'est-ce pas trait pour trait, en sa première chastêté morale de constituant, l'avocat d'Arras, l'incorruptible Robespierre?"]

86. Robespierre, *Œuvres de Maximilien Robespierre*, 10:354 ["Sur les principes de morale politique qui doivent guider la Convention Nationale dans l'administration intérieure de la République"].

87. For more on the role of emotion and sentiment during the French Revolution see Anne Vincent-Buffault's excellent book, *The History of Tears,* esp. 77–97. Vincent-Buffault describes beautifully the way in which shared emotion created moral and political collectivity. Sharing tears, she shows, was a form of direct communication, a form of participation, and a form of consent (82–83). She also points out the presence of women in the myriad emotional scenes that occurred throughout the Revolution and argues that their presence signifies the importance of women's participation in revolutionary culture. See also David Denby, *Sentimental Narrative,* esp. 139–165. Denby argues convincingly for the importance of sentimental rhetoric in revolutionary political discourse. Also of interest are Margaret Cohen's brief remarks about the place of sentimentalism in the Revolution in *Sentimental Education of the Novel,* 70–76. Cohen argues that sentimental narrative attempted to reconcile the conflict between negative rights (the right to be free from state intrusion and compulsion) with positive rights (the right to participate in public life).

88. Boltanski, *Distant Suffering*, 99.

89. Smith, *Theory of Moral Sentiments*, 9.

90. Boltanski, *Distant Suffering*, 100.

91. Ibid., 37. In fact, Rousseau's conception of pity is notoriously complex and seems to shift between the second *Discourse* and the *Essai sur l'origine des langues.* In the *Discourse* Rousseau thinks of sympathy as a primordial and unmediated "internal impulsion of commiseration" (127) that precedes all reflection (which he associates with imagination): pity, he writes "is a virtue all the more universal and useful to man as it precedes the exercise of all reflection in him" (152). See the preface to "Origin and Foundations of Inequality." In other cases he argues that the imagination is vital to the activation of pity: "Pity, although natural to man's heart, would remain eternally inactive without imagination to set it in motion. How do we let ourselves be moved to pity? By transporting ourselves outside ourselves. . . . Think how much acquired knowledge this transport presupposes! . . . How could I suffer when I see another suffer if I do not even know that he suffers, if I do not know what he and I have in common? Someone who has not reflected cannot be clement, or just, or pitying" (Rousseau, "Essay on the Origin of Languages," 267–268). The status of pity in Rousseau has provoked a good deal of important criticism. See Derrida, *Of Grammatology,* 171–192.

92. Trilling, *Sincerity and Authenticity,* 53.

93. In this Fabre was a forerunner of the account Michelet gives of Robespierre's character in Michelet, *Robespierre.*

94. Aulard, "Figures oubliées de la Révolution française," 85.

95. Aulard, *La Société des Jacobins,* 5:583.

96. Many commentators have shared Fabre's view of Robespierre as hypocrite, notably Michelet and Hannah Arendt. Boltanski argues that criticizing those who denounce oppression and suffering as hypocrites who in fact seek revenge is a frequent topos of counterrevolution and is employed against Saint-Just and Robespierre (*Distant Suffering,* 72).

97. See Curtois, *Rapport fait au nom,* 52.

98. Cited in Campardon, *L'Histoire du tribunal révolutionnaire de Paris,* 1:349.

Three   Robespierre's Eye

The epigraph to this chapter has been translated by J. M. Cohen: "Since I have undertaken to reveal myself absolutely to the public, nothing about me must remain hidden or obscure. I must remain incessantly beneath his gaze, so that he may follow me in all the extravagances of my heart and into every least corner of my life. Indeed, he must never lose sight of me for a single instant, for if he finds the slightest gap in my story, the smallest hiatus, he may wonder what I was doing at that moment and accuse me of refusing to tell the whole truth" (Rousseau, *Confessions of Jean Jacques Rousseau,* 65).

1. Rousseau's exhibitionism has been discussed most notably by Paul de Man in his essay "Excuses (Confessions)"; and by Starobinski, in *Jean-Jacques Rousseau,* 203–211. David Marshall was, however, the first to formulate this compulsion in

terms of surveillance; see *Surprising Effects of Sympathy*, 135–177. Martin Jay considers Rousseau's desire for transparency as a longing for a "utopia of mutually beneficial surveillance without reprobation or repression" (*Downcast Eyes*, 92).

2. On Rousseau's relation to the Revolution, and to Robespierre especially, see Blum, *Rousseau and the Republic of Virtue;* and Swenson, *On Jean-Jacques Rousseau*.

3. Jürgen Habermas makes a similar point in his analysis of "representative publicness" (see *Structural Transformation,* 1–18).

4. Jeffery Minson makes this point in *Genealogies of Morals,* 97.

5. Foucault, "The Eye of Power," 152 (my emphasis).

6. Ibid., 147. On Claude Ledoux in relation to this problem see Vidler, *Claude-Nicholas Ledoux.* The French translation of Bentham's *Panopticon* appeared in 1791.

7. Foucault, "The Eye of Power," 152.

8. Quoted in Hunt, *Politics, Culture, and Class,* 1.

9. See, e.g., Apostolidès, *Le Roi-machine*.

10. This is one of the insights of Ettore Scola's film *La Nuit de Varennes.* In a scene analyzed by Joan Landes in *Women and the Public Sphere* the film shows a countess entrusted with the king's ceremonial attire curtseying low, nearly prostrating herself, before the dummy draped with the king's costume as she is overcome by *its* majesty. Had the king remained in costume and thus maintained character, this scene implies, the Revolution would not have toppled him so easily. And while the king's own personality, desires, and tastes certainly played an important role in the unfolding of revolutionary events, it is also true that what has been termed the desacralization of the monarch began well before the reign of Louis XVI. On this subject see Chartier, *Cultural Origins of the French Revolution;* Merrick, *Desacralization of the French Monarchy;* and Graham, *If the King Only Knew*.

11. On this problem see Wolikow, "1789–An III"; and Barny, "Démocratie directe en 1793." See also Marcel Gauchet, *La Révolution des pouvoirs*.

12. Gauchet, *La Révolution des pouvoirs,* 80–90.

13. Robespierre, "Sur la Constitution," 507.

14. On the notion of the supplement see Derrida, *Of Grammatology,* 141–157.

15. See Marshall, *Surprising Effects of Sympathy,* 164–166.

16. Huet, *Rehearsing the Revolution,* 4, 1.

17. See Jordan, *The King's Trial;* and Walzer, *Regicide and Revolution*.

18. Locke, *Two Treatises of Government,* 425–427.

19. Robespierre, *Œuvres de Maximilien Robespierre,* 9:121.

20. Ibid. Saint-Just agreed with Robespierre and made his famous maiden speech arguing against trying the king.

21. Ibid., 123. For a discussion of Robespierre's actions during the crisis of August 10, 1792, and his beliefs about the right of insurrection see Monnier, *L'Espace public démocratique,* 135–146.

22. Robespierre, *Œuvres de Maximilien Robespierre*, 9:122.

23. Rousseau, *Lettre à M. d'Alembert sur les spectacles*, 114.

24. Starobinski, *1789, ou les emblèmes de la liberté*, 31.

25. Robespierre, *Œuvres de Maximilien Robespierre*, 9:504.

26. Cited in Johnson, "Versailles, Meet Les Halles," 111.

27. Robespierre, *Œuvres de Maximilien Robespierre*, 10:279. Note the rhyme of *ténèbres* with *funèbres*.

28. Ibid., 4:82. This statement recalls James H. Johnson's insight that "a mask is not a disguise. Its physical presence—in paper, cardboard, cloth, or plaster—points to a purpose of concealment, but that very presence announces its ruse. For this reason the mask frustrates full deception. . . . Disguise, by contrast, is deceptive in its essence. . . . Masks thwart disguise. Disguise hides its 'masks'" ("Versailles, Meet Les Halles," 96).

29. Johnson, "Versailles, Meet Les Halles," 91.

30. Robespierre, *Œuvres de Maximilien Robespierre*, 10:571–572.

31. Derrida, *Of Grammatology*, 304, 305.

32. Robespierre, *Œuvres de Maximilien Robespierre*, 10:569.

33. On Robespierre's dislike of Fouché see Walter, *Maximilien de Robespierre*, 430.

34. Cited in Michelet, *Robespierre*, 361.

35. It is therefore ironic that Michelet records Robespierre's aversion for being scrutinized: "mais qui avait le sang-froid, en un tel péril, d'observer ce terrible acteur, dont le pénétrant regard pouvait être mortel à l'observateur, et qui ne craignait rien tant que d'être sérieusement regardé?" (ibid., 37). Michelet makes this comment in the context of Robespierre's conflict with Fabre d'Eglantine, who, we will remember, stared at him through opera glasses.

36. Jay, *Downcast Eyes*, 11–12. It will be the work and the achievement of Balzac's Vautrin to formulate and perfect the techniques that will allow him to resist precisely this form of visual penetration.

37. Cited in Johnson, "Versailles, Meet Les Halles," 99.

38. Robespierre, *Œuvres de Maximilien Robespierre*, 9:503.

39. Ibid., 5:291.

40. Ibid., 9:504.

41. Ibid., 5:129.

42. On Robespierre's beliefs about political representation see McNeil, "Robespierre, Rousseau, and Representation." McNeil argues that Robespierre saw deep contradictions between the tenet of popular sovereignty and the practice of political representation. Robespierre began his career as a staunch advocate of direct popular participation, but at the time of the Terror he abandoned his support of popular political participation, if not his fundamental belief in its legitimacy.

43. Robespierre, *Œuvres de Maximilien Robespierre*, 4:145.

44. Cited in Gauchet, *La Révolution des pouvoirs*, 83.

45. Cited in ibid., 99.

46. Ibid., 85. For more on the Cordeliers club see Mathiez, *Le Club des Cordeliers.*

47. Gauchet, *La Révolution des pouvoirs,* 85.

48. Robespierre, *Œuvres de Maximilien Robespierre,* 9:500.

49. In particular, he accused Jean-Marie Roland, the Girondin minister of the interior: "Que dis-je, celle même [the new hall] ou elle [the National Assembly] vient d'entrer est-elle plus favorable à la publicité et plus digne à la nation? Non; tous les observateurs se sont aperçus qu'elle a été disposé avec beaucoup d'intelligence, par le même esprit d'intrigue, sous les auspices d'un ministre pervers" (Robespierre, *Œuvres de Maximilien Robespierre,* 9:504). [What am I saying? The one into which it (the legislature) has just moved, is it more favorable to publicity and worthier of the nation? No; all the observers have noticed that it has been disposed with great intelligence by the same spirit of intrigue, under the auspices of a perverse minister.]

50. "October days" refers to the famous march to Versailles led by Parisian women who successfully demanded that the king reside in the capital.

51. Brette, *Histoire des édifices,* 90. My account of the structure and layout of the hall is based on Brette.

52. Cited in ibid., 168, 177.

53. Cited in ibid., 205.

54. *Journal de Paris,* Aug. 13, 1792; cited in Brette, *Histoire des édifices,* 251–252.

55. Robespierre, *Œuvres de Maximilien Robespierre,* 9:503.

56. Cited in Brette, *Histoire des édifices,* 233. In its October 26, 1791, edition, the *Journal de Paris* had similarly criticized deputies who seemed to wish to escape the scrutiny of their constituents:

> Il est fâcheux que quelques membres de l'assemblée actuelle aient hérité de cette haine, et qu'ils aient l'air de croire sérieusement que les représentants de vingt-cinq millions d'hommes ne jouissent pas d'une liberté bien complète, parce que des citoyens leur disent leur avis à la barre, et que cinq ou six cents autres, places dans les tribunes, osent quelquefois faire entendre le leur. (Cited in Brette, *Histoire des édifices,* 205)

> [It is annoying that some of the members of the current legislature have inherited this hatred, and that they seem to believe seriously that the representatives of twenty-five million men do not enjoy complete enough liberty because sometimes citizens speak their minds at the bar, and because five or six hundred others, in the galleries, dare sometimes to make their opinions understood.]

57. Robespierre, *Œuvres de Maximilien Robespierre,* 9:507.

58. See Cobb, *The Police and the People.*

59. Soboul, *The Sans-Culottes,* 135.

60. For more on the districts see Genty, "Pratique et théorie de la démocratie

directe." For more on the sections see Soboul's classic study *The Sans-Culottes;* and Monnier, *L'Espace publique démocratique;* for a detailed account of the inner workings and history of one Parisian section see Slavin, *The French Revolution in Miniature.*

61. Robespierre, *Œuvres de Maximilien Robespierre,* 6:350.

62. Cited in Soboul, *The Sans-Culottes,* 136. The French term translated here as "watch out" is *veillent* in the original French. See Soboul, *Les Sans-culottes parisiens en l'an II,* 550. I will add the French terms from this edition where relevant in the text. This section dealing with popular sovereignty and surveillance is deeply indebted to Soboul. Soboul's classic study of the sans-culottes, their political practices, and their aspirations is still unrivaled. Soboul argues that the sans-culottes' political vision was ultimately doomed because it did not spring from a fully developed sense of class consciousness. It could not adequately address, therefore, the problem of the relations of production. In other words, history was not yet ripe for the proletarian Revolution. Based on Soboul's own account, however, I find the sans-culottes' political vision significantly more coherent—and more relevant for our own times, in which political representation has triumphed—than does Soboul himself.

63. Cited in Soboul, *The Sans-Culottes,* 136.

64. For more on the sectional role in the practice of surveillance see Genty, *L'Apprentissage de la citoyenneté;* and Slavin, *The French Revolution in Miniature,* 244–278. For committees of surveillance outside of Paris see Rothiot, "Comités de surveillance."

65. All cited in Soboul, *The Sans-Culottes,* 119, 120, 210.

66. Cited in ibid., 125.

67. Robespierre, *Œuvres de Maximilien Robespierre,* 9:507.

68. See Soboul, *The Sans-Culottes,* 140.

69. Cited in ibid., 114.

70. Cited in Genty, *L'Apprentissage de la citoyenneté,* 204.

71. Cobb, *The Police and the People,* 188–189.

72. Cited in Buchez and Roux, *Histoire parlementaire de la Révolution française,* 23:23.

73. For a brief history of the eye symbol see Renouvier, *Histoire de l'art pendant la Révolution:* "L'œil avait été exhumé par les antiquaires Caylus et Winckelmann comme un emblème de divinité, de justice, de vigilance" (399). [The eye had been exhumed by the antiquarians Caylus and Winckelmann as an emblem of divinity, of justice, of vigilance.]

74. On the symbolism of the sun during the Revolution see Starobinski, *1789, ou les emblèmes de la liberté.* On the image of light during the Enlightenment see Bates, "Idols and Insight."

75. This is the "autel de la patrie" (the altar of the nation). For more on the origin and the practices surrounding this new kind of altar see Mathiez, *Les Origines des cultes révolutionnaires,* 30–32.

76. Robespierre successfully proposed on May 7, 1794 (18 Floréal, an II), that the National Convention promulgate a decree recognizing the existence of a Supreme Being; the festival of the Supreme Being was held in Paris on June 8, 1794 (20 Prairial, an II), just one month before Robespierre's fall. For more on the revolutionary cult of the Supreme Being see Aulard, *Le Culte de la raison;* for more on revolutionary religiosity see Mathiez, *Les Origines des cultes révolutionnaires.* For a discussion of the festival of the Supreme Being see Mona Ozouf's groundbreaking work *La Fête révolutionnaire.*

77. In the *Phenomenology of Spirit* Hegel famously called the Supreme Being "an exhalation of stale gas" from the Revolution. While the term is perhaps overly pejorative, the sense of the Supreme Being as the projection of revolutionary values seems unquestionably correct.

78. I am grateful to Catherine Gallagher for pointing out the trinitarian significance to me.

79. Robespierre, "Sur la necessité," 69. The topos of a precept of natural law written or engraved in the heart is rather common in revolutionary rhetoric.

80. I am grateful to Thomas Kavanagh for pointing out the similarity to sacred heart imagery. The revolutionary transformation of the sacred-heart symbol into the *œil de la surveillance* is particularly ironic because the sacred heart came to be the single most important symbol of royalism and counterrevolution. The sacred-heart, moreover, retained its special antirepublican association throughout the nineteenth century. For more on the political and social importance of the sacred-heart in France see Jonas, *France and the Cult of the Sacred Heart.*

81. Rousseau, *The Social Contract,* bk. 1, chap. 8.

82. Butler, *The Psychic Life of Power,* 107.

83. On this point see Balibar, "Citizen Subject."

84. See Smith, *Theory of Moral Sentiments.* Smith's book first appeared in French translation in 1764. The translation was considered defective, and the book was translated and published again in 1774–1775. The second translation was reprinted in 1782. Sophie de Condorcet famously translated *Theory of Moral Sentiments* once again in 1798. This third version was reprinted in 1820 and 1860 (see Smith, *Theory of Moral Sentiments,* 29–33). The number of translations and printings clearly indicates great French interest in this work.

85. On the role of the impartial spectator in Smith's moral philosophy see Marshall, *The Figure of Theater,* 167–192. Whereas other scholars have been interested in the notion of the spectator as impartial, Marshall is interested in the "impartial spectator as spectator" (167).

86. Ibid., 173.

87. Fouché, *Memoirs of Joseph Fouché,* 1:73.

Four   The Home and the World

The epigraph to this chapter has been translated by Maurice Cranston: "The better the state is constituted, the more does public business take precedence over private in the minds of the citizens. There is indeed much less private business, because the sum of the public happiness furnishes a larger proportion of each individual's happiness, so there remains less for him to seek on his own" (Rousseau, *The Social Contract*, 140).

1. Sara Maza discusses the means by which the affairs of private families were transformed into matters of public interest and the way in which this publicizing of the private led to the formation of a powerful, often authoritative, public opinion in *Private Lives and Public Affairs*. On bourgeois drama, in addition to the seminal texts by Diderot, see Bryson, *The Chastised Stage*.

2. Mistelet, *De la Sensibilité*, 7.

3. "De tous les côtés, il se construit des théâtres et l'on va en être inondé après Pâques. Il y en aura trente-huit" (letter from Mareux dated April 4, 1791; cited in Launay, *Une Famille de la bourgeoisie*, 107).

4. For more on the history of the Théâtre de la Cité see Louis-Henri Lecomte, *Histoire des théâtres de Paris*. Lecomte notes that the theater was so vast that it could seat its entire audience and that the décor was sumptuous. Prices ranged from fifteen sous to four livres (4).

5. The Théâtre du Vaudeville was one of the many theaters that sprang up quickly after royal regulation of the theater disappeared and freedom of the theater was officially established with the law of January 13, 1791. The Vaudeville specialized in parodies of plays, often of tragedies performed at the more elite theaters. The Théâtre du Vaudeville, whose repertoire, although not exclusively but certainly overwhelmingly made up of vaudevilles—light-hearted stories or parodies of serious plays interspersed with songs adapted to popular tunes—would be the great exception to the decreasing specialization the liberty of the theater brought about. The story of Susannah and the elders was popular in sixteenth- and seventeenth-century French theater, but it garnered less interest in the eighteenth century, as did sacred drama in general. For more on vaudeville as genre in the eighteenth century see Robinson, "Les Vaudevilles."

6. *Chronique de Paris*, no. 31, Jan. 31, 1793.

7. Cited in D'Estrée, *Le Théâtre sous la Terreur*, 177. Hébert is best known as the creator of the highly scabrous and ultrarevolutionary newspaper *Le Père Duchesne*.

8. *Révolutions de Paris*, no. 186, Jan.–Feb. 1793.

9. Ibid.

10. Cited in Carlson, *Theatre of the French Revolution*, 144: "Vous êtes ses accusateurs, vous ne pouvez pas être ses juges." Carlson's interpretation concurs with those in D'Estrée, *Le Théâtre sous la Terreur*, 176; Welschinger, *Le Théâtre de la Révolution*, 340; and Hérissay, *Le Monde des théâtres pendant la Révolution*, 133.

11. Kennedy et al., *Theatre, Opera, and Audiences,* 4.

12. Carlson notes the quick alteration of the line to "Accaron, Barzabas, vous ne pouvez pas être ses juges" (2.2) [Accaron, Barzabas, you cannot be her judges] and dates the change to sometime before January 10, 1793 (Carlson, *Theatre of the French Revolution,* 144–145). But he believes that the line change occurred as a result of the complaint brought to the Commune. However, the *Chronique de Paris* (no. 31, Jan. 31, 1793) reports that Delpeche went to the Commune on January 29, 1793. In fact, the line Carlson cites was changed in response to immediate objections, but the play remained deeply troubling. Evidently, something beyond simple allusion was at stake.

13. The duel to the death between Girondins (whose name derives from the name of the department, la Gironde, from which many of the leading Girondins hailed) and Jacobins is one of the great themes in French Revolution historiography. Two recent excellent works on the Jacobins are Higonnet, *Goodness beyond Virtue;* and Jaume, *Le Discours Jacobin de la démocratie.* Higonnet emphasizes the two groups' commonalities and goes so far as to call the Girondins "Girondin Jacobins." He argues that what distinguished the two was their divergent sense of how far the Revolution could or should go. The Girondins, he explains, wanted to bring the Revolution to a halt earlier than did the Jacobins.

14. Historians typically claim that the Jacobins were free-marketers at heart who conceded market controls unhappily in order to win over the masses.

15. In addition to the plays I discuss here see, e.g., Chastenet, *L'Intérieur d'un ménage républicain,* discussed below, which was performed forty-six times and spawned a sequel; Piis, *La Nourrice républicaine, ou les plaisirs de l'adoption,* which ran for a healthy thirty-seven performances; Laugier, *Les Épreuves du républicain,* nine performances; Rézicourt, *Les Vrais sans-culottes,* forty-eight performances. In response to an earlier version of this essay presented at the annual meeting of the American Society for Eighteenth-Century Studies (Nashville 1997), Dena Goodman pointed out the significance of generic distinctions to the ideological work performed by these plays. It is not incidental that critique found its home at the Vaudeville theater—the site for parody and clownishness—while drame, a form invented in the mid-eighteenth century precisely to explore and expose the private, served as the vehicle for the representation of surveillance. I thank Goodman for her comment.

16. I do not mean to use *domestic* and *private* synonymously but rather to follow Jürgen Habermas's usage: Habermas considers domestic life to constitute a sort of private sphere within the private sphere. Habermas argues that there was a "doubling of the private sphere." On the one hand, the private sphere was the sphere of the market and of exchange—that is, the sphere of civil society; on the other hand, the family constituted another sphere, which he sometimes terms the "interior domain" or the "intimate sphere." I think it is a sign of the radical saturation of life by politics that these plays choose to focus on the most intimate sphere. See Habermas, *Structural Transformation,* 28–29.

17. Maurin de Pompigny, *L'Époux républicain,* 1.9. Interestingly, Franklin also claims that marriage is good for women. Married women, he claims, achieve full equality, whereas unmarried girls are still subject to what he terms "gêne," a kind of hindrance or bother. Many of the plays I discuss in this chapter seem to express something akin to an obsession with and compulsion for what we would now think of as normative heterosexual marriage. Certainly we see an ardent embrace of a new sentimental conception of companionate marriage and a rejection of everything associated with the sexual "corruption" of the Old Regime. But the very fact that these plays so vociferously push marriage raises the question of the actual practices of the period. Did the Revolution, for example, see a rise in the numbers of unmarried cohabitating couples (Marat and his companion, Simone Evrard, would have been a well-known example) or of other nonnormative households with the decline in the authority of the church?

18. Ibid. The law of February 13, 1790, abolished monastic vows and freed monks and nuns to leave their convents.

19. See D'Estrée, *Le Théâtre sous la Terreur,* 261. Emmet Kennedy lists Pompigny as the revolutionary decade's fifteenth most popular playwright with 835 performances of his plays during the period. See Kennedy, *Cultural History of the French Revolution,* 394.

20. See, e.g., Desan, "'War between Brothers and Sisters.'"

21. *Les Spectacles de Paris* (1794): 155. *La Veuve du républicain* ran for a respectable twenty-four performances.

22. Boardinghouses were particularly subject to the surveillance of sectional officials. See Slavin, *The French Revolution in Miniature,* 244–277.

23. For a groundbreaking analysis of the relation between domestic architecture and conceptions of privacy and the public sphere see Marcus, *Apartment Stories.*

24. *La Veuve du républicain,* 1.9.

25. See Roland, *Memoirs of Madame Roland.* For more on the political and cultural significance of breast-feeding in the wake of Rousseau see Badinter, *L'Amour en plus;* and Sheriff, "Erotic Mothers."

26. Soboul, *The Sans-Culottes,* 143. My argument here owes a great deal to Soboul and to Lucien Jaume's excellent discussion of denunciation in *Le Discours Jacobin et la démocratie,* esp. 203–209.

27. Soboul, *The Sans-Culottes,* 145.

28. There is some dispute about the authorship of this play. In *Theatre, Opera, and Audiences* Kennedy et al. attribute the plays published under the name Citoyenne Villeneuve to François Cizos-Duplessis. I have not come across any contemporary documents that challenge the authorship of Villeneuve, however, who was married to one of the primary actors in the Théâtre de la Cité's troupe and whose son appeared in the play.

Before enacting the laws that extended rights to illegitimate children, the legislature had already passed laws ending primogeniture and ensuring that girls inherited equally with their brothers. For more on the family in French revolutionary law and culture see Traer, *Marriage and the Family;* Goodheart, "Adoption in the Discourse of the French Revolution"; and Desan, "'War between Brothers and Sisters.'" On the representation of the family in theater see McDonald, "The Anxieties of Change."

29. This play was performed thirty-seven times at the Théâtre du Vaudeville, and the *Spectacles de Paris* called it a "brillant succès" (2:26). Piis wrote twelve plays during the revolutionary period that were performed at the Vaudeville and at the Opéra-Comique. Piis collaborated frequently with Pierre-Yves Barré, one of the triumvirate responsible for *La Chaste Suzanne* and one of the Vaudeville directors.

30. In the context of this song it is slightly eerie that Robespierre's father, François Robespierre, abandoned his four small, motherless children in Arras and moved to Germany. For more on Robespierre's life see the definitive biography, Gérard Walter's *Maximilien de Robespierre.*

31. Cited in Jaume, *Le Discours Jacobin et la démocratie,* 192.

32. On transparency and obstacle see Starobinski, *Jean-Jacques Rousseau.* On the revolutionary will to render all things transparent and the role of revolutionary journalism in the publicizing project see Baecque, *The Body Politic,* 209–247. In *The Cultural Origins of the French Revolution* Roger Chartier argues that the Revolution sought to "exorcise the dangers of the private sphere" through publicity (196).

33. *L'Intérieur d'un ménage républicain.* First performed at the Théâtre de l'Opéra-comique de la rue Favart, 15 Nivôse, Year II (Jan. 4, 1794).

34. *Le Moniteur,* no. 114, 24 Nivôse, Year II (Jan. 13, 1794).

35. Cited in Hunt, *Politics, Culture, and Class,* 1.

36. The Civil Constitution of the Clergy (July 12, 1790) made clergymen state-salaried functionaries elected in district electoral assemblies. Clergy were required to take an oath to the nation, the law, the king, and the constitution; those who refused were called non-juring priests. Eventually, in the summer of 1793, non-juring priests were subject to deportation.

37. *L'Intérieur,* sc. 8. Emmet Kennedy, in his discussion of abdications from the priesthood, argues convincingly that many priests took advantage of the Revolution to leave a profession into which they had been pressured or even forced. Kennedy's examples use the same term, *prejudice,* to describe the institution of the priesthood: "Clerics alleged that they never wanted to be priests, that they never believed what they preached, that they no longer wanted to stand apart from the general citizenry, that the priesthood represented a 'prejudice' which they renounced in favor of philosophy and reason" (*Cultural History of the French Revolution,* 341).

38. Marriage appears to be the metaphor, or psychic structure, most readily available to figure the process of forming a new nation of fraternal citizens. It would be interesting to speculate on the degree to which the obsession with mar-

riage reveals an underlying anxiety about "fraternity" and its effects on the ordering of both sexuality and gender in the Republic. It also seems important to consider the republican anxiety about "family values" in relation to the depiction of homosexuality as an aristocratic vice and sign of the corruption of the Old Regime.

39. See Buchez and Roux, *Histoire parlementaire de la Révolution française,* 23:23.

40. *La Chaste Suzanne,* 1.4. It seems that the playwrights have conflated this bath with the *mikvah,* the ritual bathing of Jewish women after menstruation, which was indeed a sacred rite from which men (although not other women) were barred.

41. Lemaistre de Sacy, *La Sainte Bible,* Dan. 13:4. Lemaistre de Sacy's seventeenth-century translation was published often throughout the eighteenth century.

42. Ibid., Dan. 13:6.

43. Radet and Desfontaines, *Chaste Suzanne,* 1.2.

44. It is probably no coincidence that Accaron bears the same sobriquet—the incorruptible—that Robespierre did.

45. And the Jacobins seemed particularly annoyed by the play. The *Chronique de Paris,* no. 29, Jan. 29, 1793, includes the following extract of the procès-verbal of the January 26 meeting of the Paris Jacobin club:

Sur la dénonciation répétée faite à ladite assemblée des allusions et sentiments d'incivisme que renferme la pièce dite la *Chaste Suzanne,* jouée au théâtre du Vaudeville, elle a arrêté que derechef des commissaires porteraient au Conseil-général l'invitation d'empêcher la représentation de cette pièce aristocratique, motivée sur l'impudence avec laquelle les valets de la ci-devant cour y ont applaudi hier soir aux allusions criminelles qu'elle renferme.

[On the repeated denunciations lodged with this assembly of the antipatriotic allusions and sentiments contained in the play called *La Chaste Suzanne,* performed at the Théâtre du Vaudeville, the assembly declared that the sectional commissaires should ask the General Council (of the Commune) to forbid the performance of this aristocratic play based on the impudence with which, last night, the lackeys of the former court applauded the criminal allusions it contains.]

46. Cited in Buchez and Roux, *Histoire parlementaire de la Révolution française,* 23:25.

47. *Révolutions de Paris,* no. 186, Jan.–Feb. 1793.

48. The theme of Susannah and the elders posed a problem for painting, Michael Fried argues, because "beholding, specifically illicit beholding, belonged to its theme. It therefore threatened to call attention to the actual beholder and in effect to implicate him along with the elders" (*Absorption and Theatricality,* 96). Fried argues that implicating the beholder, acknowledging the presence of the beholder, theatricalizes painting.

49. *Révolutions de Paris,* no. 186, Jan.–Feb. 1793.

50. Much recent scholarly work has examined the central place of Marie-Antoinette in the revolutionary imagination. See especially Hunt, *Family Romance of the French Revolution.* Hunt argues that the queen came to stand for the dangerous sexual power women could wield over men. Hunt also points out that it was Hébert, the procureur who sided with the fédérés and against *La Chaste Suzanne,* who brought the infamous charge of incest against Marie-Antoinette. And for an account of the popular revolutionary depiction of Marie-Antoinette as dangerous libertine see Thomas, *La Reine scélérate.*

51. Thomas, *La Reine scélérate,* 79.

52. Edmund Burke offers the best-known *admiring* account of Marie-Antoinette as spectacle:

> It is now sixteen or seventeen years since I saw the queen of France, then the dauphiness, at Versailles; and surely there never lighted on this orb, which she hardly seemed to touch, a more delightful vision. I saw her just above the horizon, decorating and cheering the elevated sphere she just began to move in,—glittering like the morning star. (Burke, *Reflections on the Revolution in France,* 169)

Burke's chivalrous attitude toward the victimized queen could be seen as bearing out the revolutionaries' assumption that public women necessarily exercise power by acting on and through men. Rousseau argues repeatedly in the *Lettre à M. d'Alembert* that beauty endowed women with an "empire" over men. Analysis of the gender dynamics during the Revolution and of revolutionary sexuality is beyond the scope of this study; it is clear, however, that although both women and men could be characterized as surveillants in these plays, women had a privileged position as objects of the gaze, and this position made them seem especially threatening to some. In other words, the position in which power was thought to inhere (subject or object of the gaze) was unstable. As we will see, *La Chaste Suzanne* seems to take the position that the object of the gaze does not exert a dangerous power over its onlookers. But if this aspect of my analysis of surveillance does, nonetheless, seem to support an orthodox argument about gender and the gaze (i.e., that the beholder is constructed as male and the object of beholding as female), another aspect of my argument undercuts these traditional arguments. Indeed, another way to read this material in relation to gender is to point out that in insisting on the integration of the home and the world, the Jacobin culture of surveillance understood women to be participants in the Republic. Ultimately, one could argue that surveillance amounted to, among other things, a preemptive action against the division of lived experience into home and world and thus an action against the relegation of women to the private.

53. Lemaistre de Sacy, *La Sainte Bible,* Dan. 13:32.

54. On the fear of a specifically female power to petrify men, that is to castrate

them, and the role this masculine fear plays at moments of political turmoil, see Hertz, "Medusa's Head."

55. Starobinski, *Jean-Jacques Rousseau*, 119.

56. To add insult to injury, *La Chaste Suzanne* mocked this fear of theatricality: the only characters who fear the power of Suzanne's spectacular appearance and who feel its deleterious effects are the degenerate, criminal, and comical elders.

57. See Sennett, *Fall of Public Man*, 1–122.

58. See Poovey, *Uneven Developments;* and Marcus, *Apartment Stories.*

59. Marx, "On the Jewish Question," 166.

60. Ibid., 168. I am indebted to conversations with John Ehrenberg for this discussion of Marx.

61. "Le patriote n'a rien de personnel, il rapporte tout à la masse commune: les jouissances, les sentiments douloureux, tout est épanché par lui dans le sein de ses frères, et voilà la source de la publicité qui distingue le gouvernement fraternel, c'est-à-dire républicain" (cited in Jaume, *Le Discours Jacobin et la démocratie,* 206).

62. The play was first performed on 5 Fructidor, Year II (July 9, 1794), at the Théâtre de la rue Favart (L'Opéra-comique), and then was revived a year later. In a long preface the author explains that "[m]ettre sur la scène les Jacobins de l'Inquisition, c'est y mettre les Jacobins de Paris, puisqu'il existe entre eux la plus parfaite ressemblance" [to represent Jacobins of the Inquisition on the stage is to represent the Jacobins of Paris since there is a perfect resemblance between the two]. Lebrun-Tossa condemns especially Collot-d'Herbois, Billaud-Varenne, and Barère. Although Lebrun-Tossa wrote several other plays during the revolutionary decade, only his *La Folie de Georges III* was a success. *Les Jacobins de Goa* signified the Inquisition and religious fanaticism throughout the eighteenth century.

63. On the idea of totality see Jay, *Marxism and Totality,* esp. 21–81.

▮ Bibliography

Primary Works

Newspapers

Année littéraire et politique (Repr., Geneva: Slatkine, 1966)
La Chronique de Paris
Le Courrier des 83 départements
Le Journal de Paris
Le Journal des théâtres
Mercure français
Le Moniteur
Les Révolutions de France et de Brabant (Collected in Desmoulins, *Œuvres*)
Les Révolutions de Paris
Les Spectacles de Paris, ou Calendrier historique des théâtres

Plays, Pamphlets, Essays, Memoirs, and Speeches

Archives parlementaires. 1ère série. Paris, 1867–.
Aulard, François-Alphonse. *La Société des Jacobins: Recueil des documents.* 6 vols. Paris, 1895; Repr. New York: AMS, 1973.
Bailly, Jean-Sylvain. *Mémoires de Bailly.* Ed. Berville and Barrière. 2 vols. Paris, 1822.
Buchez, P.-J.-B., and P.-C. Roux. *Histoire parlementaire de la Révolution française.* 40 vols. Paris, 1836.
Cailhava, Jean-François. *Les Causes de la décadence du théâtre et les moyens de le faire refleurir.* 1772. Repr., Paris, 1790, 1807.
Chastenet, Armand-Marie-Jacques de. *L'Intérieur d'un ménage républicain.* Paris, Year II (1794).
Chénier, Marie-Joseph. *Caius Gracchus.* Paris, 1793.
———. *Charles IX, ou l'École des rois.* Paris, 1790.
———. "De la liberté du théâtre en France." Published as an appendix to *Charles IX, ou l'École des rois.* Paris, 1790.
———. "Discours prononcé devant MM. les représentants de la commune," Aug. 23, 1789. Published as an appendix to *Charles IX, ou l'École des rois.* Paris, 1790.

————. *Fénélon, ou les religieuses de Cambrai.* Paris, 1793.

Collin d'Harleville, Jean-François. *L'Optimiste, ou l'homme content de tout.* Paris, 1788.

Condillac, Etienne Bonnet de. *Essai sur l'origine des connaissances humaines.* Paris, 1746.

————. *Traité des sensations.* Paris, 1754.

Curtois, Edmé. *Rapport fait au nom de la commission de l'examen des papiers trouvés chez Robespierre et ses complices.* Paris, Year II (1794).

Demoustier, C.-A. *Alceste à la campagne, ou le misanthrope corrigé.* Paris, 1798.

Desmoulins, Camille. *Œuvres.* Ed. Albert Soboul. 1789–1791. Repr., Munich: Klaus, 1980.

Diderot, Denis. *De la poésie dramatique.* 1758. In *Œuvres esthétiques,* ed. Paul Vernière, 183–287. Paris: Garnier, 1968.

————. *Entretiens sur le fils naturel.* 1757. In *Œuvres esthétiques,* ed. Paul Vernière, 77–175. Paris: Garnier, 1968.

————. *La Religieuse.* Paris: Gallimard, 1972.

Fabre d'Eglantine, P.-F.-N. *Lettre de M. Fabre d'Eglantine à Monsieur . . . , relativement à la contestation au sujet du Présomptueux, ou l'heureux imaginaire.* Paris, 1789.

————. *Opinion de P.-F.-N. Fabre d'Eglantine, député du département de Paris, sur l'appel au peuple.* Paris, 1793.

————. *Le Philinte de Molière, ou la Suite du misanthrope.* Paris, 1791.

————. *Protestation inédite de Fabre contre les comédiens.* Bibliothèque de l'Arsénal, collection Rondel, Rf18.038, Paris.

Fouché, Joseph. *The Memoirs of Joseph Fouché, Duke of Otranto.* 2 vols. London, 1825.

Framéry, Etienne Nicholas. *De l'Organisation des spectacles de Paris, ou Essai sur leur forme actuelle.* Paris, 1790.

Lafitte, Jean-Baptiste. *The French Stage and the French People as Illustrated in the Memoirs of M. Fleury.* Ed. Theodore Hook. 2 vols. London, 1841.

La Harpe, Jean-François. *Discours sur la liberté du théâtre prononcé par M. de la Harpe, 17 décembre 1790, à la société des amis de la constitution,* B.N., Lb40 565. Paris, 1790.

————. *Répertoire de la littérature.* Paris, 1825.

Laugier, Marie. *Les Epreuves du républicain, ou l'Amour de la patrie.* Paris, Year II.

Laya, Jean-Louis. *L'Ami des lois.* Paris, 1793.

Lebrun-Tossa, Jean-Antoine. *Arabelle et Vascos, ou les Jacobins de Goa.* Paris, Year III (1795).

Léger, François. *L'Auteur d'un moment, comédie en un acte, en vers et en vaudevilles.* Paris, 1792.

Lemaistre de Sacy, Isaac, trans. *La Sainte Bible.* Paris, 1846.

Lesur, Charles-Louis. *La Veuve du républicain, ou le Calomniateur.* Paris, Year II (1794).

Marmontel, Jean-François. "Apologie du théâtre, ou Analyse de la Lettre de M. Rousseau, citoyen de Genève, à M. d'Alembert, au sujet des spectacles." In *Œuvres complètes*, 5:721–783. Geneva: Slatkine, 1968.

———. *Œuvres complètes de Marmontel*. Paris, 1824.

Maurin de Pompigny. *L'Époux républicain, drame en deux actes et en prose*. Paris, 1794.

Millin de Grandmaison, Aubin-Louis. *Sur la liberté du théâtre*. Paris, 1790.

Mistelet. *De la Sensibilité par rapport aux drames, aux romans, et à l'éducation*. Amsterdam, 1777.

Molière. *Le Misanthrope, ou L'Atrabilaire amoureux*. In *Œuvres complètes*. Ed. Georges Couton. 2 vols. Paris: Gallimard, 1983.

Palissot, Charles. "Considérations importantes sur ce qui se passe, depuis quelques temps, au prétendu Théâtre de la Nation, et particulièrement sur les persécutions exercées contre le sieur Talma." Paris, 1790.

———. *La Critique de la tragédie de Charles IX*. Paris, 1790.

Piis, P.-A.-A. de. *La Nourrice républicaine, ou les plaisirs de l'adoption*. Paris, 1794.

Quatremère de Quincy, Antoine-Chrysostome. *De la liberté du théâtre*. Paris, 1790.

Radet, Jean-Baptiste, and Georges Desfontaines. *La Chaste Suzanne, pièce en deux actes melées de vaudevilles*. Paris, 1793.

"Rapport des MM. les commissaires nommés par la commune relativement aux spectacles." Paris, 1790.

"Relation de ce qui s'est passé à la Comédie française dans la nuit du vendredi 23 au 24 juillet, ou Déstruction de la cabale du ministre Farcy-Guignard, dit St. Priest." Paris, 1790.

Rézicourt, Jean-Baptiste. *Les Vrais sans-culottes, ou l'Hospitalité républicaine*. Paris, Year II.

Robespierre, Maximilien Marie Isidore. *Œuvres de Maximilien Robespierre*. 10 vols. Paris: Presses universitaires de France, 1910–1967.

———. "Sur la Constitution." In *Discours et rapports à la Convention*. Paris: Union Générale d'Editions, 1965.

———. "Sur la necessité de révoquer le décret sur le marc d'argent." In *Robespierre: Textes choisies*. Ed. Jean Poperen. Vol. 1. Paris: Editions sociales, 1974.

Roland, Marie-Jeanne. *The Memoirs of Madame Roland: A Heroine of the French Revolution*. Trans. and ed. Evelyn Shuckburgh. Mount Kisco, NY: Moyer Bell, 1989.

Rousseau, Jean-Jacques. *Les Confessions*. Ed. Jacques Voisine. Paris: Garnier, 1964.

———. *The Confessions of Jean Jacques Rousseau*. Trans. J. M. Cohen. Baltimore: Penguin, 1954.

———. "Discourse on the Origin and Foundations of Inequality among Men." In Rousseau, *The Discourses and Other Early Political Writings*, 113–231.

————. *The Discourses and Other Early Political Writings.* Ed. Victor Gourevitch. Cambridge, UK: Cambridge University Press, 1997.

————. *Du Contrat social.* In Rousseau, *Œuvres complètes,* 3:349–470.

————. "Essay on the Origin of Languages." In Rousseau, *The Discourses and Other Early Political Writings,* 247–299.

————. *Lettre à M. d'Alembert sur les spectacles.* 1758. In Rousseau, *Œuvres complètes,* 5:1–184.

————. *Œuvres complètes.* 5 vols. Paris: Gallimard, Bibliothèque de la pléiade, 1995.

————. *The Social Contract.* Trans. Maurice Cranston. London: Penguin, 1968.

Smith, Adam. *The Theory of Moral Sentiments.* Ed. D. D. Raphael and A. L. Macfie. Oxford: Oxford University Press, 1976.

Villeneuve, Citoyenne. *Le Mari coupable.* Paris, Year III (1795).

————. *Plus de bâtards en France.* Paris, Year III (1795).

Watelet, Claude-Henri. "Grimace." In *Encyclopédie,* ed. Jean le rond D'Alembert and Denis Diderot, 7:948. Paris, 1757.

Secondary Works

Apostolidès, Jean-Marie. *Le Roi-machine: Spectacle et politique au temps de Louis XIV.* Paris: Editions de Minuit, 1981.

Arasse, Daniel. *The Guillotine and the Terror.* Trans. Christopher Miller. London: Penguin, 1988.

Arendt, Hannah. *On Revolution.* London: Faber and Faber, 1963.

Aulard, François-Alphonse. *Le Culte de la raison et le culte de l'être suprême.* Paris, 1894.

————. "Figures oubliées de la Révolution française: Fabre d'Eglantine." *Nouvelle Revue* (1885): 59–85.

Badinter, Elisabeth. *L'Amour en plus: Histoire de l'amour maternel (XVIIe–XXe siècle).* Paris: Flammarion, 1980.

Baecque, Antoine de. *The Body Politic: Corporeal Metaphor in Revolutionary France, 1770–1800.* Trans. Charlotte Mandell. Stanford, CA: Stanford University Press, 1997.

Baker, Keith Michael. *Inventing the French Revolution: Essays on French Political Culture in the Eighteenth Century.* Cambridge, UK: Cambridge University Press, 1990.

Balibar, Etienne. "Citizen Subject." In *Who Comes after the Subject?* ed. Eduardo Cadava, Peter Connor, Jean-Luc Nancy, 33–57. New York: Routledge, 1991.

Barish, Jonas. *The Antitheatrical Prejudice.* Berkeley: University of California Press, 1981.

Barny, Roger. "Démocratie directe en 1793: Ambiguité d'une référence théorique." In *L'An I et l'apprentissage de la démocratie,* ed. Roger Bourderon, 71–87. Saint-Denis: Editions PSD, 1995.

———. "Molière et son théâtre dans la Révolution." *Bulletin d'Histoire de la Révolution française* (1994–1995): 43–63.

Bates, David. "Idols and Insight: An Enlightenment Topography of Knowledge." *Representations* 72 (2001): 1–23.

Besterman, Theodore, ed. *Studies on Voltaire and the Eighteenth Century.* Geneva: Droz, 1964.

Bingham, Alfred Jepson. *Marie-Joseph Chénier: Early Life and Ideas (1789–1794).* New York: Privately published, 1939.

Blanchard, Marc Eli. *Saint-Just & Cie: La Révolution et les mots.* Paris: Librairie Nizet, 1980.

Bloom, Allan, trans. *Politics and the Arts: Letter to M. d'Alembert on the Theatre.* Ithaca, NY: Cornell University Press, 1960.

Blum, Carol. *Rousseau and the Republic of Virtue.* Ithaca, NY: Cornell University Press, 1986.

Boltanski, Luc. *Distant Suffering: Morality, Media, and Politics.* Cambridge, UK: Cambridge University Press, 1999.

Boncompain, Jacques. "Théâtre et formation des consciences: L'Exemple de *Charles IX.*" *Revue d'histoire du théâtre* 41 (1989): 44–48.

Bourdieu, Pierre. "The Uses of the 'People.'" In *In Other Words.* Stanford, CA: Stanford University Press, 1990.

Brasart, Patrick. *Paroles de la Révolution: Les Assemblées parlementaires, 1789–1794.* Paris: Minerve, 1988.

Brette, Armand. *Histoire des édifices ou ont siégé les assemblées parlementaires de la Révolution française et de la première République.* Paris: Imprimerie Nationale, 1902.

Brooks, Peter. *The Melodramatic Imagination: Balzac, Henry James, Melodrama, and the Mode of Excess.* New Haven, CT: Yale University Press, 1995.

Brunetière, Ferdinand. "Critique de Welschinger *Le Théâtre de la Révolution.*" *Revue des deux mondes,* Jan. 15, 1881.

Bryson, Scott S. *The Chastised Stage; Bourgeois Drama and the Exercise of Power.* Saratoga, CA: ANMI Libri, 1991.

Burke, Edmund. *Reflections on the Revolution in France.* Ed. Conor Cruise O'Brien. London: Penguin, 1982.

Butler, Judith. *The Psychic Life of Power: Theories in Subjection.* Stanford, CA: Stanford University Press, 1997.

Campardon, Emile. *L'Histoire du tribunal révolutionnaire de Paris.* 2 vols. Paris, 1862.

Camus, Albert. *The Rebel: An Essay on Man in Revolt.* Trans. Anthony Bower. New York: Vintage, 1956.

Caplan, Jay. *Framed Narratives: Diderot's Genealogy of the Beholder.* Minneapolis: University of Minnesota Press, 1985.

Carlson, Marvin. *The Theatre of the French Revolution.* Ithaca, NY: Cornell University Press, 1966.

Bibliography

Censer, Jack R. *The French Press in the Age of Enlightenment.* London: Routledge, 1994.

Censer, Jack R., and Jeremy D. Popkin, eds. *Press and Politics in Pre-Revolutionary France.* Berkeley: University of California Press, 1987.

Chartier, Roger. *The Cultural Origins of the French Revolution.* Trans. Lydia G. Cochrane. Durham, NC: Duke University Press, 1991.

Clark, T. J. "Painting in the Year Two." *Representations* 47 (1994): 13–63.

Cobb, Richard. *The Police and the People: French Popular Protest, 1789–1820.* Oxford: Clarendon Press, 1970.

Cohen, Margaret. *The Sentimental Education of the Novel.* Princeton, NJ: Princeton University Press, 1999.

Coleman, Patrick. *Rousseau's Political Imagination: Rule and Representation in the Lettre à d'Alembert.* Geneva: Droz, 1984.

Court, Antoine. "Un Mélodrame d'Olympe de Gouges, ou le noir impossible." In *Mélodrames et romans noirs,* ed. Jean Sgard, 67–82. Toulouse: Presses universitaires du Mirail, 2000.

Darnton, Robert. *The Corpus of Clandestine Literature in France, 1769–1789.* New York: Norton, 1995.

———. *Forbidden Bestsellers of Pre-Revolutionary France.* New York: Norton, 1955.

———. "The High Enlightenment and the Lowlife of Literature." In *The Literary Underground of the Old Regime.* Cambridge, MA: Harvard University Press, 1982.

———. *What Was Revolutionary about the French Revolution?* Waco, TX: Baylor University Press, 1990.

Darnton, Robert, and Daniel Roche, eds. *Revolution in Print: The Press in France, 1775–1800.* Berkeley: University of California Press, 1989.

De Man, Paul. "Excuses (Confessions)." In *Allegories of Reading: Figural Language in Rousseau, Nietzsche, Rilke, and Proust.* New Haven, CT: Yale University Press, 1979.

Denby, David. *Sentimental Narrative and the Social Order in France, 1760–1820.* Cambridge, UK: Cambridge University Press, 1994.

Derrida, Jacques. *Of Grammatology.* Trans. Gayatri Chakravorty Spivak. Baltimore: Johns Hopkins University Press, 1976.

Desan, Suzanne. *Reclaiming the Sacred: Lay Religion and Popular Politics in Revolutionary France.* Ithaca, NY: Cornell University Press, 1990.

———. "'War between Brothers and Sisters': Inheritance Law and Gender Politics in Revolutionary France." *French Historical Studies* 20, no. 4 (1997): 597–634.

———. "What's after Political Culture? Recent French Revolutionary Historiography." *French Historical Studies* 32, no. 1 (2000): 163–196.

D'Estrée, Paul. *Le Théâtre sous la Terreur: Théâtre de la peur, 1793–1794.* Paris: Emile-Paul, 1913.

Doyle, William. *Origins of the French Revolution.* Oxford: Oxford University Press, 1988.

Duvignaud, Jean. *La Sociologie de l'acteur.* Paris: Gallimard, 1965.

Elias, Norbert. *The Court Society.* Trans. Edmund Jephcott. New York: Pantheon, 1983.

Ernest-Charles. "L'Action du théâtre sur l'opinion publique pendant la Révolution." *Revue d'art dramatique* (1907).

Etienne, C.-G., and A. Martainville. *Histoire du théâtre français, depuis le commencement de la Révolution jusqu'à la réunion générale.* 4 vols. Paris: An X (1802).

Eude, Michel. "Le Comité de sûreté générale de la Convention." In *L'Etat et sa police en France, 1789–1914,* ed. Jacques Aubert, Michel Eude, and Claude Goyard, 13–25. Geneva: Droz, 1979.

Farge, Arlette. *Dire et mal dire: L'Opinion publique au XVIIIe siècle.* Paris: Editions du Seuil, 1992.

Force, Pierre. *Molière ou le prix des choses: Morale, économie et comédie.* Paris: Nathan, 1994.

Foucault, Michel. *Discipline and Punish: The Birth of the Prison.* Trans. Alan Sheridan. New York: Vintage, 1979.

———. "The Eye of Power." In *Power/Knowledge: Selected Interviews and Other Writings, 1972–1977,* ed. Colin Gordon, 146–165. New York: Pantheon, 1980.

———. "*Il faut défendre la société.*" Paris: Seuil/Gallimard, 1997.

Fournel, Victor. "Le Parterre sous la Révolution." *Revue d'art dramatique* (July–Sept. 1893).

France, Peter. *Politeness and Its Discontents: Problems in French Classical Literature.* Cambridge, UK: Cambridge University Press, 1992.

Frantz, Pierre. *L'Esthétique du tableau dans le théâtre du XVIIIe siècle.* Paris: Presses universitaires de France, 1998.

Freud, Sigmund. *Totem and Taboo.* Trans. James Strachey. New York: Norton, 1950.

Fried, Michael. *Absorption and Theatricality: Painting and Beholder in the Age of Diderot.* Chicago: University of Chicago Press, 1987.

Friedland, Paul. *Political Actors: Representative Bodies and Theatricality in the French Revolution.* Ithaca, NY: Cornell University Press, 2002.

Fuchs, Max. Introduction to Jean-Jacques Rousseau, *Lettre à M. d'Alembert sur les spectacles.* Lille: Giard, 1948.

Furet, François. *Interpreting the French Revolution.* Trans. Elborg Forster. Cambridge, UK: Cambridge University Press, 1981.

———. *Penser la Révolution Française.* Paris: Gallimard, 1978.

Gallagher, Catherine, and Stephen J. Greenblatt. *Practicing New Historicism.* Chicago: University of Chicago Press, 2000.

Gauchet, Marcel. *La Révolution des pouvoirs: La Souveraineté, le peuple, et la représentation.* Paris: Gallimard, 1995.

Gearhart, Suzanne. *The Open Boundary of History and Fiction: A Critical Approach to the French Enlightenment*. Princeton, NJ: Princeton University Press, 1984.

Genty, Maurice. "1789–1790: L'Apprentissage de la démocratie à Paris." In *L'An I et l'apprentissage de la démocratie*, ed. Roger Bourderon, 37–51. Saint-Denis: Editions PSD, 1995.

———. *Paris 1789–1795: L'Apprentissage de la citoyenneté*. Paris: Messidor, 1987.

———. "Pratique et théorie de la démocratie directe: L'Exemple des districts parisiens (1789–1790)." *Annales historiques de la Revolution française* 259 (1985): 8–24.

Goldhammer, Arthur, trans. *Blessings in Disguise; or, The Morality of Evil*, by Jean Starobinski. Cambridge, MA: Harvard University Press, 1995.

Goldzinck, Jean. *Les Lumières et l'idée du comique*. Fontenay/Saint-Cloud: Ecole normale supérieure, 1991.

Goncourt, Edmond de, and Jules de Goncourt. *L'Histoire de la société française pendant la Révolution, 1789–1799*. Paris, 1869.

Goodden, Angelica. *Actio and Persuasion: Dramatic Performance in Eighteenth-Century France*. Oxford: Clarendon Press, 1986.

———. "The Dramatising of Politics: Theatricality and the Revolutionary Assemblies." *FMLS* 20 (1984): 193–212.

Goodheart, Eric Andrew. "Adoption in the Discourse of the French Revolution." PhD diss., Harvard University, 1997.

Goodman, Dena. *Criticism in Action: Enlightenment Experiments in Writing*. Ithaca, NY: Cornell University Press, 1989.

———. *The Republic of Letters: A Cultural History of the French Enlightenment*. Ithaca, NY: Cornell University Press, 1994.

Gossman, Lionel. *Men and Masks: A Study of Molière*. Baltimore: Johns Hopkins University Press, 1963.

Graham, Lisa Jane. *If the King Only Knew: Seditious Speech in the Reign of Louis XV.* Charlottesville: University Press of Virginia, 2000.

Greenblatt, Stephen. *Learning to Curse: Essays in Early Modern Culture*. New York: Routledge, 1990.

Gueniffey, Patrice. *Le Nombre et la raison: La Révolution française et les élections*. Paris: Editions de l'Ecole des hautes études en sciences sociales, 1993.

Gutwirth, Madelyn. *The Twilight of the Goddesses: Women and Representation in the French Revolutionary Era*. New Brunswick, NJ: Rutgers University Press, 1992.

Habermas, Jürgen. *Between Facts and Norms: Contributions to a Discourse Theory of Law and Democracy.* Trans. William Rehg. Cambridge, MA: MIT Press, 1996.

———. *The Structural Transformation of the Public Sphere.* Trans. Thomas Burger and Frederick Lawrence. Cambridge, MA: MIT Press, 1989.

———. *Der Strukturwandel der Öffentlichkeit: Untersuchungen zu einer Kategorie der bürgerlichen Gesellschaft.* Neuwied: Hermann Luchterhand, 1962.

Hallays-Dabot, Victor. *Histoire de la censure théâtrale en France.* 1862. Repr., Geneva: Slatkine, 1970.

Hamiche, Daniel. *Le Théâtre et la Révolution: La Lutte des classes au théâtre en 1789 et 1793.* Paris: Editions sociales, 1973.

Hamilton, James F. "Molière and Rousseau: The Confrontation of Art and Politics." In *Molière and the Commonwealth of Letters: Patrimony and Posterity,* ed. Roger Johnson Jr., Editha S. Neumann, and Guy T. Trail, 100–108. Jackson: University Press of Mississippi, 1975.

Heffernan, James A. W., ed. *Representing the French Revolution: Literature, Historiography, and Art.* Hanover, NH: University Press of New England, 1992.

Hegel, G. F. W. *The Phenomenology of Spirit.* Trans. A. V. Miller. Oxford: Clarendon Press, 1977.

Hérissay, Jacques. *Le Monde des théâtres pendant la Révolution, 1789–1800.* Paris: 1922.

Hertz, Neil. "Medusa's Head: Male Hysteria under Political Pressure." *Representations* 4 (1983): 27–54.

Hesse, Carla. "Economic Upheavals in Publishing." In Darnton and Roche, *Revolution in Print,* 69–97.

———. *Publishing and Cultural Politics in Revolutionary Paris, 1789–1810.* Berkeley: University of California Press, 1991.

Higonnet, Patrice. *Goodness beyond Virtue: Jacobins during the French Revolution.* Cambridge, MA: Harvard University Press, 1998.

Huet, Marie-Hélène. *Mourning Glory: The Will of the French Revolution.* Philadelphia: University of Pennsylvania Press, 1997.

———. "Performing Arts: Theatricality and the Terror." In Heffernan, *Representing the French Revolution,* 135–149.

———. *Rehearsing the Revolution: Staging Marat's Death, 1793–1797.* Trans. Robert Hurley. Berkeley: University of California Press, 1982.

Hunt, Lynn. *The Family Romance of the French Revolution.* Berkeley: University of California Press, 1992.

———. *Politics, Culture, and Class in the French Revolution.* Berkeley: University of California Press, 1984.

Hyslop, Beatrice H. "The Theater during a Crisis: The Parisian Theater during the Reign of Terror." *Journal of Modern History* 17 (1945): 322–355.

Jauffret, E. *Le Théâtre révolutionnaire.* Paris, 1869.

Jaume, Lucien. *Le Discours Jacobin et la démocratie.* Paris: Fayard, 1989.

Jay, Martin. *Downcast Eyes: The Denigration of Vision in Twentieth-Century French Thought.* Berkeley: University of California Press, 1993.

———. *Marxism and Totality: The Adventures of a Concept from Lukács to Habermas.* Berkeley: University of California Press, 1984.

Johnson, James H. "Revolutionary Audiences and the Impossible Imperatives of Fraternity." In Ragan and Williams, *Re-Creating Authority in Revolutionary France,* 57–78.

———. "Versailles, Meet Les Halles: Masks, Carnivals, and the French Revolution." *Representations* 73 (2001): 89–116.

Jonas, Raymond. *France and the Cult of the Sacred Heart: An Epic Tale for Modern Times.* Berkeley: University of California Press, 2000.

Jordan, David P. *The King's Trial: Louis XVI vs. the French Revolution.* Berkeley: University of California Press, 1979.

Kennedy, Emmet. *A Cultural History of the French Revolution.* New Haven, CT: Yale University Press, 1989.

Kennedy, Emmet, Marie-Laurence Netter, James P. McGregor, and Mark V. Olsen. *Theatre, Opera, and Audiences in Revolutionary Paris: Analysis and Repertory.* Westport, CT: Greenwood Press, 1996.

Lancaster, Henry Carrington. *French Tragedy in the Reign of Louis XVI and the Early Years of the French Revolution, 1774–1792.* Baltimore: Johns Hopkins University Press, 1953.

Landes, Joan B. *Women and the Public Sphere in the Age of the French Revolution.* Ithaca, NY: Cornell University Press, 1988.

Launay, Louis de. *Une Famille de la bourgeoisie parisienne pendant la Révolution.* Paris: Perrin, 1921.

Lecomte, Louis-Henri. *Histoire des théâtres de Paris: Le Théâtre de la Cité.* Paris: H. Daragon, 1910.

Liu, Alan. "The Power of Formalism: The New Historicism." *ELH* 56 (1989): 721–771.

Locke, John. *Two Treatises of Government.* Ed. Peter Laslett. Cambridge, UK: Cambridge University Press, 1963.

Lough, John. *Paris Theatre Audiences in the Seventeenth and Eighteenth Centuries.* London: Oxford University Press, 1957.

Lumière, Henry. *Le Théâtre-Français pendant la Révolution, 1789–1799.* Paris, 1894.

MacArthur, Elizabeth. "Embodying the Public Sphere: Censorship and the Reading Subject in Beaumarchais's *Mariage de Figaro.*" *Representations* 61 (1998): 57–77.

Marcus, Sharon. *Apartment Stories: The City and the Home in Nineteenth-Century Paris and London.* Berkeley: University of California Press, 1999.

Marshall, David. *The Figure of Theater: Shaftesbury, Defoe, Adam Smith, and George Eliot.* New York: Columbia University Press, 1986.

———. *The Surprising Effects of Sympathy: Marivaux, Diderot, Rousseau, and Mary Shelley.* Chicago: University of Chicago Press, 1988.

Marx, Karl. "On the Jewish Question." In Karl Marx and Frederick Engels, *Collected Works.* London: Lawrence & Wishhart, 1975.

Maslan, Susan. "Resisting Representation: Theater and Democracy in Revolutionary France." *Representations* 52 (1995): 27–52.

Mason, Laura. *Singing the French Revolution: Popular Culture and Politics, 1789–1799.* Ithaca, NY: Cornell University Press, 1996.

Mathiez, Albert. *Le Club des Cordeliers pendant la crise de Varennes et le massacre du champs-de-mars.* Paris, 1910.

————. *Les Origines des cultes révolutionnaires, 1789–1792.* Paris: Société nouvelle de librairie ert d'édition, 1904.

May, Georges. *Le Dilemme du roman au XVIIIe siècle: Etude sur les rapports du roman et de la critique.* New Haven, CT: Yale University Press, 1963.

Maza, Sara. *Private Lives and Public Affairs: The Causes Célèbres of Prerevolutionary France.* Berkeley: University of California Press, 1993.

McDonald, Christie. "The Anxieties of Change: Reconfiguring Family Relations in Beaumarchais's Trilogy." *MLQ* 55, no. 1 (1994): 47–78.

McNeil, Gordon H. "Robespierre, Rousseau, and Representation." In *Ideas in History,* ed. Richard Herr, 135–159. Durham, NC: Duke University Press, 1965.

Merrick, Jeffrey. *The Desacralization of the French Monarchy in the Eighteenth Century.* Baton Rouge: Louisiana State University Press, 1990.

Michelet, Jules. *Histoire de la Révolution française.* Paris, 1847.

————. *Robespierre.* Paris, 1899.

Minson, Jeffery. *Genealogies of Morals: Nietzsche, Foucault, Donzelot, and the Eccentricity of Errors.* London: St. Martin's, 1985.

Moffat, Mary Margaret. *Rousseau et la querelle du théâtre au XVIIIe siècle.* Paris: Boccard, 1930.

Monnier, Raymonde. *L'Espace public démocratique: Essai sur l'opinion à Paris de la Révolution au directoire.* Paris: Editions Kimé, 1994.

Montrose, Louis. "New Historicisms." In *Redrawing the Boundaries: The Transformation of English and American Literary Studies,* ed. Stephen Greenblatt and Giles Gunn, 392–418. New York: MLA, 1992.

Mornet, Daniel. *Les Origines intellectuelles de la Révolution française, 1715–1787.* Paris: Armand Collin, 1933, 1967.

Nesci, Catherine. "La Passion de l'impropre: Lien conjugale et lien coloniale chez Olympe de Gouges; Hommage à Lucienne Frappier-Mazur." In *Corps/décors: Femmes, orgie, parodie,* ed. Catherine Nesci, 45–56. Amsterdam: Rodopi, 1999.

Ozouf, Mona. *La Fête révolutionnaire, 1789–1799.* Paris: Gallimard, 1976.

————. "L'Opinion publique." In *The French Revolution and the Creation of Modern Political Culture: The Political Culture of the Old Regime,* ed. Colin Lucas, 419–434. Oxford: Oxford University Press, 1987.

Pateman, Carol. *Participation and Democratic Theory.* Cambridge, UK: Cambridge University Press, 1970.

Pitkin, Hannah Fenichel. *The Concept of Representation.* Berkeley: University of California Press, 1967.

Poovey, Mary. *Uneven Developments: The Ideological Work of Gender in Mid-Victorian England.* Chicago: University of Chicago Press, 1988.

Pougin, Arthur. *La Comédie-Française et la Révolution.* Paris, 1902.

Ragan, Bryant T., and Elizabeth A. Williams, eds. *Re-Creating Authority in Revolutionary France.* New Brunswick, NJ: Rutgers University Press, 1992.

Ratsaby, Michele. "Olympe de Gouges et le théâtre de la Révolution française." PhD diss., City University of New York, 1998.

Ravel, Jeffrey. *The Contested Parterre: Public Theater and French Political Culture, 1680–1791.* Ithaca, NY: Cornell University Press, 1999.

Redman, Ben Ray, ed. *The Portable Voltaire.* New York: Viking-Penguin, 1977.

Renouvier, Jules. *Histoire de l'art pendant la Révolution considérée principalement dans les estampes.* Paris, 1863.

Robinson, Philip. "Les Vaudevilles: Un médium théâtral." *Dix-huitième siècle* 28 (1996): 431–447.

Roche, Daniel. "Censorship and the Publishing Industry." In Darnton and Roche, *Revolution in Print,* 3–26.

Root-Bernstein, Michèle. *Boulevard Theater and Revolution in Eighteenth-Century France.* Ann Arbor: UMI Press, 1981.

Rothiot, Jean-Paul. "Comités de surveillance et terreur dans le département des Vosges de 1793 à l'an III." *Annales historiques de la Révolution française* (1998): 621–668.

Rougemont, Martine de. *La Vie théâtrale en France au XVIIIe siècle.* Paris: Champion, 1988.

Rudé, George. *The Crowd in the French Revolution.* Oxford: Clarendon Press, 1959.

———. *Robespierre: Portrait of a Revolutionary Democrat.* London: Collins, 1975.

Scherer, Jacques. *La Dramaturgie classique en France.* Paris: Nizet, 1950.

Scott, Joan W. "French Feminisms and the Rights of 'Man': Olympe de Gouges' Declarations." *History Workshop* 28 (1989): 1–21.

Sennett, Richard. *The Fall of Public Man.* New York: Knopf, 1977.

Sheriff, Mary. "Fragonard's Erotic Mothers and the Politics of Reproduction." In *Eroticism and the Body Politic,* ed. Lynn Hunt, 14–40. Baltimore: Johns Hopkins University Press, 1991.

Shuger, Deborah K. *The Renaissance Bible: Scholarship, Sacrifice, and Subjectivity.* Berkeley: University of California Press, 1994.

Slavin, Morris. *The French Revolution in Miniature: Section Droits-de-l'homme.* Princeton, NJ: Princeton University Press, 1984.

Soboul, Albert. *Mouvement populaire et gouvernement révolutionnaire 2 juin, 1793–9 Thermidor an II.* Paris: Librairie Clavreuil, 1962.

———. *Les Sans-culottes parisiens en l'an II: Mouvement populaire et gouvernement révolutionnaire, 2 juin, 1793–9 thermidor, 1794.* Paris: Clavreuil, 1958.

———. *The Sans-Culottes: The Popular Movement and Revolutionary Government, 1793–1794.* Trans. Remy Inglis Hall. Princeton, NJ: Princeton University Press, 1980. This translation is also an abridgement of the 1958 Clavreuil edition listed above.

Stael, Germaine de. *De la Littérature.* Ed. Gérard Gengembre and Jean Goldzinck. Paris: Garnier-Flammarion, 1991.

Starobinski, Jean. *1789, ou les emblèmes de la liberté.* Paris: Flammarion, 1979.

———. *Jean-Jacques Rousseau: La transparence et l'obstacle, suivi de sept essais sur Rousseau.* 1957. Paris: Gallimard, 1971.

———. *Le Remède dans le mal: Critique et légitimation de l'artifice à l'age des lumières.* Paris: Gallimard, 1989.

Swenson, James. *On Jean-Jacques Rousseau, Considered as One of the First Authors of the Revolution.* Stanford, CA: Stanford University Press, 2000.

Szondi, Peter. "*Tableau* and *coup de théâtre*: On the Social Psychology of Diderot's Bourgeois Tragedy." *New Literary History* 11, no. 2 (1980): 323–343.

Taine, Hippolyte. *Les Origins de la France contemporaine.* 3 vols. Paris: Hachette, 1875–1894.

Thomas, Chantal. *La Reine scélérate: Marie-Antoinette dans les pamphlets.* Paris: Seuil, 1989.

Thompson, E. P. *Customs in Common: Studies in Traditional Popular Culture.* New York: New Press, 1991.

Tissier, Andre. *Les Spectacles de Paris pendant la Revolution: Répertoire analytique, chronologique, et bibliographique.* Geneva: Droz, 1992.

Tocqueville, Alexis de. *The Old Regime and the French Revolution.* Trans. Stuart Gilbert. Garden City, NY: Doubleday, 1955.

Traer, James. *Marriage and the Family in Eighteenth-Century France.* Ithaca, NY: Cornell University Press, 1980.

Trilling, Lionel. *Sincerity and Authenticity.* Cambridge, MA: Harvard University Press, 1971.

Trouille, Mary. "Amazons of the Pen: Stéphanie de Genlis and Olympe de Gouges." In *Femmes savantes et femmes d'esprit: Women Intellectuals of the French Eighteenth Century,* ed. Roland Bonnel and Catherine Rubinger, 341–370. New York: Peter Lang, 1994.

Tulard, Jean. "Le Mythe de Fouché." In *L'Etat et sa police en France, 1789–1914,* ed. Jacques Aubert, Michel Eude, and Claude Goyard, 27–34. Geneva: Droz, 1979.

Vanpée, Janie. "The Trials of Olympe de Gouges." *Theatre Journal* 51, no. 1 (1999): 47–65.

Verdier, Gabrielle. "From Reform to Revolution: The Social Theater of Olympe de Gouges." In *Literate Women and the French Revolution of 1789,* ed. Catherine R. Montfort, 189–221. Birmingham, AL: Summa, 1994.

Vereker, Charles. *Eighteenth-Century Optimism: A Study of the Interrelations of Morality and Social Theory in English and French Thought between 1689 and 1789.* Liverpool: Liverpool University Press, 1967.

Vidler, Anthony. *Claude-Nicholas Ledoux: Architecture and Social Reform at the End of the Old Regime.* Cambridge, MA: MIT Press, 1990.

Vila, Anne. *Enlightenment and Pathology: Sensibility in the Literature and Medicine of Eighteenth-Century France.* Baltimore: Johns Hopkins University Press, 1998.

Vincent-Buffault, Anne. *The History of Tears: Sensibility and Sentimentality in France.* London: Macmillan, 1991.

Vovelle, Michel. *Idéologies et mentalités.* Paris: La Découverte, 1982.

———. *La Mentalité révolutionnaire: Société et mentalités sous la Révolution française.* Paris: Messidor/Editions sociales, 1986.

Bibliography

Walter, Gérard. *Maximilien de Robespierre.* Paris: Gallimard, 1961, 1989.

Walton, Charles G. "*Charles IX* and the French Revolution: Law, Vengeance, and the Revolutionary Uses of History." *European Review of History* 4, no. 2 (1997): 127–146.

Walzer, Michael. *Regicide and Revolution: Speeches at the Trial of Louis XVI.* London: Cambridge University Press, 1974.

Warner, Michael. *The Letters of the Republic: Publication and the Public Sphere in Eighteenth-Century America.* Cambridge, MA: Harvard University Press, 1990.

Wellek, René. *A History of Modern Criticism.* Vol. 1. New Haven, CT: Yale University Press, 1955.

Welschinger, Henri. *Le Théâtre de la Révolution.* Paris, 1880.

Wilbur, Richard, trans. *The Misanthrope and Tartuffe,* by Jean Baptiste Poquelin de Molière. New York: Harcourt, Brace, Jovanovich, 1965.

Wolikow, Claudine. "1789–An III: Emergence de la démocratie représentative." In *L'An I et l'apprentissage de la démocratie,* ed. Roger Bourderon, 53–69. Saint-Denis: Editions PSD, 1995.

Index